KN8

THE
PEOPLES'
COOK
BOOK

THE
PEOPLES'
COOK
BOOK

Staples, Delicacies, & Curiosities
from the Earth's Humble Kitchens

Huguette Couffignal
Translated and Adapted by James Kardon

M

Original French title *La Cuisine des Pauvres,*
© Robert Morel Editeur 1970.

This expanded English translation and adaptation including all
new material is © St Martin's Press, Inc. 1977 and further
adaptations © Macmillan London Ltd, 1978.

ISBN 0 333 24549 0

First published 1979 by
MACMILLAN LONDON LIMITED
4 Little Essex Street London WC2R 3LF
and Basingstoke
Associated Companies in Delhi, Dublin,
Hong Kong, Johannesburg, Lagos, Melbourne,
New York, Singapore and Tokyo

Published in association with Pan Books

Typeset in Great Britain by
WILLMER BROTHERS LIMITED
Rock Ferry, Merseyside

Printed in Great Britain by
LOWE AND BRYDONE PRINTERS LIMITED,
Thetford, Norfolk

Contents

To those who consider life something other than a monstrous
    belly with a golden navel for all to worship;
To those who have tasted and preferred renunciation,
    simplicity and freedom;
To those who make an art of living;
To those who cultivate poverty as a spiritual exercise,
    whatever their religion;
To those who find in each moment a life to live for;
To the unwilling poor, victims of society, property, climate,
    injustice, ignorance, overpopulation, stupidity, evil or dumb
    pride;
Because it is clear that people's kitchens all over the world have
    learned to adapt to what's available and from the nearly nothing
    at their disposal make something more than just enough to
    live on, make sturdy, simple pleasures and elemental feasts.

The Peoples' Cooking

This book is a catalogue of information and recipes from simple people's kitchens around the world. It has been assembled in a spirit very different from the usual collection of international specialities and gastronomic palate-ticklers. You will not find any recipes for caviar, pâté, truffles or fine cuts of veal in this book. Nor will you find suggestions for huge roasts or fancy stuffed birds. What you will find is an introduction to the unpretentious, delicious and natural cooking prepared in modest homes and inns, in huts and over open fires from Peru to Pakistan to Polynesia. The people of these countries can teach you how to eat well and festively for practically nothing.

Most of the world's people are poor by Western standards. This has not prevented them from making use of the resources at hand to develop cuisines that are almost always fresh and filling and often rise to true culinary distinction. As food prices rise, as land resources dwindle and as population grows, more and more affluent nations look to peasant, ethnic and Third World cooking for inspiration.

In this book we have not attempted to cull only the highest points, the most exquisite achievements of native cuisine—the court banquets and huge feasts served only on days of great celebration. We do not believe that Western cooks want to prepare huge banquets every night and doubt they have the five cooks and fifty kitchen helpers available at an Imperial Asian court. We also believe that one can have as much reverence for a humble breakfast as for a ceremonial feast: both are life-sustaining acts of different but equal import. Cooking is an attitude and a way of life. The spirit of simple cooks lies in their knowledge that they are not simply pleasing palates but also filling a basic function that is part of the will to live.

You may not be able to duplicate the flavours of foreign foods as the indigenous people know them. It is not just because some ingredients are hard to get—although in fact, more and more of them are available in foreign or health food shops, and many can be easily grown in a garden. What comes naturally, almost intuitively, to a native cook is difficult to teach yourself consciously. A sense of balance, the personality of flavours, and a relationship to the food are learned as you grow, like your accent when you speak or knowing when to smile or cry. Many foreign dishes will never seem like home cooking. And you can never translate the special associations of certain dishes. For example Greek *mayeritsa* soup can never sum up Easter to a British person the way roast turkey and plum pudding spell Christmas. A bowl of millet may never taste like a satisfying meal to you, and it may be hard for you to appreciate the intense luxury of an onion. But as you learn new possibilities, some will almost certainly find their way into your own native style of cooking, especially as you realize the exciting tastes, nutritional values, and huge economies to be realized in people's cooking. Rice and beans, bean curd and *miso* soup are not only a lot cheaper than steak, they are often a lot tastier.

The Peoples' Diet:
Famine and Feast

There are only two families in the world:
those who have and those who have not.
Cervantes, *Don Quixote*

Is there a life less enviable than that of the Mexican peasant woman, up with the dawn to spend her day finding and preparing food for her family? Making enough *tortillas* for a numerous household is hard work. She throws nothing away, using old tin cans not just to save bacon fat, but also for dishes, pots and to store water. She can't buy in wholesale quantities because there's never that much money on hand. She has to shop meal by meal. When someone's head aches she even buys aspirin pill by pill. Her life is constant work and care.

'Does the head cry for flowers when the belly cries for rice?' is an Indian proverb of universal truth. Eat or starve. Necessity is the only law. The problems of enough *tortillas*, water and *pesos*, and too much hard work in the fields dog the Mexican peasant family from dawn to dusk.

What is food to them? Usually it means morning *tortillas* washed down with a brew made from roasted maize because real coffee is too expensive; then at noon, *tortillas* with rice and tomato sauce, washed down again with maize coffee; and at dinner, *tortillas* with rice and beans, spiced with the aromatic herb *epazote* and traditional chili sauce. If the man works near the house his wife brings him dinner at four o'clock: *tortillas*, beans, sometimes meat in tomato sauce and a pint of cactus beer known as *pulque*. Supper that night consists of maize coffee and milk before bed.

Large meals are reserved for holidays. On 1 November, All Saints' Day, Mexican peasants set up a feast on the altar amid flowers and candles: loaves of pink and white sugar, cakes or *dulce*, cups of hot milk and rice, bread, *tortillas*, bananas, lemons, succulent *jicamas* and milk, milk! When the feast candles are blown out, hunger returns.

It may be true that some who have nothing lead a simple, not miserable life—contemplative, without ambitions but with elemental happiness. 'Let us suppress misery and cultivate poverty,' said Lanzo del Vasto, placing value on simplicity while fighting deprivation.

One example of this simple life can be found among the Brazilian *caboclos*, a people who mix and remix their Spanish, black, and Indian blood from generation to generation and who seem to live freely and without care. Rough but meditative people, musicians as well as dancers, the verve of their stories gave rise to a form of picaresque peasant literature, found notably at a popular little theatre in Rio de Janeiro, the Casa de Caboclo. On the coast, the *caiçara* seem to live well, satisfied with fish, manioc, and the wild fruit which usually abounds in tropical countries. They pass the time as easily as in a Polynesian paradise.

Such happy cases, if they really are happy, are bound to disappear as the modern world draws everyone to its way of consumer happiness. The other picture is one of forced indolence with its corollary, omnipresent hunger for the great mass of the world's people. There may be more free time, but how different it is in spirit. The same rhythms that delight the *caboclos* may be mere escape from misery for others, helped along by coca, *chicha*, and *pulque*—drugs and alcohol.

The descendants of the great Incas drown their hunger and weakness in pints of foamy *chicha* drawn from an earthen vat. This seemingly mild corn beer may reach a strength of 36 per cent alcohol—a stupefying drink. Such hunger-cheaters seem almost more common than food among the poor of all latitudes.

All over the world various leaves are chewed to ease hunger pangs. Little bags of dried coca leaves are offered in every country store in South America. The Indian chews the leaves all day, adding a little bit of mineral lime to draw out the alkalinity. Close to 10 per cent of the world's population chews betel—betel palm nuts wrapped in betel pepper leaves, also accompanied by lime—just to have something to chew.

'The Otomi Indian lives and works for *pulque* alone,' goes a Mexican saying. Whatever the basic reason for this, the one advanced by dieticians is no less true. This drink, which is fermented from *aguamiel*, the juice of the maguey plant (a type of agave cactus), has nutrients and vitamins otherwise missing in the daily diet. *Tezquino*, spirits made from fermented wild grains and sprouted corn, similarly compensates for common protein deficiency. *Jiculi*, brewed peyote, has much the same properties, in addition to mystical virtues.

Maguey, a useful plant whose fibres can be woven and whose leaves provide good animal feed, comes in two varieties. One, with grey-blue pointed leaves, furnishes *mezcal*, another hunger-cheater which produces psychedelic side effects. The other, with supple dark leaves and known as *Agave americana*, can be made into *pulque*. Some plants may produce up to 125 litres of *aguamiel*. Consequently, maguey fields are often called the Mexican vineyards.

The origins of *pulque*—called *neutli* by its inventors, the Aztecs —are known only from a legend in which the poor inventor's daughter becomes the beloved of the King and the mother of the 'Son of the King', who in turn becomes King. It was, however, the conquistadors who named the drink *pulque*—Spanish for bitter— in the process of stripping the native Indians not only of their gold but also of their language.

Legend and dreamy idleness are not enough to mask the sordidness of want. Such is the case in the United States, where misery has a bitterness far removed from the apparent ease of tropical life. In a land of general abundance, extreme misery exists under the shocked eyes of those who 'would never believe it'. Misery is seen in the vacant stare of a blond child standing in front of his shack in Kentucky, with skeletal arms and legs and a belly protruding under his only clothing, a shirt. Around him are scattered empty tin cans from beans, soup, condensed milk. Beans are always an essential resource of the poor. The same misery can be found all over the Deep South and Appalachia, in New England, and in all cities.

Among some peoples in the West, as well as in South America, Africa, or Asia, the spectre of starvation never departs even when the daily scramble to survive keeps poverty above the level of total misery.

Famine is an ancient companion of mankind. In China alone there have been no less than ninety-one important famines *per century* over the last two thousand years. How many victims were claimed in all that time? India has suffered one quarter of all recorded famines. Europe has been reduced more than once to eating rats, bark, and even human flesh. The ogres of fairy tales owe their name to the hordes of Hungarians who swept down on Europe from their Asian steppes without our familiar notions as to what is food and what is not. The story of Hansel and Gretel, abandoned in the woods by their parents and almost eaten by a witch, may have similar origins. France, for all its fine sauces, had fifty famines between the sixteenth and the nineteenth centuries.

During the revolution in China, the people had nothing to eat but leaves, bark and clay. Leaves sold in the market for well over £1 a kilogram. During Mao Tse-tung's famous Long March, soldiers had to be satisfied with a bowl of millet and a little cabbage, or occasionally some rice with corn bread. Some soldiers were noted for pot-bellies, due not to good living but to the swelling caused by their grass diet. When the grass was exhausted, they were reduced to eating mud to fill their bellies, mud that also caused a swelling that could prove fatal.

Geophagy is a last resort all over the world; it is practised by natives of America, Guyana, Venezuela, Siberia, New Caledonia, Thailand, Indonesia and sub-Saharan Africa. Sometimes the earth —usually clay or chalk—is prepared according to a recipe, as in the East Indies where it is mixed with water and shaped into cakes that are then roasted over a fire. A certain swamp clay mixed with fruit juice serves as jam. Thais appreciate a curious edible earth made up of silicates, aluminium and water, coloured according to the proportions of certain metallic oxides in its composition, proportions that vary from place to place. They mix the clay with water then cook it.

But earth has always been part of the human diet. The Romans at their peak were so fond of *alica*, a porridge of coarse grain mixed with a kind of earth called *creta*, that Augustus was said to have paid 20,000 sesterces for a monopoly on the product. The earth, which could be clay or chalk, came from between Naples and Pouzzoles. Equally mystifying seems the report that black people in a certain region in Texas eat, apparently for pleasure, a particular kind of red clay.

Dietary deficiencies are inextricably involved with the problem of hunger. Such enfeebling deficiencies may result from the routine seasonal gaps between harvests. In a temperate climate, the critical period is from the end of winter well into the spring; in tropical lands, the problem is worst at the end of the dry season. Even if provisions are not exhausted, there are likely to be deficiencies due to lack of vitamins in the stored foodstuffs. This is aggravated by the fact that the best and richest foods tend to be eaten first.

If the population is basically agricultural, as in the Far East and parts of Africa, even the usual diet is deficient. Farmers tend to limit themselves to high yield crops although variety is necessary for all balanced diets. In such cases, a famine may actually balance their diets by forcing them to eat ordinarily disdained worms, insects, small animals, berries, roots, and greens. Those who live exclusively on grains may make up chronic deficiencies of vitamins and proteins with these varied foods obtained by hunting and gathering. Aberrations in diet which inspire disgust, such as eating earth, carrion and even excrement, not only serve as palliatives but also help a starving person's stomach draw the maximum from meagre rations.

Deficiencies are often the result of habits or prejudices. Such is the case in the Orient where polished rice is preferred, though it lacks vitamin B1. Such is the case among many fishing peoples who throw away fish livers. These prejudices sometimes come from outside. Some people starve today because changes were forced upon them by the white men who had little idea of nutritional balance in spreading 'civilization'. When Africans ate millet, sorghum, manioc, yams, and varied local products, they did not suffer from dietary deficiencies. Now that they have assumed a Western life-style, working in factories instead of in the fields and farming only cash crops, they suffer from malnutrition. In Ceylon before World War II, the people ate an average of 8 kilograms of meat per year; in 1950, the average was down to 2.75 kilograms. On the other hand, Canadians consume around 660 kilograms and Argentinians close to 135 kilograms of meat per year.

It is easy to understand why the Chinese live almost exclusively on vegetables: animals consume too many scarce resources for what they yield. Milk returns 15 per cent of the energy consumed; eggs, only 7 per cent. Beef returns scarcely 4 per cent, truly a luxury item. This explains the importance of pork in Asia. The return of energy is about 20 per cent, and pigs can be fattened on garbage—vegetable calories not otherwise useful. Pigs make up one quarter of Asiatic livestock, the rest are made up mostly of work animals.

The alimentary geography of our planet seems to reflect the division of the world into two great systems of thought; Christianity and Islam dominate the area of meat and bread consumption, and Buddhism and Hinduism predominate in the region of boiled grains and vegetarianism. Alexis Carrel proposed a theory that carnivores are dynamic and bellicose, and vegetarians are weak and peaceful. 'Man is what he eats', is a Hindu proverb. The effects of the difference between the two diets may be seen clearly in the contrasting sizes of pastoral, meat-eating peoples and sedentary vegetarians. In India the Sikhs are taller and stronger than the Hindus. In Africa the Peulhs, Berbers, and Saras are often nearly two metres tall, towering over the Bochimans who average only just over one and a half metres.

Almost nowhere are diets based on nature's bounty alone balanced between meats and vegetables. One or the other almost always predominates, apparently according to whether the climate is hot or cold. Yakuts in Siberia live on reindeer meat, usually boiled and eaten with bread, but vegetables or fruits are very rare in the Arctic zone. Short rations of vitamins and cellulose come from tree bark, the meagre harvest of the short summer, flowers, and sometimes predigested lichen from caribou stomachs, a great delicacy. Unlike other Siberians, Yakuts eat their meat raw because they think cooking destroys the soul of foods. When weather and earth allow they are quick to cultivate cabbage, lettuce, turnips, blueberries, arbutus berries, and fucus, a seaweed that grows on rocks. Porridge, served hot like the other vegetables, is also a luxury. It is made from plantain seeds gathered by hunters from field-mouse burrows.

Shepherds of the world get little variety in their meaty diet. Some variation does come in the form of cheese and butter, usually stored in goat stomachs, which contributes to their strong smell. The milk is bitter. Sometimes there is bread and, as in the Kashmir, some *chang*, barley beer, to brighten daily life. Among the Mongolians and other pastoral peoples of the high central Asian plateau, the herd furnishes all their needs: food, clothing, fuel (fat and dung), tools (bone), and cord (tendons). Indians in America used hollow horns for goblets and used brain to tan leather for clothing and tents.

Sedentary farmers, no poorer than the shepherds, survive on different fare. Korean farmers make do with rice and corn, usually mixed and sometimes eaten with bean curd soup. Happily for them, soya, from which they make bean curd, is very rich in proteins—an excellent substitute for meat. A fair ration of meat is the biggest problem for most sedentary people. To meet this dietary requirement they eat the most varied animals, from birds of all kinds to rats and other little creatures, whatever can be found in barren regions. Pygmies delight in carrion worms, which may seem unpleasant, but supply good quality protein. Elsewhere fish supplies the protein. For instance, in Portugal the per capita fish consumption is 50 kilograms per year, and along the Asian coast rice and fish is a staple. Insects provide protein as well, as does seaweed.

Rice here, corn there, millet, sorghum, or rye—cereal grains feed the world. Northern Italians eat an average of 120 kilograms of bread a year. Many live on cereal prepared even more simply, boiled as porridge. The same gestures, the same attitudes, practically the same tools are used everywhere to prepare cereals. In Asia, Africa and America, the woman usually does the work. When a Mexican woman grinds the corn needed for the family's daily tortillas on her *metae* (a rectangular stone set on little legs on which she crushes the grain with a smooth stone roller), she repeats in all details the movements of a Ndebele woman performing the same task in Africa. Only the clothing is different. This feminine occupation is taken very seriously, even included in initiation rites, since the life of the clan depends on it.

When stones are rare or too heavy for nomadic life, as in the Hoggar of Algeria, they still use a stone roller but crush the millet on a sheepskin instead of a millstone. The peoples of Black Africa and Indonesia crush millet and manioc in hollowed tree trunks. churning with strong pestles as big as an arm.

Not all dietary imbalances or deficiencies are explained by climate and geography, or by dearth or relative abundance. There are other causes, equally disturbing, such as discrimination : not racial discrimination but discrimination within the society and within the family. In many societies the men eat first, often leaving little for the women and children. In India, Africa, and Mexico the women must sit respectfully removed from the men's table.

Sons wait until their father has started eating. Young children eat alone by the hearth. Later women eat the leftovers. In India, according to Lanza del Vasto, 'a woman eats squatting on the ground. . . . She dips her fingers in a bowl of rice and peppers and dextrously stuffs four fingers into her mouth, pushing the handful of food between her teeth with her thumb. She dips a copper cup into a large basin of water from time to time and drinks . . .'

Even the changes of modern life have not overturned these traditional imperatives. The taboos remain, strictly observed on boats, in trains and at home. These traditions are not merely a detail of underdeveloped countries; such taboos may be found in our own societies. What can we make of a society that insists that women perpetually reduce their eating, sometimes to a point of malnutrition, for the sake of some standard of beauty?

The opposition of nomadic, herding cultures and sedentary, agricultural peoples is illustrated by the dietary restrictions imposed by each group. The shepherd, afraid that the farmer might acquire some of his characteristics by eating from his herds, tries to impose on the farmer a taboo against eating beef and mutton, meanwhile prohibiting farm meats like pork and rabbit for himself. Elsewhere, herding societies deny themselves other agricultural products, especially those that have been preserved. Fermented products in particular are sometimes forbidden : cheese, breads, and drinks. Some shepherds, according to J. Claudian, 'have always been wary of the suspect magic represented by certain fermentations'.

Perception of magic is one step from the religious idealization of certain foods, occasionally leading to prohibitions such as the sacred cow of India. The notable examples for Westerners are bread and wine, already sacred to Osiris in Ancient Egypt before becoming part of the cult of Dionysus among the Greeks, and reaching us in the form of Christian communion.

Prohibitions and taboos seem to reach their peak in a practice rare these days, cannibalism. Cannibalism is usually a ritual act in which, by absorbing the dead, one hopes to impregnate oneself with his qualities and virtues. Is it perhaps for the sake of such philosophical considerations that certain destitute peoples in the Mato Grosso in Brazil throw their dead into great ponds to be eaten by large crabs that are eaten in turn?

To cure the disease of poverty, humanity must make tremendous efforts. Unfortunately this effort is too often confused with the supposed amelioration of the human lot brought about by the exportation of modern civilization—capital, microbes, and anxiety —destroying any life styles that cannot compete. Perhaps the hope is that by spreading industrial society, our familiar industrial misery will have company.

The most important problems in the war against poverty are climate and geography. More than half of mankind lives between 20° and 40° north latitude (not including Europe), precisely the same zone as the greatest area of desert. Deserts and arid zones are not likely to produce soon the miraculous harvests the Israelis have coaxed out of the Negev Desert or to blossom with the roses proudly displayed in Saharan oil fields. Man cultivates only a fraction of the land between these latitude lines, and often does so wastefully. In addition there are these problems: rains that fall or do not fall, such as the dramatic Asian monsoon on which the lives of so many depend; rivers that should flood, like the Nile, or should not flood, like the branches of the Orinoco, driving herders and their herds to leaner and leaner forage; impenetrable forests and high mountains where man lives only with titanic efforts.

Complicating a situation already made difficult by soil and climate are the systems of agricultural production developed by peoples all over the world. These systems also contribute to impoverishment. Although geographic conditions in India are not always worse than those of many other countries, India languishes because the farms yield only 22 bushels of rice an acre. Under similar conditions in Surinam an acre yields an average of 40 bushels, and in Egypt, close to 50. Archaic techniques, mediocre seeds, lack of fertilizer, and inadequate agronomic surveillance all contribute to the disparity.

On the edges of jungle in Latin America, parts of Black Africa, and in Ethiopia, farmers strip corners of earth, and farm without fertilizer until the soil is exhausted. After a few years when the harvest gives out, they move on—slash and burn, with no possibility of improvement. The tenant farmers of Brazil are even poorer. They do not even own the land they work and keep moving with their families and meagre belongings, hoping to find land that may stay good for a few years. They find an arable patch, clear it, plant, and soon move on again. However, they first sow grass that will permit the big landowner to continue to reap profit by raising cattle on land now too poor to raise people.

Adding to the misery, poor nations must often export their chief agricultural wealth in order to function in the world of commerce, while their masses die of hunger. The poor do not have enough money to buy on the world market. The only remedy is to fight ignorance and use the available resources of nature intelligently.

The world's land is poorly cultivated, and, except in Asia, the sea is also neglected. Only 1 per cent of man's food and 10 per cent of his animal protein come from the sea. Asiatics long ago solved the problems involved in using and preserving ocean products. However, we are wasting the wealth of the sea faster than we can learn how to cultivate and profit from its flora and fauna.

For many 'primitive' peoples of the world, hunting and fishing complement agriculture. But for some, like hunting for the Eskimos and fishing for some Japanese, these methods supply the only source of food. Most peoples have more sophisticated tools than the Punans in Borneo who hunt wild pig with blowguns or the Tonga islanders who capture sharks by lasso. Even so, the techniques are often insufficient to provide enough food to feed a large population. The yield from most hunting and fishing is miniscule when compared to the effort required for the activity. How do you fill the fish baskets if you fish only with a trained cormorant, a technique very common in China and Japan? The Amazon River teems with fish but those who live on its banks starve because they lack adequate techniques. The *rotos*, the very poor of Chile, live on the coastline but eat only 5 kilograms of fish per year because they do not know how to catch them.

Sometimes, however, archaic techniques are models of efficiency. For instance, leaves of appropriate size and strength, such as those of the banana, serve very well as disposable plates, pot covers and even pots for cooking over coals. Few modern cooking techniques are very distant from traditional grills, coals, and heated pits lined with stones and sealed with earth. One cooking method we no longer use was cooking by dropping red-hot stones directly into liquid food and this was a highly efficient method. American Indians who cooked this way needed only simple baskets lined with clay or well-washed bison stomachs. There was no need for clumsy pots because the vessel was never heated over a fire. A similar technique was used in Corsica to make the finest *brocciu*, a creamy goat cheese.

Of course not everybody has, as do the Maoris, hot springs close by in which to poach dinner, prepared simply in a net. At the other end of the thermometer, the mountain people of the Lebanon store snow in stone reservoirs for use through the summer.

What is most extraordinary in all this is that, in spite of such meagre resources, workers and peasants—and more especially their wives—have had the talent, ingenuity and good spirits through the ages to develop simple means of preparing foods. Their preparations respect the natural tastes of foods far better than the complex, overwrought recipes of rich cuisines and mass-marketed products. Their recipes have a simplicity which reflects the taste of food to the hungry, and is often more appealing than rich dishes. A hungry person may know better what good food is than a person with a jaded palate. These recipes help millions make feasts in the midst of want.

The Peoples' Resources

Man has learned to adapt to his environment the world over and perhaps never more so than in his ability to shape valuable foods and utensils out of his natural habitat. Many peoples' staples seem unlikely or even repugnant to the Westerner at first but, seen in context, they are the natural products of man's inventiveness and economy. Below we list many of the foods not commonly employed in the modern Western kitchen but which are basic resources in the world's fight against hunger. Recipes using many of these foods can be found in the recipe section.

Tropical Trees and Plants

THE COCONUT PALM The uses of the coconut palm are as 'numerous as the stars in the sky'. Coconut palms supply materials to build a house, then furnish it with everything from tables and chairs to cups, saucers, rugs, brooms and soap, and finally food for those who live in the house. The shade of these trees brings relief from the heat, or the trees can be burned for heat! A palm wick, burning in palm oil, in a lamp made from a coconut shell, provides light. Palm fibres can be woven to make clothing. The trunk can be hollowed out for a boat which is then fitted with sails, rigging, lines and nets made from fronds and fibres. Palm trees also provide material for a wide range of industrial uses. Four and a half

million hectares are planted with these palms, and at least 2.5 billion coconuts are used each year.

Although lacking branches and growth rings, palm trees reveal their age in the number of scars from fronds that have fallen over the years. A coconut palm reaches maturity, that is full reproductive capacity, at thirteen years of age and continues to bear fruit well into its sixties, when it begins to decline. It dies in its eighties or nineties, a life span curiously parallel to that of man. On average a coconut palm produces 70–120 nuts per year.

Coconut palms usually grow near rivers or by the sea. This fact gave rise to the theory that the tree spread around the world from its original home in south-east Asia as the nuts were carried by waves and currents across the oceans. Palms have also been found 120 kilometres from the ocean, in Guyana. In Brazil they grow in the arid Ceará in the north-east; even more amazing, they survive at almost 600 metres above sea level on the dry Borborema plateau.

Most fruit trees yield only one annual harvest, but the coconut palm provides twelve different products at any given moment. At the top the bud, which resembles cabbage with its bouquet of ivory leaves, is sometimes harvested and sold as heart of palm, which has a very fine taste. However, when the bud is cut, the tree dies. Coconut palm flowers are protected by an envelope of fibre that can be made into shoes, hats or sun helmets. Blossoming, the flowers exude a nectar with a very special taste, beloved of bees. The nuts take about ten months to develop if the flowers are not used first for other purposes. When the heads of unopened flowers are bent back and crumpled, a sweet sap flows, at a rate of up to 8 litres a day. This amber liquid, with no taste of coconut, can be boiled like maple sap for syrup and crystallized into a red sugar. The sap will also ferment rapidly, changing within several hours into a robust drink with up to 8 per cent alcohol. This drink is popular under many names throughout the tropics: *toddy* in India, *tuba* in the Philippines, *tuwak* in Indonesia and *bangui* or palm wine in Africa. Allowed to sit for a few weeks the sap turns into an excellent vinegar.

The coconut palm provides well—there are always enough flowers to produce coconuts as well as all these other riches.

After a soaking in salt water the fibres that cover the nuts, known as coir, can be woven into cloth, twisted for rope, or used for insulation or cushions. Car manufacturers cover the fibre with rubber and use it for seats. The shell itself, hard and fine grained, can be used in many different ways. A half-shell is a convenient cup. Add a handle and it becomes a ladle. Many uses are possible: spoons, ash trays, handles, toys, buttons and lamps. Charred shells are valuable not only as charcoal but also as filters for gas masks, submarines and cigarettes.

A five-month-old coconut contains 2 big cups of a fresh, sweet, crystal-clear liquid which is rich in vitamins and minerals. During World War II military doctors, both American and Japanese, used this pure and sterile liquid in place of glucose solution for intravenous injections. The coconut flesh, gelatinous at first, slowly hardens. After a year it is fully ripe. Natives grate the flesh to a pulp which can be soaked and pressed in cloth to yield coconut 'milk' for cooking. When heated the flesh yields oil for cooking, lighting, and—mixed with ash—soap.

Copra, an important item in commerce, is made by drying halves of the shelled nuts. Copra oil can be extracted from the copra, the residual material going to enrich animal feed. Copra oil has many uses in soaps and diverse toilet articles, lubricants, hydraulic fluid, paints, synthetic rubber, margarine and confectionery. Copra oil finds perhaps its most important application in India in the vegetable fat *ghee*, the principal cooking medium for the large vegetarian Hindu population.

None of the coconut palm is thrown away. The fine strands from the fronds are woven into clothes and textiles. The stems can become skewers, arrows or brooms as needed. The trunk, although mostly fibrous and particularly so at the core, can supply a few solid planks. The roots can be chewed for dental hygiene, or their extracts used in dyes and stomach medicines.

And there are no coconut trees without crabs—enough of them for their flesh to be a staple to some. The crabs are enormous and meaty. Coconut crabs display unusual intelligence in climbing the trunk, pinching a nut from its bunch and shaking the stem to make the nut drop and burst. Then the crab climbs down and feasts. When men want to catch a crab, they tie a belt of grass high on the trunk. The crab, crawling down the trunk after knocking off a coconut, lets go when he touches the grass thinking he has reached the ground. Stunned by his fall the crab is easy game.

THE DATE PALM   The date palm is the mainstay of arid

countries and equals the coconut in the variety of its uses—360 of them according to a hymn sung by Mesopotamian farmers. Dates can be eaten plain or made into honey, wine and vinegar. Dried stones are used for fuel or crushed and added to animal fodder. The tree trunk is used for small boats and timber; the fronds for brooms; and the fibres may be woven into baskets, nets and ropes. As always the bud is a delicacy for fine salads. 500 grams contain 1,300 calories: 70 per cent sugar, 2.5 per cent fat and 2 per cent protein.

OTHER PALMS   Palm trees make up a vast family. Some species, such as the central African oil palm, are grown for their oil. The carnauba, or wax palm, is a useful tree. Its seeds take the place of coffee for the poor of Brazil. The wax that seals the vast frond fans is highly prized by industry, particularly record manufacturers. Cut regularly, the fronds renew themselves after six months. The fruits are used for animal feed.

Sugar palms are useful too. All palms yield sweet sap for palm wine, but some species are richer in sugar. Notable examples are the *Borassus flabellifer* of India and West Africa, the *Arenga saccharifera* of tropical Asia and Indonesia and *Nipa fruticans* from the shores of the Far East.

The starchy marrow of the Sago Palm, when crushed and washed, is a staple through much of south-east Asia. Reduced to starch, this pith is used in puddings and stews. The fruit, cooked and roasted, can take the place of bread.

The Mauritia palm from the savannas of South America, and the Coripha from Indonesia and Malaysia also yield starch.

Betel palms provide the nut that when dried, sliced and wrapped in leaves of the betel pepper plant is chewed daily by millions as a mild stimulant.

KARITE   This tree of the African savanna, typical of the south Sudan, bears a fruit resembling a prune which when boiled yields a valuable vegetable fat known as karité butter. In Sudanese markets the butter is usually sold in 3-kilogram chunks still retaining the shape of the calabash in which it was prepared and packed in thin baskets of plaited grass. It is used not only for cooking but also for soap, light, medicine, and beauty cream.

CACTUS   We have already noted the maguey, the Mexican agave used to make a bitter beer called *pulque* (see page 5). Another cactus is the opuntia, or prickly pear, with its very sweet, juicy fruit. Once the spines are singed off, the lobes are eaten by people and animals. Opuntia is assiduously cultivated all over Latin America. *Xique-xique*, with its long arms bristling with spines, is used in the same ways.

BREADFRUIT   This originally Polynesian fruit—known as *meis* in the Marquesas, as *uru* on Maupiti, and as *Artocarpus* among botanists—provides an exceptionally valuable food for tropical populations.

The attempted transport of breadfruit trees was the mission of the voyage recounted in *Mutiny on the Bounty*. In April 1789 the plants were finally imported to the Caribbean. It was hoped that breadfruit would help alleviate the perpetual famine and dietary deficiencies that afflicted the poor inhabitants of the Antilles, the West Indies, Barbados, etc., as a result of the abusive monoculture of sugar cane. These poor people had to be maintained at least minimally to work the plantations and keep the profits from sugar cane, a cash crop, pouring in. Captain Cook, the first European to discover the prolific breadfruit, had become excited at the possibility that it could serve as a cheap way to feed the plantation populations. However, breadfruit kept the Polynesians healthy and strong only as part of a diet that included fresh fish, varied fruits and vegetables, unavailable in the crowded Caribbean. Breadfruit alone turned out not to be a balanced diet, and it was some years before profitable sugar cane land would be idled to insure a wholesome diet for the poor.

Breadfruit, despite its inadequacy as the sole food of an entire population, is a very useful plant. Like the palm tree, the bread-fruit tree provides material for everything from food to roofing, clothing to cooking pots. The flowers are prized as bait by fisher-men and used to make clothes by the beautiful young *vahines*. The seeds, too, are highly valued, resembling chestnuts in appearance, taste and preparation. The fruits themselves stay fresh for as long as eight months.

TARO   Taro, with its large round leaves swaying at the ends of long stalks, is a common plant in the tropics. The starchy roots are another of grainless Oceania's staple foods. Taro has the same uses as breadfruit and is used to make one of the most famous of the Pacific region's staples, *popoi* or *poi*.

Insects

Insects are sometimes a normal feature of diet and often a last resort in times of famine. There are people in Ethiopia who live solely on grasshoppers. No doubt we Westerners should learn to use insects for food—not only to rid ourselves efficiently of what are otherwise pests but also to utilize very nutritious substances. Crickets are 50 per cent protein when cooked. By comparison beef is only 17 per cent protein.

Insects have long been considered good food and even a delicacy. In Leviticus 11 : 22, there are details as to which varieties of locusts are proper to eat—*locusta, bruchus, ophimacus*, and *attacus*. The word *entomophagous*—insect-eating—comes from the Athenians who, although speaking with disdain of 'barbarians, cricket-eaters', used to munch grilled cicadas. Grasshoppers, termites, caterpillars, larvae, worms and so on are sought out by peoples all over the map, both 'civilized' and 'primitive'.

Arabs boil locusts in salted water and then dry them in the sun.

The Tuareg eat them raw or crushed into a fine powder. South-American Indians skewer and roast locusts or mash them into a smooth paste. Japanese, Chinese and Vietnamese eat them roasted, fried, in a sauce or sometimes in pancakes. The Burmese can boast of the supreme refinement: stuffed locust.

North-African couscous, now often served with meat, was originally made with locusts. The preparation of this dish was quite involved. First the insects were shelled, removing head, legs, and wings; then they were crushed, salted, spiced and worked into a paste with the couscous grains. The whole mixture was then set to 'cook' in the sun in an earthenware pot and stirred from time to time until a nauseating fermentation began, initiated by yeasts on grasses in the locusts' stomachs. When the fermentation was complete, the thick, odourless paste was spread on a mat of braided rushes and shaped into bread or pancakes to dry in the sun. The locust bread hardened and was soaked before eating.

Crickets and cicadas are valued as toys as well as food. Often sold in plaited reed cages in China, they are the joy of children—a sort of live transistor radio.

In Mexico unfortunate giant beetles may be eaten or sold live as toys, heavily decked with decorative stones. They provide sport as they try to escape and hide in every corner. Beetles are also used for medicine—in Malaysia, every housewife keeps some dried in a jar as a remedy for sore throats.

Sweet fat worms from palms and agaves are treats not only for the Jivaros in the Amazon jungles but also for Mexicans in cities. They are fried and sold on street corners in paper cones like hot chestnuts.

In China, the land of silk, people eat the chrysalises of silk worms. Ethiopians tear the wings from giant mosquitoes and other flying insects with bodies sometimes as big as half a thumb, impale the bodies on twigs, and roast them over coals. The whole family enjoys this treat.

Termites are also prized. In India queen termites with enormous abdomens are considered a delicacy. Amazon Indians make whole meals from soldier termites. In Africa queens, workers and soldiers are considered equally good fare, raw or cooked. The Pygmies like termites roasted black in a clay pot perched on stones over a fire. Termites are sometimes used with various caterpillars (themselves occasionally used for porridge) to enrich snail stews, heavily spiced with wild red pepper and salted with the ashes of aquatic plants.

The Bochimans gather termites artfully. Women watch from day to day for the moment of swarming. They scratch up a thin layer of earth to show where the termite corridors are and poke little wooden plugs into the holes, which are removed when the swarming begins. Then the proprietor of the termite hill surrounds the place with his family, often building a shelter in which to wait. Swarming begins at twilight. A fire is lit under a roof of leaves and branches, next to a trench dug around the termite hill. When the insects take flight they hit the roof, fall to the ground, crawl toward the fire and fall into the trench. The Bochiman woman then only has to gather them up with a scoop, lay them in a basket, and cover them with fresh leaves.

Another harvesting method which is even more curious is the simulated rain method. The termite hunters, having noted that termites leave their nests in great numbers when it rains hard,

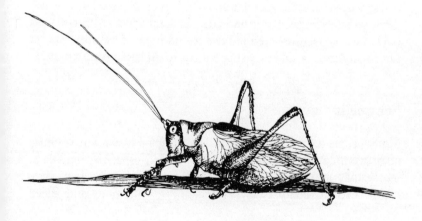

fool the insects by imitating the noise of rain. To do this they station themselves around the termite hill, which may be as tall as a man, and beat on pots. The patter must be gentle. Termites expecting a downpour stream out of their holes and are drawn to lamps held by the hunters. The hunters grill the insects with straw torches as they come out, or knock them into tubs of water with great beaters.

Grilled, crushed, shaped into sausages and rolled up in banana leaves to be poached, these insects form 'termite sausage'. Pressed and twisted inside a sack, they yield a useful oil.

The Kapapalo Indians catch butterflies, pull off their wings and munch the bodies raw like peanuts. They prefer the meatier varieties. The lice from their own unkempt heads are also appreciated.

Bees, wasps, dragonflies, crickets, ants, cicadas and more—from one corner of the earth to another—insects are a public feast. In Colombia, for instance, no one shies away from a dish of soft, fat ants, fried in butter, and served with an aperitif or whisky—a replacement for olives and other snacks. People in less exotic countries sometimes think along the same lines. A French army survival handbook advises: 'If you find yourself lost in the wild without weapons, tools or provisions, eat ants, grasshoppers and termites. These insects are edible.' Astronauts may soon be insectivores; the scientists who develop their diet are studying water fleas, which are easy to grow, cook and eat, and are a complete food. Other scientists recommend grinding insects into powder for distribution as a dietary supplement to underfed populations.

Seaweeds

Many people do not know that seaweed is good to eat, but varieties of seaweeds are appreciated in the Far East, especially in Japan, where they make up 25 per cent of the average daily diet. They can be used in many recipes, often mixed with flour and added to soups or rice, and sometimes made into noodles. For dessert, the Japanese may serve *kakimochi sembei*, small rice biscuits wrapped in seaweed.

Sargasso seaweed, a yellow brown algae with seemingly limitless branching, floats on the ocean by means of air nodules. It grows without roots, at the whim of the currents. Other seaweeds reach great size, like the giant seaweeds of the California coast, sequoias of the deep. Rooted 15–18 metres deep by suction cups, the soft but solid stems may reach a length of 45 metres. Their 'leaves' are thick and heavy, similar to those of rubber trees. Double rows of air nodules, sometimes with a buoy the size of a grapefruit, keep them vertical and floating. Some are long-lived whilst others are annuals reaching monstrous size within the space of a few months. These huge seaweeds form submarine jungles supporting a host of parasite plants.

The seaweeds called wrack and goemon are used as fertilizer in Brittany, for example. There are several types: flotsam goemon, which is either ripped loose by tempests or comes in the form of a loose-fitting annual and so is easily harvested; black shore goemon, harvested live by shore communities from flats and rocks exposed by the receding tide; marl, the accumulation of certain calcareous seaweeds, dredged up and then ploughed into fields; and bottom goemon, growing 30 metres deep, harvested year round as a cash crop with varied industrial uses. American seaweed farmers have even developed an underwater harvester, with a giant blade to cut the seaweed and a conveyor belt to bring it aboard the ship.

Edible species of seaweed are numerous. In Japan the *asakusanori*, from the Tokyo bay area, are among the most prized. This red porphyra seaweed is commonly called purple laver and cultivated in fields 2 metres deep that are uncovered at low tide. They can be gathered at any season. It is indigenous to North American as well as Japanese coastlines. Their floating 'leaves' are dried before packing. They are prepared by strong heating to harden them; in the course of heating the colour goes from red to very

deep green. This and other laver or *nori* seaweed are used primarily for wrapping *sushi*, as garnishes or to flavour and enrich soups, sauces and varied dishes.

Another type of *nori*, *amanori*, gathered in Yeso and Waya-hama bays, is dried on the spot, then quickly taken to factories inland to be processed. There the seaweed is washed, pounded and spread outside, even on dry winter days, to bleach in the sun. Then it is boiled at low heat until mucilage rises to the surface. This is skimmed off and cooled. The result is a translucent, thick gel which can be cut into ribbons, shavings, and flakes not unlike tapioca, and is used in the same way. This *amanori* is used in desserts under the name *kanten*. It is also known as *agar-agar* and, in Japan, *thao*. (*Agar-agar* is also sometimes made from kelp.) *Amanori* is used by the Asian swift to build its nest, the same nest used for the famous bird's nest soup—it is easy to guess how agar-agar can be used to counterfeit this precious dish.

Kombu, dried kelp, is also prized in Japan (and also common off British coasts). Gathered, washed, dried and cut into thin noodles, *kombu* can be eaten dry, as it is, or tenderized in hot water. Other preparations may use the same name—*kombu* comes in many forms. Sometimes these kelps are soaked in vinegar before drying; sometimes they are 'peeled' with a knife. The dried pulp may be pulverized or just cut up. In Japan *kombu* is used in soups and stews; its 'heart' is used as a seasoning. *Kombu* can even be brewed into a kind of tea.

Wakame, or lobe-leafed seaweed, is enjoyed as a main ingredient in Japanese soups and stews.

Other peoples besides the Japanese use seaweed, though not so extensively. There are old Breton recipes for dried seaweed ribbons cooked in milk or stock. The Scottish, Welsh, and Irish continue to prepare sea lettuce or cabbage (*Ulva lactuca*); and Irish moss, also known as carrageen (*Chondrus crispus*), is still gathered by a few who live on the west coasts of Britain. The Welsh use seaweed to make very filling laver bread which is still sold commercially. It consists of a purée of laver seaweed, rolled in oatmeal and fried in bacon fat. The sweet, cartilaginous stems of Scottish badder-locks and Irish murlins—members of the *Alaria* family, common in the North Sea—are also eaten. *Rhodymenin palmata* or dulse has also been eaten for centuries by the Irish. It can be eaten steamed, sautéed with other vegetables or served raw in salads. Chileans also appreciate seaweed, especially a variety called *coch-ayuyo*. They gather it on tidal flats and prepare it in every which way: in soup, fried, puréed or in pâté.

Herds and Game

MUTTON, YAK, CAMEL AND COW   In Mongolia, a land of
yurts (felt tents which are the homes of nomadic pastoral people),
the staple is meat. This diet is common among all pastoral peoples.
Mongolian sheep and yaks are the daily foods of meat and milk.

A fat animal is the choicest. It is cut in two, boiled without
being boned or butchered, and served with knives. When time
and weather permit, the animal is put on a spit whole and grilled
over an open fire. Blood is collected and dried in a sheep's intestine,
then cut into slices, fried and served. This preparation is also
common in the Chinese Gobi Desert. Extra meat is dried. In this
form it is called *bortse* and served as an appetizer before the boiled
meat, together with *shinju*, peppers preserved in bitter brine. The
meat is washed down with *airag*, fermented mare's milk. A bowl
of *sootei tsai*, a mixture of tea and milk simmered for a long time
by the dung fire, warms the winter chill.

In Tibet every part of a sheep is prepared to the best advantage.
The stomach is boiled and sliced into ribbons, seasoned, and served
as a salad. Kidneys are grilled whole without cutting away the
surrounding fat, on an open fire. Lungs, a delicacy, are fried.

Cooking in Tibet, as in Mongolia, is done with yak butter, preserved in sheep stomachs and sold by the slice. This strong butter
is used to flavour tea. Tibetan yak liver and meat, like the best
parts of a sheep, are grilled or roasted.

In Ethiopia much of the population subsists on grains, but there
are Ethiopian herders who live mainly on meat. A sheep is roasted,
whole or quartered, on a bed of *teff* (a type of millet) pancakes
which soak up the juice. Eating beef raw is not an oddity for the
cultured Ethiopian palate—it is a regular feature of their wedding
feasts. Even the viscera of cattle are eaten raw. Camel meat, however, is roasted and the blood adds its savour to the sugared and
peppered wedding cakes.

As a consequence of eating raw meat, Ethiopians often suffer
from tapeworm. For two days a month the Ethiopian herders rest

and take the dried flower of the *kusso* tree as a purgative to dislodge the parasite.

SEAL, CARIBOU AND AUK   Eskimos are meat eaters by necessity. They generally eat animal flesh raw—narwhale blubber, for instance—cutting off chunks at their lips with a hunting knife.

Seal liver is served sliced and smeared with fresh grease. The intestines and stomach may be grilled. Even the eyes are prized. The heart is boiled—the same preparation used for snow hares, bear, and some caribou meat. Apart from meat and innards fit for eating, seals and walruses provide fat prized as a source of oil to burn in lamps. The Eskimos pass their rest periods comfortably installed on seal skins, munching slices of walrus dried during the sunny months earlier on simple lattices of branches raised on stakes. Chunks and slices thus preserved are stored away in a reindeer skin sack until a time comes when they will be appreciated.

When hunting is successful Eskimos eat caribou. Boiled leg of caribou, swimming in grease and served on a wooden plate, with its hot bones cracked for the marrow, is a real feast. Dried meat, marrow and caribou make up a three-course banquet. Caribou also provide dessert. Their stomachs are often filled with a green grey mousse of partially digested lichen, which can be eaten as it is or with some frozen berries.

The hunt is not limited to these beasts alone. Sometimes, with luck from the weather, wild geese fly by; they are delicious when roasted over oil lamps. Sometimes auks arrive in great numbers. Some are eaten immediately, but the rest must be preserved for the more difficult season ahead. The birds are wrapped in fatty seal skin and buried under a pile of stones. In the spring the 'preserves' are ready to eat. The decomposed birds come out soaked in seal fat; they are purple, strong-smelling, and taste something like mature cheese. The Eskimos also eat frozen duck eggs.

ELEPHANT   Together with monkeys, buffalos and antelope, elephants are an excellent source of protein. But not only are elephants a protected species so that usually one is allowed to kill only three a year, they are also hard to catch. Not all people hunt with guns—some Africans still use ancestral methods. The hunters, smeared with elephant dung, encircle the huge beast. At the psychological moment they run under the elephant and jab at his entrails with keen poisoned lances. They then trail the elephant as he runs berserk in his struggle with death.

The animal is usually butchered on the day following the kill. The intervening time is spent driving stakes and trimming palm branches to erect wide racks a metre or so from the ground for the elephant barbecue. The barbecue itself takes at least two days. Seven or eight racks are necessary, with good-sized fires underneath each one, to cook the meat. The trunk alone may weigh well over 100 kilograms. The fat, particularly from around the heart, is precious. It is essential for cooking during the long months before the next successful hunt.

The scramble begins: cut, hack and slice. So many people are working and climbing over the bloody mass that much is butchered at random. Machetes fly, flies swarm. In the torrid heat the stench rises to fill the jungle. Other men, called by tom-tom, arrive to barter chickens, rice or maybe tobacco for the meat.

Roast or boiled meat, raw or boiled manioc, then more meat— 10 kilograms of meat per person per day per glutting: a good hunt.

Small Animals

GUINEA PIG   Guinea pig (cavy), or *cuy*, is one of the meats of the poor in South America. It is sold already roasted in the markets of Cuzco, either in a very hot tomato and pepper sauce or with sautéed onions. Often *cuy* is served with rice. Everyone raises chickens and guinea pigs in his backyard, the way rabbits are raised for food in many parts of the world.

HEDGEHOG   The *niglo*, a hedgehog coated with clay and baked between hot stones, is practically the Gypsy national dish. When cooked, the hardened clay shell can be cracked with a stone; the animal is ready to serve, skinned with no effort. Gypsies use the same procedure for chicken and other fowl, which need not be plucked because the feathers will come away with the clay shell.

In Argentina both male and female hedgehogs are valued. Gutted, then marinated without being skinned, the hedgehog is cooked in its carapace. When it is done even the spines can be eaten.

LIZARDS   Like all things that live and move, lizards can satisfy a hungry person. Australian aborigines grill lizards by a camp fire.

The fat lizards of North Africa, the *dobs*, are a delicacy for children, who pick out the meat with their fingers after opening up the belly. These same *dobs* also provide eggs—there are no chickens in the Sahara. In Malaysia they grill lizard eggs and serve them with pepper. These are called *tjitjiaks* and taste as good as any hard-boiled chicken eggs.

Natural Fermentation

INDIAN MASATO OR MANIOC BREW   Among others, the Indians of the Amazon enjoy this special drink. The women prepare it.

First manioc is cooked. The women sit in a circle around a calabash and chew the manioc, mouthful by mouthful, then spit it into the pot. The mash is left to ferment until the festival day when it is welcomed by all.

KAVA   The natives of the Windward Isles in Polynesia use the same process as the Indians of the Amazon above, replacing manioc with *kava*, the root of the pepper tree. The preparation of this precious liquor is a job for men, and young men at that.

The *kava* roots are soaked in water. The youth of the village sit in a circle and chew the roots as long as possible, often for hours. The well-salivated mash is then spit into a tub. They add water and continue the mashing by hand, then filter it through a clump of fibres. The fermentation begins and continues until the drink is ready.

CHICHA   A similar process, starting with maize, is used in South America. The Indians chew the grains of corn and spit them into a bowl set in the middle of the chewers. The mash is then left to soak for 15 days. The resulting foamy *chicha* is bottled in jars, corked with mint leaves and served in Andean *casitas*, local taverns, usually in rough glasses. Fermented twice, this liquor sometimes reaches 36 per cent alcohol content. Its appearance resembles beer.

There is also a darker drink, *chicha morada*, made from sweet violet maize called *morado*.

BAIGA   This northern Chinese drink from the Gobi Desert is very strong. It is made from curious ingredients: millet and pigeon droppings. These are mixed together and heated in little metal pots. The mixture becomes very alcoholic with fermentation.

Baiga is better if the pigeons have been well fed. It is the feast beverage that washes down the New Year's *chiao-tzu* or dumplings.

Guide to Ingredients and Utensils

Grains

All grains can be eaten whole, cut up small, or ground into coarse or fine flour. Whole grains keep well over long periods of time if stored in a cool, dry, ventilated place free from rodents. Stored in plastic, they may go mouldy. Whole-grain flour and polenta (maize meal) do not keep well for more than a few days and should be refrigerated. Refined white flours, available at the supermarket, keep almost indefinitely but are not as nutritious and are relatively expensive in a world where white bread is unknown or a luxury. Whole-grain flours have a fuller taste, more appropriate to the simple dishes in this cookbook. Refined flour will do in any recipe calling for flour, but, if possible, use flour that you grind fresh yourself. You can buy good quality whole-grain flours of almost every kind at health food stores, but make sure it is fresh.

Grains are ground in order to shorten the time needed for cooking and to make a softer end product. Grinding small quantities of grain is not difficult. A pestle and mortar—among the first of man's tools—will do the job but with more than a fair amount of hard work, particularly with large grains such as maize. The ideal process uses a grain mill with stone or steel grinders, but a blender or coffee grinder will do the job as long as you supervise the operation carefully. Use small quantities so as not to strain the machine and not to heat up the grain too much by long grinding. It may be necessary to sift flour or meal made in a blender. It will not have as even a texture as if it were ground in a grain mill. You can crush wheat for bulgur by grinding it for a few seconds in a blender or coffee grinder.

Grains can be grown in any garden except the postage stamp variety, but to obtain seeds, and advice on cultivation, you will need to find an agricultural merchant—in the Yellow Pages under 'Corn and Agricultural Merchants'.

Legumes:
Beans, Peas, Soya, Peanuts and Lentils

Beans and peas are the cheapest protein available. Since long before the word 'protein' was known they have formed the basis of most poor peoples' cooking, with grains. Soya beans feed the Chinese, peas and lentils (called *dhal*) replace meat entirely for vegetarian Hindus; Africans depend on the peanut and black-eyed peas; Latin Americans on beans and chickpeas (*garbanzos*); the people of the Middle East survive on lentils and beans; and Europeans and Americans fall back on beans when meat is scarce. Beans, peas and lentils are available in good quality and variety at supermarkets. Raw peanuts (best for cooking) and soya beans can be found in oriental food shops, health food stores, and sometimes supermarkets that have health food sections. Middle Eastern food shops and Indian food shops stock the greatest variety of beans and lentils. Esau sold his birthright for a mess of pottage resembling *ful medames* (see page 185).

Beans, soya beans and peas are commonly reduced to flours and ground in the same way as grains (see above). These flours can be used to enrich breads, soups and puddings.

All beans and whole peas should be soaked overnight, which reduces a long cooking time—anything from 1 to 3 hours or more, depending on the type of bean, and how long it has been stored.

They should also be rinsed and picked over for stems and stones before cooking. For pot cooking allow 3–4 parts water to 1 of beans. Do not add salt until the end, or near the end, of cooking as salt prevents the beans from softening. All beans should be cooked until thoroughly softened, so that they are easy to digest. As a rough guide, allow 45 minutes to 1 hour for split lentils or peas; 1½ hours for other beans, and 2 hours or more for chickpeas and soya beans. For a main meal allow from 50 g (2 oz) of dry beans per person.

Most peas and beans are easy to grow and will enrich the soil with nitrates. A wide variety of different seeds can be obtained from seedsmen such as Thompson & Morgan Ltd., Ipswich IP2 oBA, or just save and plant the beans from your larder (split peas do not grow).

Soya beans, lentils, whole peas and, best of all, mung beans can be sprouted to make a crunchy, delicious fresh vegetable. Soak a small quantity (2–3 tablespoons) overnight and drain. Place in a gauze-covered jar in a warm dark place for 3–6 days, rinsing and draining every day, until completely sprouted.

Milk, Cheese and Curds

Milk from any animal is a rich colloid of fats and proteins. Natural ferments, rennet—an enzyme from calf's stomach—or an acid like vinegar can precipitate most of these particles as curds, which separate from a rich clear liquid called whey. Natural ferments and acids produce a soft curd fairly slowly; this can be drained to make fresh cheeses such as cottage cheese and some ricotta. These cheeses are often salted or enriched with cream. Rennet speeds the curdling process and produces a harder curd that is generally used for aged and cured cheeses. These curds are generally cooked slowly at low temperatures and drained before being used simply, like mozzarella; or they are left to ferment quickly like Camembert, or cure slowly like Emmenthal. Taste and texture depend on the milk, the method of curdling, the kind of cooking and pressing, the cultures used and atmospheric conditions.

Whey can be used in breads or in making whey ricotta or gjetost, a Scandinavian cheese with an unusual taste.

Cheddar cheese is satisfactory when a recipe calls for fresh cheese. Hard cheeses of any kind can be used when grated cheese is called for, although these cheeses come in a wide range of tastes and textures. Where specified use the cheese recommended. Avoid processed and mass-marketed packaged cheeses. Fresh mozzarella picked out of a tub of whey in an Italian food shop makes a better pizza than the plastic-wrapped cheese sold in supermarkets.

The Indians often cook with curds made by natural fermentation —they let milk stand warm for a few hours until it sours. They use it as it is, or drain it in cloth to separate the more solid curds from the whey. Pasteurized milk, which is what the milkman delivers, does not sour naturally— it only spoils. It can be soured by adding some acid such as vinegar or lemon juice—about 1 tablespoon per 300 ml (½ pint)—and letting the mixture stand for 10 minutes or so. (Soured milk should thicken to about the consistency of buttermilk.) This procedure is adequate for making sour milk to use in baking but is not suitable for making curds, since they will be too sour. The simplest procedure for making your own curds is to add 1 tablespoon of buttermilk to 300 ml (½ pint) of boiled milk and leave it to stand at room temperature until it reaches the approximate consistency of yoghurt. This mixture is identical to 'clabbered milk' (see Drinks and Desserts section). To obtain curd suitable for crumbling or frying, drain this liquid mixture through cheesecloth.

Raw milk, available from some health food stores, will sour naturally.

Buttermilk, originally the liquid produced in churning butter, is made nowadays by souring milk with bacterial cultures. It can be substituted whenever curds or soured milk are called for, but it should be added at the last minute because it tends to curdle further and separate if heated too much. Yoghurt, another good substitute for curds and important in its own right in Near and Middle Eastern cooking, is made like buttermilk by adding a bacterial culture to milk and incubating it. The taste and texture depend on the culture used and the conditions of incubation. Yoghurt is a true health food. Its role in the good health of Balkan and Caucasian mountain people led to the discovery of several important vitamins. The bacteria apparently aid digestion too.

All milk products can be made from the milk of any animal that gives milk. The majority of common cheeses and soured milks are made from cow's milk; but sheep and goat cheeses are useful and readily available here in delicatessens, especially Greek goat cheese like feta, and fine French cheeses.

Meat and Fish

The meats available in our butchers' shops are not the same as those that most people eat from time to time. There are animals we do not eat, such as lizards, guinea pigs and turtle doves; animals we do not eat often, such as rabbits and game; and part of familiar animals we do not prize, such as lungs and chicken feet. Even familiar meats are different—our grain-fed beef has a different texture and taste from the meat from the thin cattle slaughtered by the poor; and our broiler chicken is a different bird from the scrawny yard-fed bird familiar to Africans and Italians.

A good butcher can usually supply on request all kinds of offal and soup bones which you may not see in a supermarket. Unusual, cheaper cuts and offal are flavourful once you get to know them. High-class butchers stock game but it is very expensive and really only qualifies as people's meat if you hunt it yourself.

The kind of fish cooked by different peoples depends on what is plentiful off nearby shores. The British tend to confine their taste to a fairly narrow range of fish, but almost all fish and sea animals

are edible and eaten somewhere. A Greek fishing village dines on
whatever they catch that day. Small fish, dried or fresh, can be
used to enrich a soup or season a sauce.

There is little reason to be shy about eating every soft part of
seafood. Fish cheeks generally have a taste finer than that of the
fillets, and the Chinese prize fish eyes.

If you live in a city with a Chinese community you will find
that Chinese food shops sell a far wider and more exotic assortment of fresh seafoods, including eels and sea cucumber, than the
average fishmonger. Japanese shops also sell fine seafood for their
raw fish luxuries. Italian food shops always sell *bacalao* (dried cod),
but Chinese ones offer a far greater variety of dried fish. Fish that
you catch yourself taste best because they are absolutely fresh.

Animal Fats and Vegetable Oils

Animal fats and vegetable oils account for much of the taste and
character of different nations' foods. They are also an important
element in nutritition—fat is a concentrated form of energy for
people who do not overeat.

Olive oil is vital to Italian, Spanish, Greek and Middle Eastern
cooking. It is much more expensive than other cooking oils, but
has the finest flavour, and without it Mediterranean dishes lose
much of their character. Note that the olive oils of different nations
have different tastes. Olive oil does go stale when exposed to air
so buy it and store it in small bottles.

Peanut oil does not have a strong taste but is generally the best
choice for frying, especially Chinese foods. Other light vegetable
oils can be substituted freely.

Ghee, either clarified butter or a substance made from coconut
and other vegetable oils, is an important component in many of
India's regional cuisines. When we refer to *ghee* in the recipes in
this book, we are talking about the product which is sold under
that name in Indian food shops—it is also more widely used

among the average people in India than butter. Fine and rich, it gives body to the lively spices of curries. If this type of *ghee* is unavailable, you could substitute a mixture of coconut and peanut oils, or plain peanut oil; or indeed that other form of *ghee*, clarified butter.

Sesame oil is more truly a flavouring than a cooking oil because it is so strong and so expensive. Use it sparingly, but it is especially good in Chinese food and also in some Middle Eastern and Mexican dishes.

The animal fat most commonly used in cooking is *pork fat*, either in the form of *lard* or *bacon fat*. In Mexico, South America, and Europe it is the most inexpensive and consequently most popular frying medium. Lard is rendered fresh pork fat and is available in most supermarkets or at your butcher's, or use that left over from cooking bacon or other salt pork.

Many peoples, especially Moslems and Jews, have dietary laws against eating any part of the pig, thus mutton or lamb fat and chicken fat take the place of lard in their cooking. Hindus cannot eat any animal fats and replace them with *ghee* or oil. Here many people use margarine or oil in place of lard or any other animal fat because it is lighter, keeps well and does not burn as readily. Also, being low in, or entirely free from, cholesterol, it is considered more healthy. However, lard and bacon fat, and indeed chicken and lamb fats, have their characteristic tastes and should be used if called for to better approximate the taste of certain dishes.

Recipes from pastoral areas such as the Middle East and central Asia often call for mutton or lamb fat. Mutton is not commonly available in Britain, but what we call lamb is much older than what a shepherd generally chooses to call lamb. With either mutton or lamb, simply use the dripping from roasts or chops, or render pieces of fat cut from the meat or bought from your butcher. To render fat, chop it into small pieces and heat it over water, occasionally mashing until most of the fat has melted. Strain out the membranes and fibres.

Chicken fat, obtained by skimming soups, collecting dripping or rendering the pieces of fat generally found along the backbone, is often used in Eastern European cooking, particularly by Jews whose dietary laws prohibit the use of lard and milk products such as butter with meat dishes.

Suet, rendered beef fat, is common in British cooking, usually in prepared, packeted form.

Butter varies in taste according to the breed and diet of the animal that supplies the milk. However, because it is perishable and subject to strong health regulations, there is relatively little variety available in the West. Clarified butter, melted butter from which the sediment has been removed, is also good for general cooking purposes because it does not burn as readily.

Spices and Herbs

Spices and herbs are what give food shops, except for supermarkets which are scented at best with aerosols, their characteristic smells. Together with cooking oils, spices and herbs also supply much of the characteristic national flavour to dishes. Historically used as preservatives they are employed most freely in the cooking of tropical areas such as India, Mexico, Africa, and the Middle East where foods spoil most readily and where most of the sharpest-flavoured spices happen to grow. Using spices and herbs well is a question of experience and imagination. You learn what harmonizes and what the dishes should taste like, remembering that on native tables some exotic blends are as familiar as salt and pepper.

Herbs are unquestionably best when fresh and are generally easy to grow on the borders of gardens or in window boxes. Thyme, marjoram, mint, tarragon, basil, parsley, sage, rosemary and dill should be standard garden herbs. Fresh coriander, also known as *cilantro* or Chinese parsley, with its highly distinctive, somewhat

bitter flavour, is important in Indian, Mexican, and Chinese cooking, and should be available in shops selling their foods. It is also
worth cultivating, as is *epazote*, a Mexican herb. Both can be
grown in a warm, sheltered spot; coriander seed is widely available
but *epazote* may be hard to find.

Spices, like herbs, are best when fresh, but the freshest you can
usually get them is 'fresh' from the store. They lose their fragrance
over time and in the air, especially when ground, so it is best to
buy spices whole and in small quantities. Indian food shops, which
have a good turnover in spices, are probably the best suppliers. In
addition, their stores are exciting places to visit; you will never
smell more variety. Other sources of supply are health food stores,
delicatessen shops and, surprisingly, Boots the Chemist.

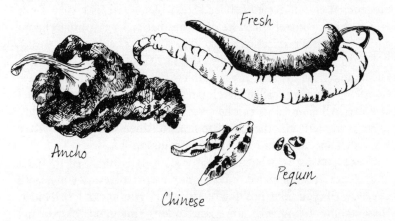

For maximum freshness, grind whole spices each time you need
them. The traditional tools for this are a pestle and mortar. These
can be bought at specialist kitchen shops or from Culpeper Ltd, 21
Bruton Street, Berkeley Square, London W1X 7DAX. (Details are
available on their price list, which also gives the addresses of their
other shops, and mail order prices of herbs and spices.) They come
in a fine assortment of shapes and materials. You can grind large
quantities with less effort in a coffee grinder or a blender, but most
whole spices are soft and easy to crush by hand.

One of the most important spices is hot pepper, the usually dried fruit of *Capsicum* bushes. The hottest pepper is *cayenne*, a small red pepper, usually powdered, and used, for instance, in African cooking. It also serves well for Indian curries, although Indians generally prefer hot fresh green peppers. The Mexicans are the greatest experts on hot peppers, called *chilis*, which can be ground, used whole or prepared for *molé* (see page 247). Seeds and inside membranes should always be removed before use; they are too fiery even for Mexicans to eat.

Mexican *chilis* vary greatly in taste, ranging from the sweet *ancho chilis* to very hot, tiny red *pequins*. Any of the hot *chilis* are appropriate in recipes calling for powdered chilis. Commercial chili powder is a blend of ground hot peppers and cumin or oregano; it is not recommended. Such blends are not very fresh and you can control the taste of dishes better by crushing chosen *chilis* with other spices yourself. The Chinese make their dishes hot with fresh hot green peppers (sold in Chinese food shops) and with ginger. They also use a milder spice, not related to these *Capsicum* peppers, called Szechuan pepper, which has overtones of anise. All *Capsicums* can be grown from the seeds fairly readily in your garden, but they tend to cross-fertilize so that results are unpredictable, and your *anchos* may come up hot.

Curry powder is a blend, usually stale. It is not used in India and is not recommended. Make your own curries starting with cayenne (if you like hot food), turmeric, cumin, and coriander, then adding fenugreek, anise, cardamon, cinnamon, cloves and ginger as desired and as appropriate. The blend should match the dish. Some of the spices have a bright, sweet aroma, such as cardamom, cinnamon, cloves and ginger. Others are slightly sour, such as turmeric and fenugreek. Cumin and coriander have solid, full tastes. You do not need to use much, no more than 1 or 2 tablespoons of ground spice blend in a dish for four people, to get a distinctive but still delicate taste. Indians generally fry the spices when they begin cooking, which develops the flavours—but be careful not to burn the spices as they may get bitter. For

Malaysian curries add lemon grass (*sereh*) to the seasoning, if you can get it.

Saffron, the pistil of the crocus flower, is important in Spanish cooking and is used in almost every other country as well. It is expensive, so use it sparingly—3–4 pistils for a dish—and grind or soak it first, using the liquid, so that the taste and colour are distributed throughout the food. Pistil saffron is preferable to the powdered variety, which is often adulterated.

Garlic is a critical part of many dishes. Use fresh garlic, which has a finer flavour, or cloves from a dried garlic bulb, rather than garlic powder. Its characteristic taste need not overwhelm a dish—it often serves to enhance the other tastes. Usually it is browned whole or chopped in oil in the pan before adding the other ingredients; sometimes it is chopped finely and added at the very end of cooking.

Ginger is also much better fresh, or at least dried whole, rather than powdered. Two or three thin slices give a fine edge to many Chinese and Indian dishes and practically any fish. The succulent roots can be bought at oriental food shops and delicatessens. The only problem is their tendency to go mouldy and spoil. To preserve a ginger root, scrub the skin with a stiff brush and store submerged in dry cooking sherry in a cool place. It should keep well for weeks.

Special Products

Soy sauce is made from soya beans fermented in water, aged and mixed with sea salt. There are three kinds available: thin, stocked by most supermarkets and on the table in Chinese restaurants; thick, which is stronger, heavier and less salty and available mainly at oriental food shops; and tamari, which has less salt and a stronger soya flavour and is available at health food stores and Japanese food shops. Quality varies according to the quality of the mash and length of time aged, so it is worthwhile to experiment.

Thin soy sauce is what is most commonly used and is appropriate for the recipes in this book. Soy sauce should be added shortly before cooking is done, as too much heat affects the flavour. A similar concentrate is *miso* paste, made from fermented soya beans and barley, and used in much the same way.

Tahina, or sesame paste, can be made by crushing hulled sesame seeds in a pestle and mortar and adding a little sesame or olive oil to give it the desired consistency. It is bottled, and available at Middle Eastern and Indian food shops.

Coconut cream, the concentrated extract of coconut flesh, can be used as a substitute for coconut milk when thinned with water (see Basic Stocks and Sauces). It is available canned, bottled or frozen in Indian food shops.

Water chestnut powder is used by the Chinese instead of cornflour to thicken soups and sauces.

Peanut paste or butter, made by crushing plain roasted peanuts, is used as a flavouring and cooking medium in Africa and other regions. Commercial peanut butter is crushed peanuts mixed with hydrogenated peanut oil and tends to have a more cloying taste than the natural paste.

DRIED FOODS
Dried mushrooms, used extensively in European and Asian cooking, are available in far greater variety and are often more fragrant

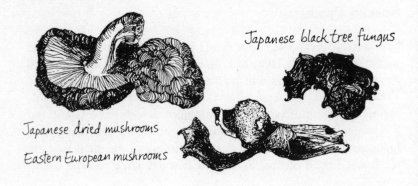

Japanese black tree fungus

Japanese dried mushrooms

Eastern European mushrooms

than fresh mushrooms. The most aromatic dried mushrooms come from eastern Europe, with the Italian ones not far behind. Use them in dishes of appropriate nationality. Chinese and Japanese mushrooms tend to be more delicate. Some, like Japanese black tree fungus, are prized mainly for their texture. Prepare dried mushrooms by soaking them until soft. If the mushrooms are cut or broken up, soaking for 30 minutes may suffice, but soaking overnight does not hurt. Use the liquid in which they soak, too. Italian and sometimes Japanese dried mushrooms are available in good delicatessen shops, but the best selection and quality can be found in Italian, Chinese and Japanese food shops. Dried mushrooms have a different texture and should not be substituted indiscriminately for fresh ones.

Most people who depend on fish have developed techniques for preserving them since they spoil quickly. The most common method is drying. Dried fish, like dried mushrooms, do not completely replace fresh fish but have characteristic tastes and textures that are good in their own right.

Cod, formerly one of the most plentiful seafish, is one of the most common dried fish. Also known as *bacalao*, dried cod is often sold in Italian and Oriental food shops or delicatessens. To use dried fish soak it in cold water overnight or, depending on size, for a few hours, changing the water from time to time. Drain, add cold water to cover, heat to a boil and simmer gently for 15 minutes. Drain, saving the stock for use in sauce. Fry the fish or cook in a sauce. Oriental food shops stock many other kinds of dried seafoods prized for their more concentrated taste. All are prepared by soaking thoroughly, which may take as little as 20 minutes for small shrimps or overnight, depending on thickness and toughness of the fish.

Like Portugal, Japan is a maritime country and a great consumer of fish. Since transportation and conservation are crucial problems, drying is a useful, if unvarying, way to treat fish. Cleaned, dried *bonito*, a variety of tuna, are opened like books to dry gently in the sun; they can be seen strung on cords in the markets ready for sale. These bonito, known as *katsuobushi*, are grated and added to soups and sauces for flavour, body, and to give a lovely yellow colour. The dried fish is also used for fish sausages.

Dried meats, such as jerky or *charqui*, can be: 1) crushed and used as a flavouring and enriching agent in sauces; 2) eaten plain and salted; 3) cooked in sauce; 4) eaten as a salad with oil and vinegar like Swiss *Bundenfleisch*. Dried meats can be found in some delicatessens. The finer raw hams, like *prosciutto crudo*, are basically dried and salted pork with a concentrated taste and tough texture that necessitates thin slicing.

Dried seaweeds are vital components of Japanese soup stocks and stews, serve as flavouring agents in rice dishes and are often used as garnishes. There are three main varieties of Japanese dried seaweed available in oriental (and some health or natural foods) shops: *kombu* or kelp, which is used in stock and for flavouring; *nori* or laver, used for wrapping *sushi* and as a garnish; and *wakame*, a lobe-leafed seaweed used as an ingredient in soups and stews.

Irish moss or *carrageen* is a dried seaweed used by New Englanders, the Welsh and the Irish. It can be found in health food stores.

Utensils

The most useful foreign utensil called for in this book is the famous oriental *wok*. Made from heavy iron, it is a wide, round-bottomed pot with handles. The *wok* is well adapted for sautéing or Chinese stir-frying, deep frying and boiling rice. It can be fitted out with bamboo trays and a high cover for steaming. *Woks* can be obtained from kitchen supply stores and from Habitat. Choose an iron *wok*, usually sold coated with grease to prevent rust (stainless steel or aluminium woks are not as satisfactory) and get a wok ring as well—this is essential to support the wok on a Western stove. 35 cm (14 in) is a good size.

To prepare a wok for use, remove the protective grease with detergent and dry well. Then carefully wipe on a thin coat of cooking oil, heat for 10 minutes in a 200°C, 400°F or gas 6 oven, wipe with a damp cloth, dry, wipe on another thin layer of oil, and heat again. You can then cook in the wok, which will blacken after repeated use. Never wash a seasoned wok, or any other iron pot, with detergent. Simply brush out, rinse with hot water, then dry quickly with a towel or over heat. When cooking in a wok, use wooden utensils such as chopsticks or tongs instead of metal spoons or forks which may scratch the seasoned surface. Use a wire mesh ladle for deep frying.

Chinese and Japanese cooks also pride themselves on their good knives, which are usually heavy, rectangular, very sharp steel implements. Hold the vegetable or meat to be cut with your knuckles and cut by chopping gently, pivoting the knife forward from the heel of the blade, guiding it with your knuckles. Do not chop hard or saw. Like woks, these knives are useful for all kinds of cooking.

Other oriental utensils of note are Chinese clay soup pots for slow, even cooking and Japanese iron pots, used for the same purpose. Note that clay, unlike metal, does not impart a metallic taste to the food. It is, however, fragile and susceptible to cracking if heated or cooled rapidly. Clay pots also must be seasoned because otherwise they will give a clayey taste to the food. Heat them gently with oil or fill them with a mixture of 2 parts water to 1 part vinegar and heat gently until the liquid boils away. Clay pots should generally not be used over an open flame.

Useful South American utensils include the molcajete, a large, rough stone mortar good for grinding grains, beans, chilis and spices; the comal, a flat, seasoned iron or clay griddle for cooking tortillas or pancakes; and the wide deep clay dishes used for paellas.

A tortilla press, like an Italian pasta machine, saves hand labour and produces a more even product.

The Indian *tawa* (or *tava*), a concave iron disc, is recommended for cooking flat Indian breads.

Electric appliances, such as blenders, should be used according to instructions. In particular, when blending pastes such as *hummus*, be sure there is enough liquid so that the blades do not get stuck. In grinding grains, take care that the grains and the blender do not heat up too much.

RECIPES

Unless otherwise indicated, most of the recipes in this book will yield about four servings. We have not usually specified the number of servings because (1) most of the dishes do not easily divide themselves into categories such as starters, main meals or side dishes, and so on; and (2) it is in the nature of most simple foods to be easily and almost infinitely expandable. Leftovers from almost any recipe in this book will be good the next day, or usable in new, equally delicious dishes—bread or grain puddings, refried beans and so forth.

Imperial equivalents for metric measures are given throughout—always use either one or the other, never a mixture of both. A metric teaspoon and tablespoon hold 5 ml and 15 ml respectively; their Imperial equivalents are fractionally bigger.

BASIC STOCKS AND SAUCES

Tomato Sauce

The following is a basic recipe for tomato sauce. Vary the spices and vegetables to match the other tastes in the recipe in which it will be used. For a stronger tomato taste you may want to add tomato paste, in which case simmer the sauce for longer than you would otherwise.

> 1 carrot
> 1 onion
> 1 celery stalk
> 2–3 cloves garlic
> Salt, pepper, thyme, and basil
> 500 g (1 lb) tomatoes (use canned Italian plum tomatoes if fresh tomatoes are too expensive or unavailable)
> Vegetable oil

Chop the carrot, onion, celery, garlic, and herbs, and brown in oil. Add the chopped tomatoes and simmer very gently for 40 minutes. Add salt and pepper. Strain and purée or liquidize. Makes about 2 cups.

Stock

Stocks contribute mightily to the character of dishes. There are two ways to approach the use of stock: one is to make a standard tasty stock (see below) wherever stock is called for, using familiar vegetables that may not be a part of every country's cooking; another is to make a simpler stock that can be flavoured to harmonize with a particular recipe.

STANDARD MEAT STOCK

    1 chicken, cut up, or 2 kg (3–4 lb) chicken backs, necks, and
       feet or 2 kg (3–4 lb) short ribs of beef
       or 2.5 kg (5 lb) marrow and knuckle bones
    2 stalks celery
    1 large carrot
    2 onions
    2–3 cloves garlic
    1 small turnip
    2 bay leaves
    6–8 peppercorns
    4 cloves
    A pinch of whole mace
    Marjoram or thyme
    4 litres (6 pints) water

Cut up the vegetables; the onions and garlic can be left whole.
Put all the ingredients into a large, heavy stock pot. Add water
to cover. Bring to a boil slowly and leave to simmer gently and

evenly without interruption for 2½ hours. Drain carefully.

Store in the refrigerator, protected by the fat that solidifies on the surface, or freeze. Skim the fat before using. If you want to store stock in the refrigerator for a long time, boil it up every few days.

This standard stock is good for European, East European, and Mexican recipes. For Middle Eastern, African, and Asian recipes make a simpler stock using only the meat, adding, if desired, a few vegetables or spices that will match those of the planned dish or will at least mingle well with the taste of that country's cooking.

Vegetable stocks should also be varied according to the nationality of the cooking you wish to approximate. Here is a standard recipe:

STANDARD VEGETABLE STOCK

3 stalks celery
2–3 onions
2 carrots
1 turnip
1 parsnip
2–3 cloves garlic
1 bay leaf
6 peppercorns
1 pinch mace
Thyme or marjoram
3 litres (5 pints) water

Chop the vegetables; the onions and garlic may be left whole. Put all the ingredients into a heavy stock pot. Add water to cover. Bring slowly to the boil and simmer for 1½ hours. Drain and use. Vegetable stock is generally not kept, but if you need to store it, freezing is the best method.

Other vegetables, such as cabbage, leeks, cauliflower, chickpeas, and grains such as wheat and barley, can be used for stock, as well as other spices, but cooking times vary. Note, too, that starchy vegetables, like potatoes, peas and beans will thicken stock considerably.

Coconut Milk

In many Third World cuisines, coconut milk serves the same function as stock does in Western cooking—as the base for soups, stews and main dishes. It is an essential ingredient in south-east Asian, Pacific, and some African and South American cooking, and if you are at all interested in the food of these regions, you should learn how to make and cook with this extremely versatile and tasty milk. Making it is neither difficult nor expensive and will prove rewarding.

Coconut milk is made by soaking grated fresh coconut flesh in water and pressing it through cheesecloth to extract the flavour, nutrients and oils from the pulp. The first step in this process is opening the coconut. Puncture holes in two of the three 'eyes' of the coconut by hammering an ice pick or screwdriver into them; extract the liquid sap inside (this is *not* coconut milk but almost pure water; it can be added to the soaking water or served as a drink as it is); then pound the shell of the coconut with a hammer or the back of a cleaver, constantly rotating the shell until it cracks. A messier way is to start off with the cracking process right away, keeping a bowl nearby to catch the liquid as it spills, although sometimes you may be fortunate enough to remove the cracked outer shell without actually breaking the inner nut.

Pry off the coconut flesh from the hard shell by inserting a screwdriver between the two. Take the inner flesh, cut or break into pieces, and peel off the brown skin with a vegetable peeler. Now either grate the flesh or put it through a vegetable chopper or grinder (easier), or use a blender (see complete blender instructions below). There are three methods of soaking:

Soak the grated flesh in 500-750 ml (about 1 pint) water and coconut sap for an hour at room temperature.

Pour 500-750 ml (about 1 pint) boiling water and coconut sap over the grated flesh and leave for 20 minutes.

Pour 500-750 ml (about 1 pint) cold water and coconut sap over the coconut flesh and bring just to the boil, remove from heat, and leave for 20 minutes.

The blender method is as follows :

Place whole pieces of peeled coconut into the blender along with 500-750 ml (about 1 pint) water and coconut sap (heated or not). Blend at high speed for a minute, then scrape down sides of blender, and blend again. Press through the cheesecloth, as below.

The last part of the process involves pressing the coconut/water mixture through cheesecloth. You will want to squeeze hard, since the last drops are the richest ones, so a double or triple layer of cheesecloth is essential. Discard the remaining coconut pulp— it is now tasteless and without nutrient value. Coconut milk keeps for about five days if it is covered and refrigerated.

Coconut milk, like fresh cow's milk, separates if it stands for a while, and a rich coconut cream rises to the surface. You can skim and save this to use as a flavouring in soups and stews or to make sweets. Or mix the cream back into the milk.

You can make a thinner version of coconut milk using dried grated coconut bought in supermarkets, but you will have better results buying canned or frozen coconut cream (available at Indian, Filipino and some oriental stores) and thinning it with water.

When cooking with coconut milk, heat gently and leave the pot uncovered, otherwise the milk may curdle.

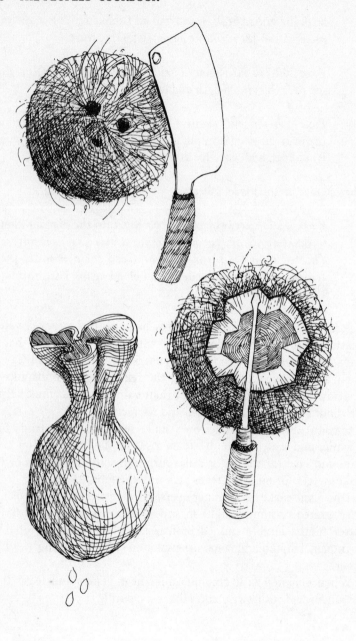

BREADS AND PANCAKES

Indian Breads

Contrary to some Western assumptions, India is by no means strictly a rice-eating country. The use of cereal grains varies considerably according to available water: rice is the grain of wet regions, while wheat and millet are the staples of dryer areas. Indian curries are served with rice in some places and with breads in others.

These Indian breads, like most breads from the Third World, have little in common with Western breads. There are three main types: *chapatis*, *parathas*, and *pooris*. There are also breads made from peas and beans.

Indians use two kinds of wheat flour: *atta* or whole wheat flour; and *maida* or white flour. In the south breads are made out of rice. Both Moslems and Hindus make whole wheat *chapatis* with only slight differences. Both cook the rolled thin cakes on a *tawa*, a gently curved pan without a handle; Hindus use the *tawa* convex side up, and Moslems use it convex side down.

The most common stove, the *enghati*, is portable so that *chapatis* and other dishes can be prepared as easily on the road as in the house. The fuel can be coal, charcoal or dung. The fire is fanned with the aid of a leaf from the versatile palm tree, cut with the handle about 60 cm long and the leaf about a metre long, then folded like an accordion, bent over, tied back on the handle. Modern stoves, particularly electric stoves, do not perfectly replace the traditional *enghati* since *chapatis* must be grilled, in part, over an open flame. An open gas burner will serve the purpose, however.

Wheat Chapatis

> 250 g (8 oz) *atta* (whole wheat) flour
> Approximately 250 ml (½ pint) water
> Salt

Mix and knead into a firm dough. Leave to stand for ½ hour. Divide into 6–8 egg-sized pieces and roll out thinly. Cook quickly on both sides on a hot ungreased *tawa* or heavy griddle over a high flame. Then grill quickly on both sides over an open flame, using tongs, so that the *chapatis* puff up.

Rice Chapatis

> 250 g (8 oz) rice flour
> Approximately 250 ml (½ pint) boiling water
> Salt

Follow the recipe for wheat *chapatis* above but use boiling water, and leave to stand for 1 hour. Divide into egg-sized pieces and roll out thinly between folds of linen or other clean cloth. Cook as above.

Parathas

> 500 g (1 lb) *atta* (whole wheat) flour
> 250 g (8 oz) *ghee* (see page 38) or butter
> Salt
> Approximately 250 ml (½ pint) water

Mix the flour, salt, and a tablespoon of *ghee* or butter with enough water to make a firm dough. Knead and leave to stand for ½ hour. Divide and roll out, as with *chapatis*.

Brush each cake with melted *ghee* and fold over on itself. Brush with *ghee* again and fold over once more into a quarter circle. Roll out thinly (pancakes should retain the triangular shape), and cook on an ungreased *tawa*, or thick griddle, over a high flame.

Stuffed Parathas

Uncooked *parathas*
Cooked, diced vegetables—one kind or mixed (zucchini, celery, cauliflower)

Place vegetables or other filling on a *paratha*. Cover with another *paratha* and pinch the edges closed. Cook several minutes on both sides.

Dhal Bread

Dhal, a general name for several varieties of peas and beans, is used in India in many ways: dry, whole, cracked, milled, etc. *Dhal* is often used in breads, mixed with spices and condiments, minced onions and peppers, or even *asafoetida*, one of the strongest and strangest of the Indian spices. The method is the same as for *chapatis*, using flour and *dhal*, and mixing in the other ingredients.

200 g (8 oz) *dhal* (or dried split peas)
100 g (4 oz) flour
Salt, pepper
1 teaspoon anise
½ teaspoon cumin
Approximately 250 ml (½ pint) water

Soak the *dhal* for 6 hours, drain thoroughly, and mash. Add the *dhal* to the other ingredients and work into a firm dough. Roll small pieces of dough very thin and fry.

Dosa
Rice and Dahl Pancake

This very popular south Indian dish is served all over India.

750 g (1¾ lb) rice
400 g (1 lb) *urid dhal* (white, unshelled *dhal*—see page 310)
Salt

Soak both the rice and *dahl* for about 3 to 4 hours. Wash well and blend in a mixer (or mash in a *molcajete* or other stone mortar) until very fine. Add water to make the paste the consistency of milk.

Leave the dough overnight to rise (or add 1 teaspoon yeast). Add salt to taste. Make a very thin pancake on the griddle or *tawa*. Serve hot with chutney (see below).

Coconut Chutney

100 g (4 oz) shredded fresh coconut
2–4 fresh or dry, soaked hot chilis
1–2 slices fresh ginger
½ teaspoon salt
250 ml (½ pint) yoghurt

Mix the coconut, chilis, ginger and salt together with the yoghurt in a blender, or mash the dry ingredients first in a mortar and add to the yoghurt.

Pooris

250 g (8 oz) *atta* (whole wheat) flour, or *dhal* flour (see page 310) mixed with white flour
Approximately 250 ml (½ pint) water
Salt

Knead together into a firm dough, divide, and roll into thin discs, slightly smaller than *chapatis*. Roll even thinner.

Deep fry in very hot fat, basting the top side when the *poori* floats. Fry for only about 30 seconds, turn and fry for a further 30 seconds. Serve hot.

Khasta Pooris

250 g (8 oz) *atta* (whole wheat) or *dahl* flour (page 310)
50 g (2 oz) butter or *ghee* or oil
Approximately 250 ml (½ pint) curds (see 'Ingredients') or yoghurt
Salt

Mix and knead into a firm dough. Roll out and cook like *pooris* above.

For less rich *khasta pooris*, reduce the amount of butter and mix water with the curds or yoghurt.

Malay Bread

300 g (10 oz) flour
1 egg
Approximately 75 g (3 oz) lamb fat
Salt, water
Lamb fat or margarine to fry

Make a hole in the mound of flour. Break the egg into the hole and work it into the flour. Add salt, moisten with a little water and knead into a firm dough. Divide into 3 pieces. Roll out into thin discs.

Brush the discs with melted lamb fat. Stretch the dough even thinner by hand until transparent. Fold and refold the edges into the centre. Roll out into a long rectangle. Roll up the band of dough on itself, then roll out thin again.

Cut into 15 cm (6 in) discs and fry on both sides in hot fat or margarine.

Chinese Breads

The Chinese cook the greatest variety of breads, using many grains in different ways: baked in ovens, steamed, grilled in pans, browned in oil, or braised. The breads take many shapes, from large loaves to *brioches*, and are even stuffed with widely varying ingredients: pork, soya noodles, dates, etc.

The peasants in the regions bordering the Gobi Desert eat large, round and flat wheat loaves called *gaokwei*. Little more than 2.5 cm (1 in) thick and almost 45 cm (18 in) in diameter, sometimes sprinkled with *colza* oil (coleseed oil, common in northern China), this bread needs very little cooking. First the peasants mix up a big pile of dung and straw on the bare ground. They fire the pile so that it smoulders overnight. The next morning they put the dough into special moulds that fit together and close tightly. The moulds are then slid into the cinders and buried. Cooking takes about an hour, and one oven can cook seven loaves. The principle is not unlike that behind the French *pain de mie*.

Man T'ou
Chinese Steamed Rolls

It is in this very filling form that wheat most often takes the place of rice in northern China.

500 g (1 lb) flour
15 g (½ oz) fresh yeast
400 ml (¾ pint) warm water

Mix the yeast with the water. Add the flour, kneading into a firm dough. Divide into approximately 16 pieces and shape into balls. Leave to rise for 40 minutes until they feel light. Arrange on a metal or bamboo steamer that fits into a pot or wok. The Chinese use a cauldron fitted into a sort of stove built into the ground with an opening at ground level for feeding the fire. Whether using such a stove or an ordinary cooking stove, the pot, cauldron, or wok should be tightly covered. Steam for 20 minutes.

VARIATION   Stuff the dough balls with dried pork or ham and minced garlic and steam as above.

Chinese Pancake

250 g (8 oz) flour
Salt
Approximately 180 ml (6 fl oz) water
Sesame oil
Garlic shoots or spring onions

Mix the flour, salt, and water. Knead. Divide and roll out into large, thin pancakes. Brush with sesame oil. Cook on both sides on a heavy griddle. Wrap around garlic shoots or spring onions and eat.

Rice Pancakes

These are a Chinese speciality.

> 125 g (4 oz) rice or rice flour
> 125 g (4 oz) wheat flour
> Approximately 125 ml (¼ pint) water
> Salt

Soak the rice for 12 to 36 hours, changing the water from time to time. Drain and dry in the sun or in a low oven. Then mash the rice.

Add the wheat flour and salt. Moisten slowly with the water to make a dough that can be rolled. Roll thin, cut into 20-cm (8-in) discs, and steam for 5 to 10 minutes.

(Prepared rice pancakes may be bought in oriental groceries. They must be moistened before use with beaten eggs or a sprinkling of water.)

The pancakes may be stuffed and rolled and sautéed in oil in a heavy frying pan.

Latkes
Potato Pancakes

These pancakes are a traditional treat at Hanukah, the 8-day Jewish festival of lights.

> 500 g (l lb) potatoes.
> 1–2 onions, chopped
> 1–2 eggs
> 1 carrot, grated
> Salt, pepper
> 1 teaspoon baking powder
> Vegetable oil

Grate the raw potatoes coarsely and mix with the onions, eggs, carrot, salt, pepper, and baking powder. Fry on both sides in a little vegetable oil.

Serve hot with apple sauce or sour cream. Potato pancakes are usually served directly from the pan on to waiting plates, so each batch is different. The best is the one currently being eaten and the worst is the one when you have eaten too many.

Manioc Pancakes

These large pancakes, made in all manioc countries from South America to Oceania by way of Africa, take the place of bread, sopping up sauce and filling stomachs. Manioc is also commonly known as cassava or yuca.

Some types of manioc have roots that can be eaten directly after roasting. Others require additional preparation of the roots which would otherwise be poisonous. After preparation the roots are grated and left to ferment, then pressed. The pulp is used for large cakes.

The juice yielded by pressing manioc drops a sediment of starch grains, used familiarly as tapioca.

75 g (3 oz) manioc meal
125 ml (¼ pint) water
2 tablespoons vegetable oil
Salt

Mix the manioc flour, water, oil and salt into a thick batter and pour carefully on to a thick griddle over a medium-high heat. The pancake should be about the size of a water lily leaf. Brown on both sides. Africans and Jivaro Indians of the Amazon cook these on an earthen plate supported over the fire on three carefully chosen stones.

Buckwheat Flapjacks

These are an old American favourite.

125 g (4 oz) sifted white or whole wheat flour
500 g (1 lb) buckwheat flour
1 teaspoon salt
1 tablespoon dried yeast
1 litre (1¾ pint) warm water (40°C or 110°F)
3 tablespoons dark brown sugar
1 teaspoon bicarbonate of soda
1 tablespoon vegetable oil

Combine the flours and salt. Dissolve yeast in warm water; dissolve 1 tablespoon sugar in remaining water; cool to lukewarm. Add liquid mixtures to flour, stir well and leave to rise (several hours or overnight) at room temperature. Make sure the bowl is large enough to handle the batter doubling in bulk.

When ready to cook the pancakes, knock down the batter and add the remaining sugar, soda and oil. Blend and bake on a lightly greased hot griddle. Brown on both sides, turning only once. Serve hot with butter and honey or black treacle.

Yufka
Nomadic Turk Pancakes

125 g (4 oz) plain flour or fine semolina
About 250 ml (½ pint) water

Mix the flour with water by hand on a worktop to make a batter. Cook on an ungreased heavy griddle or frying pan. In Turkey these fine flour pancakes are prepared on an earthen disc heated on the coals of an open fire. In Iran they put the batter into an oven which is little more than a hollow in a stone, heated red hot. The pancakes cook almost instantly.

Taguella
Millet Pancakes

These flat cakes of millet, or less often wheat, replace bread in parts of the Sahara.

250 g (8 oz) millet flour
About 250 ml (½ pint) water
Salt

Mix flour, water and salt to make a firm dough. Knead well. Divide and flatten into thin pancakes. Grill on both sides on an ungreased heavy griddle.

Ethiopian Indjera
Millet Pancakes

These large grey cakes are made not with wheat flour but with a flour made from *teff*, a kind of millet peculiar to Ethiopia. The *teff* is harvested by sickle and laid in stacks which are protected from the 'evil eye', and perhaps the wind, by cattle hides draped over stakes. The harvest is threshed by treading oxen, and winnowed in the air in the ancient manner.

Indjera is the Ethiopian national dish.

250 g (8 oz) millet flour
½ tablespoon yeast or baking powder
875 ml (1½ pints) water

Mix the flour, raising agent and water to make a semi-liquid paste. Allow to stand for one hour if using yeast. Cook in a heavy, ungreased frying pan. The cakes will rise as they cook, and bubbles will burst on the surface.

Indjera are enjoyed most when torn up and dipped in a pot of wot (see page 186) placed in the midst of the diners.

Mexican Tortillas

This staple of Mexico is eaten at every meal. A man going off to work in the fields may eat 25 for breakfast. Since most households are well-populated the cook has to prepare more than a hundred at the start of each day. At other meals fewer tortillas are eaten if other foods, such as vegetables and sometimes meat in a sauce, are available.

The maize meal is usually milled the evening before because fresh meal does not work as well. If the cook has a hand mill, she does not have to work as hard as when she has to grind the grain on a *metate*, a rectangular millstone with a roller. The dry grains of corn are boiled with lime before milling. Even those who can afford to buy ready-ground meal prefer to make sure of the quality by grinding it a little more themselves on their *metate*.

> 250 g (8 oz) *masa harina* (fine maize meal)
> 350 ml (12 fl oz) warm water
> Salt

Mix the *masa harina* and salt with enough water to make a dough that can be shaped into a ball. Knead until it is no longer sticky; at least 5 minutes. Divide into a dozen equal pieces and leave for 20 minutes.

Flatten the pieces into pancakes either by slapping them between your palms, Mexican-style, which is difficult and takes practice, or with a rolling pin on a table dusted with flour, or with a tortilla press. Trim the edges. Cook on both sides on a *comal*, a flat earthen plate, or in a heavy, ungreased pan.

The poor use simple tortillas like the ones above. It is possible to make richer tortillas using half wheat flour, half maizemeal flour, egg, oil, salt and water. These tortillas are cooked in the same way as the plain ones.

STUFFED TORTILLAS These can be found in almost any Mexican market. Women prepare them sitting on the bare ground next to a small market stall on which they have set out bowls with dough and cooked stuffings—tortilla sauce, minced peppers, and sometimes mixtures of vegetables. They brown the tortillas on small stoves, little more than simple sheets of metal propped over a fire on three rocks. They are often eaten with pieces of grilled pig skin and the maize beer *chicha*.

Here is one suggestion for tortilla sauce:

Tortilla Sauce

Epazote, also known as Jerusalem oak or wormseed, can be found fresh or as a seed in some Italian delicatessens.

  1–2 hot, fresh or dried, chili peppers
  1–2 chopped onions
  1 kg (2 lb) tomatoes, chopped
  Epazote to taste
  Salt and pepper
  Lard or oil

Remove stems and seeds from chili peppers, and, if using dried ones, soak in a little hot water for 30 minutes. Chop.

Sauté the onions in lard or oil. Add the tomatoes and chilis. Simmer for 5–10 minutes and season to taste. Since the sauce should be smooth, mash it in a pestle and mortar or a *molcajete*— the typical Mexican stone or baked earth mortar–or purée in a blender.

Tacos

These stuffed meat tortillas can be served as a main dish.

  750 g (1 ½ lb) lean chopped beef
  2 chopped onions

2–3 tomatoes, cut up
2 cloves garlic
Crushed chilis
Seasoning to taste : coriander, oregano, cumin, basil, salt
Prepared tortillas (see page 74)
Grated Cheddar cheese

Sauté the meat. When it is pale all over add the onions and leave to soften; add tomatoes, garlic and chilis. Season to taste.

Cook the tortillas, stuff them with the meat and sprinkle with grated cheese. Serve as they are or heat briefly under the grill to melt the cheese before serving.

Chilaquiles
Cheese Tortillas

12 tortillas
100 g (4 oz) grated Cheddar cheese
Seasoning (thyme, basil, oregano, chili)
1 egg, beaten
450 ml (¾ pint) tortilla sauce (see page 75)

Spread the tortillas with cheese. Fold over on themselves, coat with egg and fry. Serve hot with tortilla sauce.

VARIATION   Alternate layers of tortilla sauce, fried tortillas and cheese in a casserole. Top with cheese and bake for 30 minutes at 175°C (350°F) or Gas 4 until the cheese has melted.

Arab Leavened Bread

25 g (1 oz) fresh yeast
450 ml (¾ pint) warm water

Salt

1 kg (2 lb) fine semolina

Mix the yeast with the water. Add the salt and semolina. Knead into a supple but firm dough.

Shape into 2 or 3 flat cakes. Dust with flour, cover with cloth, and leave to rise in a warm place.

Once the loaves have risen, cook them over medium heat in a *tadjin*, or grooved, heavy-bottomed pan (an ungrooved heavy pan will do, but won't produce the pattern typical of this bread), pressing the dough down firmly so that it takes on the pattern of the pan bottom. Cook on both sides for approximately 20 minutes.

You may also bake in oven for 35–40 minutes at 175°C (350°F) or Gas 4. When done the bread will make a hollow sound if tapped on the bottom.

Arab Unleavened Bread

When there isn't much time, this bread is quickly kneaded and cooked.

4 tablespoons oil

up to 250 ml (½ pint) water

500 g (1 lb) semolina

Salt

Beat the oil with some of the water and mix with the semolina and salt. Knead, moistening the dough as necessary to make it supple. Shape into a ball.

Roll out to about 1 cm (½ in) thick. Cook in a heavy frying pan over a medium heat for about 15 minutes, or bake for 20–30 minutes at 175°C (350°F) or Gas 4. This bread is absolutely delicious when served still warm.

Matzah
Jewish Unleavened Bread

Jews eat matzah at Passover. It became the wafer of Christian communion by way of the Last Supper which was a passover *seder* (ceremonial meal).

Matzah, made properly, must not rise at all. This is insured by a ritual procedure involving careful selection and storage of whole wheat flour to keep it dry. Wild yeasts begin to grow wherever they find nourishment, such as in damp flour. Once the flour is mixed with pure, cold spring water, the kneading and rolling must proceed continuously—the whole process, including baking, should take little more than 20 minutes.

> 350 g (12 oz) whole wheat flour
> 225 ml (8 fl oz) water

Mix the water and flour and knead thoroughly. This is best done by dividing the dough into tennis-ball-sized pieces and kneading each steadily for 1–2 minutes. Then roll thin on a clean, dry board—ritually it is wrong to sprinkle the dough with flour, and as a consequence, lifting the rolled dough from the board may be a delicate operation. Wrap the dough around a rolling pin to lift the dough. Score the dough with parallel cuts and perforate the cuts. Then slide dough into a 300–400°C (600–800°F) brick oven and bake for 2–3 minutes. Or bake on a baking sheet in a very high oven.

The matzah should be crisp and light.

Blintzes
Pancakes Stuffed with Cheese

An important dish in Jewish dairy cooking, blintzes are very popular.

PANCAKES:
3–4 eggs
250 ml (½ pint) milk
125 g (4 oz) flour
Salt

FILLING:
500 g (1 lb) Cheddar cheese, grated, or dry cottage cheese
1 egg
1 tablespoon melted butter
1 teaspoon grated lemon peel

To make the pancakes, beat the eggs with the milk and mix in the flour and salt. Pour a couple of tablespoons of the batter on to a medium-hot buttered griddle and spread to make a very thin pancake. Cook until bubbles appear on the top. Remove from heat and stack, cooked side up, separating the pancakes with greaseproof paper.

To make the filling, mix the cheese, egg, butter and lemon peel. If desired, add a tablespoon of sugar.

Place a few tablespoons of the filling in the centre of the pancake, cooked side up. Fold the sides in over the filling and roll to make a cylinder. Fry in butter on both sides, or bake for 10–15 minutes at 175°C (350°F) or Gas 4 to brown.

Serve hot with sour cream or dusted with sugar and cinnamon.

SWEET BLINTZES   Replace the filling with the following:

500 g (1 lb) apples, peeled, cored and grated
2 tablespoons sugar
1 egg
½ teaspoon cinnamon

Mix together and fill pancakes. Cook as above.

Serve hot with sugar and cinnamon or sour cream.

Pizza

> 15 g (½ oz) fresh yeast
> 250 ml (½ pint) lukewarm water
> 375 g (12 oz) flour
> ½ teaspoon salt
> 4 tablespoons olive oil
> 50 g (1 lb) chopped, peeled ripe tomatoes
> Oregano, salt, pepper
> Optional: chopped garlic, crushed dried red pepper
> 250 g (8 oz) mozzarella cheese

Mix the yeast with the water and leave to froth for 5 minutes. Then mix with the flour and salt. Knead for 8–10 minutes. Cover with a cloth and leave to rise away from draughts for 2–3 hours until it triples in volume. Punch down and divide into 2 even balls. Leave to rise under a cloth for another 1–1½ hours.

Preheat the oven to 240°C (475°F) or Gas 9. The hotter the oven the better.

Stretch and press each ball to make a thin, rimmed disc 25–30 cm (10–12 in) in diameter. Brush with olive oil to within 1 cm (½ in) of the rim. Spread each crust with chopped tomatoes, sprinkle with oregano, salt, pepper and chopped garlic and crushed dried red pepper. Grate or chop the mozzarella cheese and sprinkle generously over the tomatoes.

Pizzas should be baked on hot stone—if you have a good flat, heat-resistant stone, or a *comal* for a small pizza, preheat the stone along with the oven, dust it with corn meal, slide the pizza in, and bake at the highest temperature your oven will reach for 20–25 minutes until the crust is browned. If you have no flat stone, use a lightly oiled baking sheet and bake on the lowest shelf.

Proja
Yugoslavian Maize Bread

Traditionally this is served with *kajmak* sheep's milk cheese (see page 231).

> 500 g (1 lb) maize meal
> 375 ml (12 fl oz) milk
> 2–3 eggs
> 150 g (5 oz) lard
> Salt

Mix the maize meal with a little of the milk and the eggs. Beat until smooth; add the softened lard and salt. Mix well, then add the rest of the milk. Pour into a greased square or rectangular baking tin and bake for ½ hour at 175°C (350°F) or Gas 4. Cut into squares and bake for another ½ hour.

Usually served hot, *proja* is also very good cold.

Hush Puppies

Hush puppies are one of the Virginia colonists' adaptations of native American cuisine. They are considered especially good with fried fish.

> 350 g (12 oz) maize meal
> 1 teaspoon baking powder
> 1 teaspoon salt
> 125 ml (¼ pint) milk
> Seasonings (optional): basil, chives, parsley

Stir together the maize meal, baking powder and salt, pressing out lumps. Add seasonings if using. Beat together the eggs and milk, then stir into the dry ingredients, forming into balls about

2.5 cm (1 in) across. Cook in hot deep fat, until golden brown. Drain on kitchen paper and serve hot.

Spoon Bread

This bread is another American creation.

> 175 g (6 oz) maize meal
> 750 ml (1¼ pints) milk
> 1 teaspoon salt
> 2 tablespoons butter or margarine
> 4 eggs

Cook the meal in milk until thick—about 5–7 minutes after it comes to a boil. Add the salt and butter and cool to lukewarm. Meanwhile separate the eggs. Beat whites until stiff and yolks until creamy. Stir the yolks into the lukewarm mixture; fold in the whites. Pour into a large greased baking tin and bake in a 175°C (350°F) or Gas 4 oven for 35 minutes, until firm and slightly brown. Serve hot.

Hominy Bread

Hominy is dried, hulled sweet corn kernels and was first introduced to Virginia colonists by Indian women who used ashes and water to remove the skins. Hominy grits—broken pieces of dried hominy—can be bought commercially, or prepared at home by soaking dried whole sweet corn kernels in bicarbonate of soda and boiling for 6–10 hours.

> 375 g (13 oz) cooked hominy grits
> 1 tablespoon butter
> 2 eggs, beaten
> 500 ml (a scant pint) milk
> 150 g (5 oz) maize meal

While the grits are still hot stir in the butter. Add the eggs, stirring rapidly to prevent bits of cooked egg from forming. Gradually stir in the milk and maize meal. Place in a greased baking tin and bake at 175°C (350°F) or Gas 4. This 'bread' is really a savoury pudding.

Boston Brown Bread

This classic steamed bread is usually served with baked beans.

>   500 ml (a scant pint) buttermilk
>   175 ml (6 fl oz) black treacle
>   200 g (7 oz) raisins
>   250 g (8 oz) rye flour
>   125 g (4 oz) whole wheat flour
>   150 g (5 oz) maize meal
>   2 tablespoons bicarbonate of soda
>   1 teaspoon salt
>   2 tablespoons brown sugar
>   2 tablespoons butter, softened

Beat together the buttermilk and treacle; add the raisins. Stir together the flours, the bicarbonate of soda, salt and brown sugar and add to the first mixture. Beat in the softened butter. Pour into greased 500 g (1 lb) coffee tins or similar containers, filling no more than ⅔ full. Cover with foil and tie with string. Steam for 2 hours in a large pan; cool for 10 minutes before removing from the tins. Makes 2 loaves.

Sally Lunn
Old American Bread

This was a common bread in England and in early colonial

American kitchens. It is coarse in texture, as it only rises once, but when eaten fresh it is tender and moist.

15 g (½ oz) fresh yeast
500 ml (a scant pint) warm milk
4 eggs, well beaten
4 tablespoons butter
500 g (1 lb) white flour

Mix the yeast with a little of the milk and leave to froth for 5 minutes. Add the eggs and butter to the flour and beat well; add the milk and the milk mixed with yeast gradually and beat out any lumps. Place it in the pan in which it will be baked and leave to rise for about an hour. Bake in a moderate oven 175°C (350°F) or Gas 4 for about 40 minutes, or until it is crusty and brown. Brush the top with melted butter and serve warm.

Sally Lunn

Salt Risin' Bread

STARTER:
500 ml (a scant pint) milk
250 g (8 oz) white flour
1 tablespoon maize meal
1 teaspoon salt

Stir together all the ingredients and leave them to rise for about 24 hours (covered with a towel and left in a warm place). The batter should be light and bubbly, with a light crust on the surface. Stir in :

1 tablespoon margarine
1 teaspoon sugar
500 g (1 lb) flour

Knead the flour into the mixture; knead thoroughly until the dough is smooth. Divide into 2 small loaves and leave to rise until almost double in bulk. Bake in a 175°C (375°F) or Gas 4 oven for about 45 minutes, or until brown on the top.

Oatmeal Bread

Early American housewives believed that bread to which oatmeal had been added would keep longer, and they might have been right.

500 ml (a scant pint) milk
250 g (8 oz) rolled oats
2 tablespoons honey
1 tablespoon salt
2 tablespoons butter or margarine
2 tablespoons yeast

125 ml (¼ pint) warm water
750 g (1½ lb) white flour

Scald the milk (by bringing just up to boiling point). Stir in the oats, honey, salt and butter. Remove from the heat and cool to lukewarm. Dissolve yeast in warm water; place in large bowl. Add the milk mixture and the flour to the yeast. Beat vigorously with mixer or wooden spoon, scraping the sides, until the batter is smooth. Stir in as much flour as you can, then turn the dough out on a floured board and knead in the remaining flour (adding as necessary). Knead until the dough is smooth and silky; about 10 minutes. Place in a lightly greased bowl; turn dough over to grease the top.

Leave to rise, covered, in a warm place until doubled in bulk; about 1 hour. Punch down and let rise again until nearly doubled; about ½ hour.

Divide the dough into 2 parts, shape into loaves and place on a baking sheet or in greased loaf tins. Leave to rise until almost doubled; about 1 hour. Bake in moderate oven 175°C (375°F) or Gas 4 for about 40 minutes. Cool slightly before removing from the tins.

Austrian Sourdough Rye Bread

This is a firm bread with a crisp crust. It is a staple of the Tyrol.

STARTER:
125 ml (¼ pint) milk
125 g (4 oz) white flour
15 g (½ oz) fresh yeast

Stir all the ingredients together in a crock or jar and leave, uncovered, at room temperature for 3–5 days: it should be frothy and taste sour. Cover and refrigerate until ready to use (within 10 days or it may degenerate). To replenish the starter, do not wash the container which it was kept in; simply add equal parts of flour and milk and leave to stand at room temperature without a lid while bread is first rising. Cover and refrigerate until ready to use again.

BREAD:
250 g (8 oz) rye flour
250 g (8 oz) white flour
250 g (8 oz) starter (see above)
2 teaspoons salt
500 ml (a scant pint) water

Stir these ingredients together in a large bowl. Cover with a cloth and leave to stand in a warm place, overnight or for about 8–12 hours. At the end of this time add:

125 g (4 oz) rye flour
125 g (4 oz) white flour
1 teaspoon bicarbonate of soda

Knead together the original bread batter and the 3 new ingredients until the dough looks silky. Form a large round loaf and place on a floured baking sheet. Leave to rise, uncovered, until doubled in bulk; about 2–3 hours. Bake at 190°C (375°F) or Gas 5 for about 45 minutes.

Yorkshire Oatcakes

Although Scotland is thought of as the land of oats, these cakes have long been a traditional staple in the north of England.

1 teaspoon sugar
1 tablespoon yeast
500 ml (a scant pint) milk or buttermilk
40 g (1½ oz) oat flour

    1 teaspoon salt
    125 g (4 oz) porridge oats

Dissolve the sugar and yeast in lukewarm milk. Stir in the flour, salt and oats. Stir gently and leave in a warm place for 30 minutes. Stir again and cook on a griddle or in a large heavy frying pan as you would a large pancake. Cut into wedges or *farls*, and eat buttered while still warm.

Bannock
Scottish Oatcakes

In name and form these Scottish cakes curiously resemble *banik*, Eskimo wheat cakes made with leavening and seal fat. Bannocks, however, are served crisp.

    250 g (8 oz) oat or barley flour
    250 ml (½ pint) soured milk (see page 36) or buttermilk
    1 teaspoon bicarbonate of soda
    Salt

Mix all the ingredients together to make a loose dough. Shape by hand into 6-mm (¼-in) discs. Cook on both sides on a medium hot, buttered griddle, or bake on a greased baking sheet for 10–15 minutes at 200°C (400°F) or Gas 6.

Serve hot with butter or cheese.

To vary the texture, replace half the flour with rolled oats.

BOILED MILLET

This is the staple food of the people of central Asia, central and West Africa, and part of Eastern Europe. Pasternak recounts in *Dr Zhivago* how it saved millions of Russians from starvation in 1917, just before the Revolution. In Sudan boiled millet, together with manioc, is the daily diet, accompanied by a bit of scraggy chicken fried in palm oil. In north China a bowl of millet replaces the bowl of rice eaten in the south, accompanied for the poorest only by braised cabbage. Like rice, millet should be cooked so that the grains remain separate.

Millet Bread

This is good with vegetables and soups, especially borscht.

> 250 g (8 oz) millet
> 500 ml (a scant pint) milk
> Butter, salt, pepper
> 2–3 eggs

Simmer the millet in milk for 10–15 minutes until it thickens. Season and add a nut of butter for taste. Leave to cool.

Separate the eggs. Beat the whites until stiff. Mix the yolks and beaten whites with the millet, then pour into a buttered baking tin. Bake for 20 minutes at 175°C (350°F) or Gas 4 until cooked through.

Sorghum Bread

Although the staple grain in many parts of the world, sorghum is not marketed commercially in the Western world for human consumption. Nevertheless, it is available from many animal feed dealers, at less than a third of the cost of the lowest priced corn. If you buy it from grain dealers, you must be sure that it is free from pesticide residue (if marketed as poultry feed it usually is).

To make flour use a grain or flour mill—many natural food stores will grind it for you.

> 250 g (8 oz) finely ground sorghum grain
> 1 teaspoon salt

500 ml (a scant pint) buttermilk
2 eggs
1 teaspoon bicarbonate of soda

Stir together sorghum flour, salt and milk in a saucepan. Cook over low heat, stirring frequently, for 5–10 minutes or until stiff. Remove from the heat and cool to lukewarm. Beat the eggs and stir into the cooled mixture. Sprinkle the bicarbonate of soda over this and fold in.

Preheat oven to 230°C (450°F) or Gas 8. Place a 25-cm (10-in) oiled skillet or muffin tin in oven for 5 minutes before baking. Pour sorghum mixture into pan; return to oven and bake for 20–25 minutes, or until a skewer inserted in the centre comes out clean. Bake muffins for 10–15 minutes. Split and spread with butter, or use as a base for a creamed entrée.

Tunisian Droo
Buckwheat Bread

250 g (8 oz) buckwheat flour
125 ml (¼ pint) water
125 ml (¼ pint) oil
Salt
1 tablespoon sugar

Mix together the flour, water and oil. Add salt and sugar and mix well. Leave to stand for several hours.

Turn into a greased heavy frying pan or mould. Bake for 20 minutes at 175°C (350°F) or Gas 4.

Bread Couscous

500 g (1 lb) dry bread
3 tablespoons oil

Grate dry bread into small crumbs the size of couscous or cracked wheat. Moisten with cold water and toss with two forks. Moisten more if necessary, but do not soak. Mix in the oil.

Put into a steamer and cook like couscous (see page 104).

This is a very common dish in North Africa, often served with tchakchuka (see page 234).

Aragon Migas
Bread and Sausage Fry

This Spanish dish is often served for breakfast although it can be served with other meals.

Chorizo sausage can be obtained at good delicatessens.

650 g (1¼ lb) bread, dry, cubed
2 cloves garlic, whole
125 g (4 oz) diced bacon
125 g (4 oz) diced ham
250 g (8 oz) diced *chorizo* (Spanish sausage)
Olive oil
2 tomatoes, chopped
Salt and cayenne

The night before moisten the bread lightly with water. Cover with a cloth and leave overnight.

Brown the garlic cloves, bacon, ham and sausage in oil. Remove the garlic and add the bread. Stir, then add the chopped tomatoes and seasoning. Simmer a few more minutes and serve.

GRAIN DISHES

Bulgur

This is a very common (and practical) way to prepare wheat in the Middle East. (You can also buy ready-made bulgur in most natural food and Middle Eastern food shops.)

> Whole grain wheat
> Salt

Wash and pick over the wheat. Boil in abundant lightly salted water. When the grains begin to burst, drain and leave for at least 1 hour. Dry in a very low oven. The grains will harden.

When the dried wheat cools, grind it coarsely. Sealed in a tight box it will keep for many months.

Bulgur, also known as *burghul*, can be prepared hot or cold.

Hot Bulgur

> 500 g (1 lb) bulgur
> 250 ml (½ pint) water

Mix the bulgur with water, bring to the boil, cover and simmer over a low flame, like rice, for about 10 minutes. The liquid should be completely absorbed. Serve with strong grated cheese.

Bulgur can also be used as a stuffing: add herbs and crushed, cooked or fresh vegetables, maybe some minced lamb or mutton, and bind with an egg.

There are many other uses for bulgur:

Cooked in water and served with milk, honey, or raisins, it makes a good breakfast.

Browned in oil, then cooked with water (or stock) as above, it can replace rice pilaf or kasha (see page 100).

It is often served with vegetables or meat, or added to stews. Milled very finely, bulgur can be used in place of flour in brioches, pancakes and other delicacies, or for thickening sauces and soups.

Bulgur Salad

> 250 ml (½ pint) hot water
> 500 g (1 lb) bulgur
> 4 tablespoons olive oil
> Black olives
> Fresh mint and/or basil
> Cumin and anise

Pour the hot water over the bulgur and sprinkle with oil. Mix well. Leave to soak and cool. All the liquid should be absorbed.

Add olives, herbs and spices and serve cool. This is a refreshing dish in hot weather.

Tabooleh
Grain Salad

This cold North African dish is made from bulgur or uncooked couscous.

> 250 g (8 oz) bulgur or couscous (semolina)
> 2 finely chopped spring onions
> Fresh parsley and mint
> 500 g (1 lb) ripe tomatoes
> Juice of 2 lemons
> 6 tablespoons olive oil
> Salt
> Vine leaves or lettuce

Mix the grain, onions, parsley, mint, tomatoes, lemon juice and oil in a salad bowl. Add salt and leave to soak for several hours. Cool.

Serve the *tabooleh* accompanied by a plate of supple vine or lettuce leaves. Each person can then roll some of the preparation on a leaf and eat it whole.

Tibetan Tsampa
Barley Porridge

This dish is the Tibetan favourite. They serve it with strong, rancid yak butter which has been stored in sheep stomachs. It is considered good hospitality to serve butter so strong that the guest gags. Real Tibetan *tsampa* is strong and smelly but, other than that, the dish is not unlike oatmeal porridge.

  100 g (4 oz) barley or whole wheat grains
  500 ml (a scant pint) hot tea
  Butter

Grill the barley or wheat, then grind to a more-or-less fine flour. Mix with hot tea and add the butter.

Turkish Barley

  125 g (4 oz) prunes
  250 g (8 oz) hulled barley
  500 ml (a scant pint) water
  Saffron (3–4 pistils dissolved in 1 tablespoon hot water)
  Salt, pepper
  2–3 sliced sweet peppers
  Oil (olive oil is best)
  Chopped fresh parsley
  125 g (4 oz) sliced almonds

Soak the prunes, then simmer them for 10–15 minutes. Remove stones and chop prunes coarsely. Soak the barley for 1 hour then drain. Add water and cook for 15–20 minutes until all the water is absorbed. Add saffron, salt and pepper. Sauté the peppers in oil.

  Mix all the ingredients together, including the almonds and parsley. Serve hot or cold.

Asink
Crushed Millet Porridge

This is the staple of the Tuareg people of the Sahara.

> 250 g (8 oz) crushed or ground millet
> 750 ml (1¼ pints) water
> 250 g (8 oz) fine millet flour

Boil the crushed millet for 2 hours to make a thick soup. Gradually stir in the flour with a wooden paddle or spoon. (The Tuareg use an *esseroui*, a wooden paddle special to this dish.) Simmer for 20 minutes until firm. Serve hot with milk or butter.

Tibik
Roasted Millet

This is the principal food of *meharists*, desert camel drivers, and is always made from millet.

> Millet
> Dried dates

To cook the millet in the desert, *meharists* pour the crushed, winnowed and washed grain into a large wooden plate, the *tarrahout*, and bury heated stones in the grain to grill it lightly. A more convenient Western method is to shake the millet in a heavy frying pan over a low heat until lightly cooked.

Add dried, stoned dates and grind the mixture to a powder. The powder is eaten as it is.

Millet with Pumpkin

This is a common dish in Slavic countries. Pumpkin is served with grain in most cereal-eating countries. The poor in corn countries such as Spain, Italy and France prepare recipes similar to this with corn instead of millet.

> 500 g (1 lb) pumpkin flesh
> 500 ml (a scant pint) milk
> 5 tablespoons millet or corn meal
> Salt
> 2 tablespoons sugar
> 2 tablespoons butter

Mince the pumpkin and simmer for 20 minutes in the milk along with the millet, salt and sugar. Mash or put through a strainer and serve with butter.

VARIATION   Use proportionately more milk to make a soup.

Indian Millet

Although we usually associate rice with Indian cooking, millet is an equally important staple.

> 1 onion, chopped
> Butter or *ghee* (see page 38)
> 250 g (8 oz) millet
> 500 ml (a scant pint) vegetable stock (see page 57) or hot water
> Cheese

Brown the onion in *ghee* if possible. Add the millet and sauté for 3–5 minutes. Add the stock and simmer for 20 minutes.

Serve with sautéed vegetables or onions, and sprinkled with cheese.

VARIATION   Add a cup of diced vegetables, such as cauliflower, okra or courgettes, or a mixture of these, to brown with the onion. Finish as above.

Millet with Dried Mushrooms

Dried mushrooms are a common feature of Slavic cooking.

15 g (½ oz) dried mushrooms
500 ml (a scant pint) water
250 g (½ lb) millet
1 onion, minced
Butter or vegetable oil

Soak the mushrooms overnight. Drain, saving the water to cook the millet (see page 88).

When the millet is cooked, brown the onion in butter and add the mushrooms.

Mix the millet and mushroom-onion preparation, season well and serve with gravy.

Kasha

Buckwheat groats, known as kasha, are popular among the peoples of Eastern Europe. Kasha is traditionally served with borscht, shchi (see page 140), pork or goose. Plain kasha :

250 g (8 oz) kasha (buckwheat groats)
500 ml (a scant pint) water
Salt
Butter

Pour the kasha into boiling salted water. Add a little butter for taste. Cover and simmer. After 20 minutes the liquid should be completely absorbed. Cooked kasha should be dry and unclumped, like good rice.

VARIATION   First grill the kasha in a dry heavy frying pan over low heat. Beat an egg in quickly and continue to grill, making sure that each grain is separate and coated with egg. Add to boiling water as above. The kasha grains, when cooked, should be firm and separate.

SAUTÉED KASHA   Prepare plain kasha as above. Spread into a buttered pan and smooth over. Allow to cool. Cut into squares and sauté, browning both sides.

ROAST KASHA   Use the same ingredients as for plain kasha. Grill the groats in a dry frying pan, stirring constantly. Pour into a buttered baking tin and add boiling water, salt and butter to taste. Cover and bake at 175°C (350°F) or Gas 4 for ¾ hour.

Kasha with Beef Marrow

15 g (½ oz) dried mushrooms
350 ml (12 fl oz) water
Butter
250 g (8 oz) kasha (buckwheat groats)
125 g (4 oz) marrow from beef bones

Soak mushrooms in the water for at least 1 hour (overnight if possible). Drain, saving the water. Sauté the mushrooms in butter. Cook the kasha in the water. When almost done, spread it in layers in a baking tin, alternating with layers of marrow and mushrooms. Top with marrow.
    Cover and bake for 20 minutes at 175°C (350°F) or Gas 4.

Fettucine al burro
Italian Noodles with Butter

2 eggs
½ teaspoon salt

    1 tablespoon water
    200 g (8 oz) flour
    2 litres (4 pints) lightly salted water
    100 g (4 oz) melted butter
    75 g (3 oz) grated Parmesan cheese

Beat the eggs, salt and tablespoon of water lightly. Gradually mix into the flour. Knead for 10 minutes. Add more flour if necessary, for a firm dough. Leave for at least 1 hour, then divide into 2 pieces. Roll each as thin as possible on a floured board, stretching the dough over the rolling pin. Hang on a line to dry for 20 minutes or so, then roll up into a cylinder and slice diagonally into strips 5–10 mm (¼–½ inch) wide. Shake loose.

Bring to a boil at least 2 litres (4 pints) of lightly salted water. Add the fettucine. These fresh noodles cook almost instantaneously —they are done only 30 seconds to a minute after the water returns to a boil (and they have floated to the water's surface) depending on how thick they are. Be careful not to overcook them. Drain and rinse quickly with cold water. Mix thoroughly with melted butter and about half the cheese. Serve immediately with the rest of the cheese alongside.

Serves 2–3.

Reshta
North African Noodles

These semolina noodles take little time to prepare. They are served with *tchakchuka* (see page 234), and sometimes with chicken or mutton in chickpea soup.

    250 g (8 oz) fine semolina
    125 ml (¼ pint) water
    Salt

Work ingredients together gradually to make noodle dough. Split up into balls and roll out as fine as possible. Dust the roller with flour from time to time. Slice into fine noodles.

Steam and serve with melted butter.

Couscous with Meat

This is a feast version of the classic North African dish. For a simpler meal the meatballs can be eliminated and a vegetable sauce substituted for the soupy meat given here. Cracked millet or wheat may be substituted for store-bought couscous, which is usually semolina. The *harissa* powder called for is hot spice blend, usually available in Middle Eastern stores, but at a pinch you could substitute chili pepper or cayenne.

COUSCOUS:
350 g (12 oz) couscous (semolina)
Salted water
1½ litres (3 pints) water or soaking liquid from chickpeas (see below)
Olive oil

MEAT SAUCE:
1 kg (2 lb) lamb shoulder, cubed; or 1 chicken cut-up
Oil
Seasoning: garlic, basil, cumin, parsley, cayenne
700 g (1½ lb) stew vegetables (carrots, celery, turnip, etc.)
175 (6 oz) dry chickpeas, soaked overnight
1–1½ kg (2–3 lb) courgettes, peppers, tomatoes or other fresh vegetables
Water

MEATBALLS:
500 g (1 lb) minced beef

3–4 cloves garlic, crushed
1 egg
Flour
Oil

GARNISH:
700 g (1½ lb) Spanish onions
100 g (4 oz) raisins
1 teaspoon *harissa* powder

THE COUSCOUS About half an hour before cooking put the couscous into a big bowl and sprinkle with salted water. Aerate by tossing with 2 forks. Pour into the couscous maker—the real one is called a *keskes* or *couscoussière*; but a simple strainer, steamer, or cheesecloth-lined colander which fits closely into a large pot will do. Steam the couscous over boiling water or chickpea stock for 10–15 minutes until the grains swell considerably.

Turn out of the steamer on to a big working plate with a flat bottom—this is called a *kesra* in North Africa. Aerate again by hand, breaking up any clumps. Sprinkle with salted water and a little oil. Return to the colander or *couscoussière* and steam for another ½ hour maximum; 15 minutes should suffice.

To serve, put the couscous in a big serving plate and aerate once more by hand. Add butter to taste.

MEAT SAUCE Cut up the lamb or chicken and brown in oil. Drain and season to taste. Put in a large pot with stew vegetables and soaked chickpeas. Cover with cold water, bring to a boil and simmer for 2½ hours. Skim the foam and excess fat during the cooking process. Add the courgettes, peppers, tomatoes or other fresh vegetables 20 minutes before serving.

MEATBALLS Mix the minced beef with the crushed garlic. Season and bind with an egg. Divide into balls and dust with flour. then brown in oil and drain.

GARNISH   Slice the onions. Sauté and season. Soak the raisins for at least 1 hour, then simmer in a small amount of the meat stock for 15 minutes. Dissolve a very little *harissa* powder in a ladle of stock.

TO SERVE   Shape the couscous into a mound in the middle of a large plate and surround with the raisins and onions. Serve the meat and vegetables in their sauce in a separate bowl, surrounded by the meatballs. Serve the *harissa* in a separate sauce bowl.
   Serves 6–8

Mamaliga
Maize Porridge

Mamaliga, also called *malai*, is the principal dish of poor Rumanians. This solid porridge takes the place of European-style bread, which is eaten only as a dessert or on Saints' days.
   Mamaliga can be eaten hot or cold, usually cut into slices with a wire. The poorest often make a whole meal of it, with perhaps an onion and some wine. If there is a guest, they may enrich the dish with some grated cheese known as *brunza alba*.

   250 g (8 oz) maize meal
   Salt
   1 litre (1¾ pints) boiling water

Stir the maize meal and salt into the boiling water. Simmer for at least 20 minutes until it thickens. Press into a large round bowl previously rinsed out with water. Turn out of the bowl on to a plate immediately.
   Fancy *mamaliga*: Press cooked *mamaliga* into a greased baking tin. Spread with sliced onions, browned first in lard or margarine. Cover with a few lightly poached eggs. Bake for no more than 5 minutes at 175°C (350°F) or Gas 4. Do not overcook the eggs.

Polenta

This solid maize porridge, similar to *mamaliga*, replaces bread and pasta in parts of northern Italy. The basic recipe can be enriched by adding butter, cheese, onions or whatever.

> 250 g (8 oz) coarse maize meal
> 1 litre (1¾ pints) boiling water
> Salt

Stir the maize meal gradually into the boiling salted water. Simmer and continue to stir until the *polenta* is dry enough to come away smoothly from the sides of the pot. Shape into a mound on a serving plate.

Serve hot with Bolognese or Milanese (meat or tomato) sauce, or serve cold.

> VARIATION
> *Cooked polenta*
> 5 tablespoons butter
> 5 tablespoons grated Parmesan cheese

Remove the polenta from the heat and stir in the butter and cheese. Pour into a deep dish, to a depth of about 2.5 cm (1 in). Smooth over and allow to cool.

Cut in squares and sauté in butter.

Another possibility is to lay the squares in a greased baking tin, sprinkle with additional cheese, and bake for 10 minutes at 200°C (400°F) or Gas 6 until brown.

Cooked Hominy Grits

Hominy is treated, soaked, de-skinned sweet corn (maize) kernels, and hominy grits are broken pieces of dried hominy. 'Grits' are a classic dish of poor Southerners, white and black.

1 litre (2 pints) water
1 teaspoon salt
250 g (8 oz) dried hominy grits

Bring the salted water to a boil. Sprinkle in the grits, stirring
constantly, then cover the pan and lower the heat to simmer.
Cook for 10–20 minutes, or until all the water is absorbed (check
quickly and replace lid so that not too much steam escapes). If the
grain is not tender at the end of that time turn off the heat and
leave the pan, covered, for 10 more minutes to complete cooking.

Tamales
Sweet Corn Husks Stuffed with Maize Dough and Meat

The poorest of the poor in Mexico, such as the Tarasques, live
almost exclusively on sweet corn or maize, sometimes cooked as
tortillas, sometimes as *atole*—a simple porridge occasionally mixed
with cocoa. Atole without the cocoa is similar to *polenta*. The
Tarahumaras also eat *pinole*: maize simply grilled and milled.
The Otomis, like the Tarasques and Tarahumaras, cannot often
afford the luxury of pork in their *choclo pastel* (see page 110). They
supplement their diets with lizards, doves, and agave worms.

The husks from the sweet corn are not wasted but used as a
wrapping in which to cook *tamales* (see illustration). They are
prepared for use by cutting off the pointed tips and thick rounded
bottoms. *Tamales*, like *tacos* (see page 75), are good with a wide
variety of fillings, depending on what is available: pork (*cuche*),
chicken, and so on. This Mexican dish is common all over Latin
America.

DOUGH:
500 g (1 lb) maize meal
1 litre (1¾ pints) water
250 g (8 oz) lard

2 tablespoons baking powder
Salt

FILLING:
500 g (1 lb) minced pork
1–2 hot green fresh chilis, chopped; or
   1 teaspoon chili powder and a pinch of cayenne
1 teaspoon allspice
3–4 pistils saffron dissolved in water
1 teaspoon cumin
Lard
1 dozen fresh sweet corn husks
Meat or vegetable stock

Begin the filling by browning the pork and chilis, allspice, saffron, and cumin in lard. Set on one side.

To prepare the dough mix the maize meal with boiling water to make a thick porridge. Allow to cool, then knead in the lard and baking powder. Add salt and roll out fairly thinly.

Blanch the sweet corn husks, drain and dry. Trim as described above. Cut the dough into 12 and lay a piece on each corn husk.

Fill with 1 tablespoon of the pork filling, and fold to make a little packet, being sure the dough covers the meat filling. Fold the sweet corn husks as shown and secure with cotton or fine string.

Lay the *tamales* in a pot and cover with stock. Cover and cook in the oven at 175°C (350°F) or Gas 4, or simmer over a low flame, for about 45 minutes. When done the *tamale* dough should peel easily from the husks which are not eaten.

TAMALES CHIAPANECOS   Add chopped prunes to a reduced amount of pork stuffing and prepare the *tamales* as above.

Humitas or Choclotanda
Stuffed Sweet Corn Husks

These are found all over Latin America. The sweet corn, called *choclo* by the Indians, must be fresh.

    12 ears of fresh sweet corn, with husks
    4 chopped onions
    Lard
    1–2 fresh chopped chilis; or 1–2 dried, soaked chilis; or 1
       teaspoon chili powder
    Suggested seasonings: thyme, coriander, salt, pepper
    500 ml (1 pint) tomato sauce (see page 55)
    250 ml (½ pint) boiling milk

Husk the corn and grate the kernels. Wash the husks and soak in hot water.

Sauté the onions in lard, add the grated sweet corn, herbs and seasonings. Add the tomato sauce and boiling milk. Simmer, stirring constantly, until it thickens to a stiff paste.

Drain and dry the sweet corn husks. Put one or two tablespoons of the paste on each huck and roll closed. Tie with thread if necessary.

Steam or poach for ½ hour. Drain, pat dry, and serve hot. As with tamales you do not eat the husks.

VARIATION   Add grated cheese to the stuffing.

Cheese Humitas

12 ears fresh sweet corn, with husks
1 egg
2 tablespoons lard
Pinch of baking powder
250 g (8 oz) Cheddar cheese, grated
Salt and suggested seasonings: chilis, oregano, thyme

Wash and soak the sweet corn husks. Grate the kernels. Separate the egg and beat the white until stiff.

Mix the grated sweet corn with the softened lard, the egg yolk, the beaten egg white and baking powder. Add the cheese and season to taste.

Put some of the paste on each husk. Trim the husks as for *tamales* and fold to envelope the stuffing. Tie with thread if necessary.

Steam in a strainer or colander for ½ hour. As with *tamales* you eat the stuffing off the husks, not the husks themselves.

Choclo pastel
Sweet Corn and Meat Pie

SWEET CORN:
1 minced onion
8 ears fresh sweet corn
250 ml (½ pint) milk

Salt and pepper
Pinch of chili powder
Suggested seasoning : thyme, coriander, basil, oregano
1 egg
Sugar

STUFFING :
3 minced onions
Vegetable oil
250 g (8 oz) chopped pork
100 g (4 oz) black olives
75 g (3 oz) raisins
2 hard-boiled eggs, sliced
Salt and pepper

To prepare the stuffing brown the onions in a little oil and add the meat. Cook gently for 15 minutes, then mix in the other stuffing ingredients. Spread out in a greased baking tin.

To prepare the sweet corn brown the onions and strip the corn kernels from the cobs. Add them to the pan, with the milk. Season and simmer, stirring steadily. Separate the egg and beat the white until stiff. Remove the corn mixture from the heat; mix in the yolk and beaten white. Pour the mixture evenly over the stuffing and sprinkle with a little sugar. Bake for 15 minutes at 230°C (450°F) or Gas 8 until browned.

Creole Maize with Giblets

500 g (1 lb) giblets
Oil
250 ml (½ pint) tomato sauce (see page 55)
150 g (5 oz) maize meal
Water or stock

Brown the giblets in oil. Wet with tomato sauce, adding water or stock if necessary to cover. Simmer for 10 minutes. Remove the giblets from the sauce and drain. Stir the maize meal into the sauce. adding more stock if desired. Simmer for 15–20 minutes to thicken. Return the giblets to the corn mush and cook, stirring, for another 5 minutes.

VARIATION : Add sautéed onions.

Afghan Kitchiri
Rice and Sweet Corn Porridge

Along with *palao* or *polo*, a variation of *pulao*, this is a staple of Afghanistan, where it is served with strong Afghan *kuruti* cheese (made from dried sheep or goat curds) and chopped or boiled local herbs.

> 125 g (4 oz) rice
> 125 g (4 oz) dried sweet corn kernels
> ¾ litres (1¼ pints) water
> Fresh coriander, parsley and mint
> 125 g (4 oz) dry sheep or goat cheese (Greek *kefalotiri* or
>   *pecorino*)

Boil the rice and sweet corn for 1–1½ hours until they soften to a thick porridge. Mash and mix in the chopped fresh spices. Serve with grated or crumbled cheese.

Rice

Rice feeds a vast part of Asia and much of the rest of the world. Its preparation varies almost as much as do the people over this vast and diverse terrain. When Indians boil rice they use a full pot of boiling water, then drain and dry it in a low oven. The popular Chinese method is to cook the rice in water that will be completely absorbed by the time the rice is cooked. But the result is the same: each grain remains separate and firm. We must add to these simple boiled rices the various methods of frying rice before boiling it: the *pilafs*, *pulao*, *palaos* and other recipes common in the Middle East, India and central Asia.

Indians say rice must be aged at least 5 years before it is good. They like to enrich it with almonds, fried onions or raisins. For festivals they colour it red, green, yellow or brown. When means permit, meat or fish is added to the rice as it is cooked.

In India rice is usually fried first, then boiled and served with meat and vegetables. In China it is boiled first and then fried with meat and vegetables.

Indian Rice

> 250 g (8 oz) rice
> 1½ litres (2¾ pints) water
> Salt

Add the rice to the boiling, salted water. Simmer for 15 minutes until the rice is cooked but still firm. Drain. Rinse with cold water and drain thoroughly. Spread the rice on a baking sheet and dry slightly in a low oven, turning the rice from time to time.

Chinese Rice

> 500 g (1 lb) rice
> ¾ litres (1¼ pints) water
> Salt

Put the rice in the water, add salt and bring to the boil. Cover and simmer for 12–15 minutes until all the water is absorbed. Dry for 10 minutes over a very low heat.

On the subject of Chinese rice: the pigeons of Peking were famous carriers of rice stolen from the Imperial granaries. After careful training, they were justly called 'bearers of life'. The pigeons flew to the granaries, gorged themselves on rice, and upon their return were given a mild emetic so that they would spit up the rice. After washing the rice was sold. One good pigeon could pilfer a good 250 g (8 oz) of rice a day.

Rice and Fish

These comprise the daily meal for many in Asia, from China to Indonesia.

> 350 ml (12 fl oz) water
> 500 g (1 lb) fish—cleaned whole fish or fillets
> 150 g (5 oz) rice
> Suggested seasonings: cardamom, saffron, pepper, garlic

Boil the water. Add the fish, then throw in the rice and seasonings. Simmer for 15 minutes. Mix together and serve.

VARIATION   Add 250 ml (½ pint) more water for a rice and fish soup.

Tibetan Dresi
Sweet Rice

The Tibetans use yak butter in this recipe. Stored Mongol-style in yak bellies it has a strong taste and often has yak hairs in it. Use plain rice or sweet rice, a glutinous variety sold in oriental food shops.

125 g (4 oz) raisins
250 g (8 oz) rice
425 ml (¾ pint) water
2–3 tablespoons butter
1–2 tablespoons sugar

Soak the raisins, preferably overnight. Boil the rice with the water, then cover and simmer for 12–15 minutes until very dry. Put on a serving plate and add the butter. Stir in the sugar and raisins.

Serve with *momos*, large meat-stuffed ravioli not unlike Chinese *chiao-tzu* (see page 242).

Indian Yellow Rice

2 minced onions
Ghee (see page 38) or vegetable oil
1 teaspoon turmeric
1 pinch cumin
250 g (8 oz) rice
Salt
500 ml (a scant pint) water

Brown the onions in *ghee* or vegetable oil. Add the spices and fry for a few minutes. Add the washed and drained rice and salt. Brown for a few minutes before adding hot water, covering the rice not much more than 2.5 cm (1 in) deep. Cover and simmer for 12–15 minutes until all the liquid is absorbed.

Indian Kichri
Rice with Peas

This dish can also be made with fresh peas or diced vegetables.

2 minced onions
Ghee (see page 38) or vegetable oil

Suggested spices: cardamom, cloves, cumin, saffron, cinnamon
250 g (8 oz) rice
500 ml (a scant pint) hot water
250 g (8 oz) soaked dhal (see page 65), split peas or lentils
Salt

This dish lent its name to a different dish—Anglo-Indian kedgeree. It appears that since *kichri* often accompanies fish, the English thought it was a mixture of rice and fish. Actually *kichri*, which means hotchpotch, is rice cooked with *dhal* (peas or beans) not fish.

Brown the onions in *ghee* or vegetable oil and add the spices. Fry. Add the rice and brown it before adding the water. Mix in the *dhal*. Cover and simmer for 30–45 minutes until the *dhal* is cooked.

Pulao
Indian Fried Rice

1–2 minced onions
Ghee (see page 38) or vegetable oil
Suggested spices: curry or cumin, cardamom, turmeric, saffron, cloves, cinnamon
250 g (8 oz) rice
500 ml (a scant pint) hot water
Optional: 75 g (3 oz) raisins, soaked; 50 g (2 oz) almonds
Salt

Brown the onions in *ghee* or vegetable oil. Add the spices, fry, then add the rice. Brown the rice, then add the water. Cover and simmer for 12–15 minutes, until all the liquid is absorbed. If desired, sauté almonds and raisins separately in *ghee* and add them to the cooked rice before serving.

Burmese Rice

1 coconut or 75 g (3 oz) dried, grated coconut
500 ml (a scant pint) water
2 minced onions
Ghee (see page 38) or vegetable oil
250 g (8 oz) rice

Crack open the coconut, grate the flesh and cover with half the water. Strain through cheesecloth to press out the coconut milk. Mix the rest of the water with the coconut pulp and press again. The final squeezes yield the richest milk. You can also make coconut milk in a blender (see page 59).

Brown the onions in *ghee* or vegetable oil. Add the rice and simmer for 12–15 minutes. When all the liquid is absorbed the rice is ready to serve.

Chow Farn
Chinese Fried Rice

5–6 tablespoons peanut oil
1 tablespoon sesame oil
Salt
2 eggs
675 g (1½ lb) cold, cooked rice
1 bunch of spring onions, minced
1 tablespoon soy sauce

Heat the 2 oils together and pour in salted beaten eggs, stirring briskly until cooked. Add the rice. Stir quickly. Heat, adding spring onions and soy sauce just before serving.

VARIATION   Fry bits of ham, bacon or shrimp with the eggs.

Chinese Fried Rice II

A version of the preceding recipe, used by more prosperous Chinese.

    4–5 tablespoons peanut oil or pork fat
    1–2 teaspoons sesame oil
    2 eggs
    500 g (1 lb) cold, cooked rice
    Salt
    125 g (4 oz) cooked, minced pork
    50 g (2 oz) dried shrimps, soaked and drained
    1 teaspoon soy sauce
    1 bunch spring onions, finely chopped

Heat the oil in a wok or frying pan and stir in the beaten eggs. Before the eggs are completely cooked add the rice and salt. Mix in the pork and shrimps. Add the soy sauce and onions just before serving.

If desired chicken or beef may be substituted for pork.

Nasi goreng
Malaysian Fried Rice

Like the Chinese the Malaysians often use cold, cooked rice.

Malaysians who are Moslem never eat pork so their recipe uses chicken. The Chinese in Malaysia, on the other hand, who love pork, use chopped ham and bacon along with the traditional dried mushrooms.

    250 g (8 oz) fresh shrimps, unshelled
    5–6 tablespoons peanut oil
    3 minced onions
    3 sweet red peppers, sliced

Salt
700 g (1½ lb) cold, cooked rice
250 g (8 oz) diced chicken
4 chicken livers
1 teaspoon soy sauce
2 eggs

Boil the shrimps for 5 minutes. Drain and save the liquid. Shell the shrimps, brown in oil and set aside.

Sauté 1 minced onion with the sliced peppers. Season with salt. Add the rice and then the shrimps, chicken and livers. Stir well. Add the soy sauce and some of the water used to boil the shrimps. Stir and simmer for 5 minutes. Stir in one egg and cook for 3–4 more minutes. The rice should be firm and dry.

Beat the remaining egg. Fry, roll up and cut into narrow strips. Fry the remaining onions.

Put the rice on a plate and garnish with strips of egg and onions. If desired, garnish further with sliced cucumber or minced raw spring onions.

Indonesian Rice

2 minced onions
Suggested spices : coriander, cardamom, turmeric
250 g (8 oz) cold, cooked rice
2–3 slightly green bananas or plantains
3–4 eggs

Brown the onions, then add spices as desired, and the rice.

Meanwhile slice the bananas lengthwise and fry in one pan. In another pan cook the beaten eggs as an omelet (it should be quite dry). Cut into strips.

Serve the rice piled on a plate, surrounded by the bananas and egg strips.

Mexican Rice with Frijoles
Rice and Beans
This is the daily food of poor people in Mexico.

> 250 g (8 oz) red, black, or pinto beans
> 1–2 minced onions
> 250 g (8 oz) rice
> Salt
> Bits of dried meat or a bone
> ¾ litre (1¼ pints) water
> 1–2 dried or fresh chilis, or chili powder

Soak the beans (*frijoles*) overnight; then simmer for 2–2½ hours in plenty of *unsalted* water. Drain. Brown the onions. Add the rice, beans and salt. Remove seeds and stems from chilis. (If using dried chilis, soak for 20 minutes in warm water.) Chop and add with the meat to the rice and beans. Add water, bring to a boil, cover and simmer for 12–15 minutes. There should be enough water so that there is some gravy after cooking, naturally thickened with starch from the beans.

Rice and Tomato

This is another of the daily foods of Mexico.

> 250 g (8 oz) rice
> Oil, lard or butter
> Salt
> Suggested spices: chili, saffron, cumin, garlic
> 2 chopped onions
> 500 g (1 lb) tomatoes, chopped

Fry the rice. (Mexicans use lard for frying because oil and butter are too expensive.) Add salt and spices, then the onions and tomatoes. Pour in water to cover. Cover and simmer for 15 minutes, as with any pilaf.

This rice can be enriched with some cubed dried or salted meat, bacon or ham, with fresh cooked corn in season or sautéed chicken livers.

Moors and Christians
Rice and Beans

This is the name the Cubans give their daily meal : rice and beans.

> 250 g (8 oz) black beans
> 2 chopped onions
> 1–2 dried or fresh chilis, or powdered chili
> 250 g (8 oz) rice
> 125 g (4 oz) diced ham
> Garlic, salt
> 500 g (1 lb) chopped tomatoes

Soak the beans overnight, then simmer for 1½–2 hours in plenty of *unsalted* water.

Brown the onions. Remove stem and seeds from the chili. (If using dried chilis, soak for 20 minutes.) Chop and add to the onions. Add the other ingredients, including the beans, and water to cover. Bring to the boil, cover, and simmer for 12–15 minutes. Add more water, if necessary, so that some liquid is left as gravy when cooking is finished.

In Haiti this dish is served, whenever possible, with a fish or meat sauce.

Spanish Spring Rice

> 500 g (1 lb) fresh spring vegetables (cauliflower, peas, artichoke hearts, etc.)

¾ litre (1¼ pints) water
125 g (4 oz) diced ham
Vegetable oil or lard
250 g (8 oz) rice
Suggested seasonings: garlic, salt, pepper, saffron

Gently boil the vegetables in water for 7 minutes. Drain, saving the water. Brown the diced ham in lard or oil and add the rice. Season (remember that spices are not generally used heavily in Spanish cooking).

Add the water saved from cooking the vegetables. Bring to a boil, then add the vegetables. Simmer for 15 minutes until the liquid evaporates or is absorbed. Dot with butter and finish drying in the oven, at the lowest setting.

Arroz a la Cubana
Rice with Garlic

Despite the name this is a Spanish dish.

250 g (8 oz) rice
2 cloves garlic, whole
2 cloves garlic, crushed
Olive oil
Salt
Suggested seasonings: bay leaf, saffron

Gently cook the rice with the whole garlic cloves and an abundance of water in a covered pot for 12–15 minutes. Drain and rinse in cold water.

Fry the minced garlic gently in oil. Add the rice. Cook, stirring, for a few minutes. Season.

Serve with: fried eggs, fried tomato slices and sliced *chorizo* (Spanish sausage).

Turkish Pilaf

Rice is the staple of Middle Eastern countries. They cook it in large round copper pots, called *djindjeres*. The rice is often soaked a short time in heavily salted water before being cooked with lots of butter or mutton fat.

The poor often eat no more than rice with perhaps some olives and raw onions.

    1–2 onions, chopped
    Oil, butter, or lamb fat
    Suggested spices : saffron, cumin, cinnamon, dill
    Salt
    250 g (8 oz) rice
    500 ml (a scant pint) boiling water
    100 g (4 oz) sliced almonds
    100 g (4 oz) prunes, soaked and stoned

Brown the onions in oil, butter or lamb fat. Add the spices, salt and rice. Brown, then add the water. Cover and simmer for 12 minutes. Fry the almonds and prunes separately and mix in with the rice.

Serve garnished with hard-boiled eggs cut in half.

Greek Pilaf

With bread, rice is the staple of poor Greeks. Like bread it is often served with fat black olives and *feta* or goat cheese.

    3 tablespoons butter, lamb fat or olive oil
    1¼ litres (2¼ pints) boiling water
    Salt
    250 g (8 oz) rice, preferably long grain

Melt the butter. Add the boiling water and salt. Add the washed and drained rice, carefully turned to avoid clumps.

Cook on a high flame for 5–10 minutes until most of the liquid boils off, then cover the pot tightly and simmer gently for a further 8–10 minutes.

Press the rice into a salad bowl then quickly turn it out on to a plate. Serve sprinkled with melted butter.

This pilaf is often served with one of the following sauces:

GLAZED TOMATOES
500 g (1 lb) tomatoes; or
a 396 g (14 oz) can of peeled tomatoes
1 tablespoon sugar
Butter

Peel the tomatoes and boil gently in a little water; canned tomatoes will just need heating. Add sugar and butter to taste. Simmer gently to reduce, occasionally basting the tomatoes.

PEAS AND HAM
100g (4 oz) ham
100 g (4 oz) fresh peas
Olive oil or butter

Cube the ham and sauté with fresh peas in olive oil or butter. Serve mixed with the pilaf.

Risotto
Italian Pilaf

Rice is to the northern provinces of Italy what pasta is to the south. It is prepared in a different way from the Asian, American and Middle Eastern methods and almost never served alone.

1 minced onion
15 g (½ oz) butter
250 g (8 oz) short-grained (Piedmontese) rice
350 ml (12 fl oz) white wine and 750 ml (1¼ pints)
    water, or 1 litre (1¾ pints) stock
Salt and pepper

Brown the onion in butter in a heavy frying pan. Stir in the rice.
Add the wine and simmer, stirring until it is completely absorbed.
Then add water gradually. (If using stock, add bit by bit, stirring
constantly.) Season and simmer, stirring, for another 15–25
minutes.

Risotto in Salto
Italian Rice Pancakes

500 g (1 lb) cold, cooked *risotto*
1–2 beaten eggs
Breadcrumbs
Oil

Shape the *risotto* into thick pancakes and dip in egg and breadcrumbs. Fry on both sides until golden, taking care when turning.
Use a moderate flame.

Serve with butter and cheese.

Suppli
Rice and Cheese

This is another excellent use for cold *risotto*

2 eggs
500 g (1 lb) cold, cooked *risotto*

350 g (12 oz) mozzarella cheese
Breadcrumbs
Oil

Mix the eggs into the rice. Then put large spoonfuls of rice in your hand and shape them into balls around small pieces of mozzarella. Be sure the rice envelopes the stuffing. Dip in breadcrumbs and fry in oil.

The melted cheese stretches into long strings as the ball is bitten into–which is why the dish is called *suppli al telefono*.

VARIATION Replace the mozzarella with mortadella sausage or ham.

Risi e bisi
Venetian Rice and Peas

1 chopped onion
Butter
125 g (4 oz) ham
500 g (1 lb) fresh peas
1 litre (1¾ pints) stock or water
500 g (1 lb) rice
Salt and pepper
Grated Parmesan cheese

Brown the onion in butter. Add diced ham, then the peas, and brown. Add water or stock to cover. Pour in the rice, season, and add the rest of the liquid. Cover and simmer for 15 minutes. Do not stir.

Serve with butter and grated Parmesan cheese to taste.

SOUPS

Soup is a less widespread way of preparing food than many a Westerner might think, having grown up imagining good health depended on how many bowls of soup he could swallow without flinching. The greater part of the world's population lives in tropical climates where our familiar kinds of soup are perhaps too hot and take too much cooking. China, however, knows soup well, if without the same Western psychological savour. The Chinese serve soups throughout a meal whenever it has more than one course.

Mulligatawny
Indian Lentil Soup

This is a soup from southern India. Its name means 'pepper water' in Tamil. The name applies to a soup made from black pepper and tamarind, taken as a remedy for indigestion. The following version is more filling.

> 250 g (8 oz) lentils, soaked split peas or *dhal* (see page 65)
> 500 ml (a scant pint) water
> 3 minced onions
> 2–3 cloves garlic, chopped
> Bay leaves
> *Ghee* (see page 38)
> 1–2 tablespoons curry spices, such as turmeric, fenugreek, cayenne, cumin, cloves
> 2 litres (1¾ pints) meat stock
> 200 ml (7 fl oz) thick coconut milk (see page 58)

Cook the lentils (or peas or *dhal*) for 30 minutes in the water with one of the onions and some bay leaves. Put through a strainer or food mill.

Brown the remaining onions and the garlic in *ghee*. Add curry spices and fry for a few minutes. Add the lentils and stock, season and simmer for 5–10 minutes. Add the coconut milk at the last minute and serve with a side dish of Indian rice (see page 113).

Mulligatawny with Meat

 2–3 tablespoons curry spices, e.g. turmeric, fenugreek, cayenne, cumin, clove
 Ghee (see page 38)
 1 kg (2 lb) cubed lamb
 1½ litres (2¾ pints) water
 700 g (1½ lb) stew vegetables such as, celery, carrot, cauliflower
 250 g (8 oz) lentils, soaked split peas or *dahl* (see page 65)
 125 g (4 oz) crushed almonds or walnuts
 3 minced onions
 2–3 cloves garlic
 Salt and pepper
 250 ml (½ pint) thick coconut milk (see page 58)
 1–2 lemons

Fry half the curry spices in *ghee*, then add the meat. Add the water and stew vegetables and simmer for 2–2½ hours. Add the lentils, *dhal* or peas, and almonds. Brown the onions and garlic with the rest of the spices and add to the meat.

 Simmer for 20–30 minutes until the lentils are cooked. Season, add coconut milk and serve with lemon slices.

 Serves 6–8.

Indian Fish Soup

 1 kg (2 lb) non-oily fish such as cod or coley
 Oil, preferably *ghee* (see page 38)
 675 g (1½ lb) vegetables such as akro, cauliflower, celery, carrot

2 tablespoons curry spices
Salt

Bone the fish and cut into chunks; fry in oil. Add the vegetables,
very finely chopped, and curry spices. Salt. Add water to cover
and simmer for 5–10 minutes.

Malaysian Soup

500 g (1 lb) fish fillets
500 g (1 lb) shrimps, shelled
Vegetable oil
2 minced onions
2 tablespoons curry spices such as fenugreek, cayenne,
    turmeric, cumin
Salt
250 ml (½ pint) coconut milk (see page 58)
Lemon

Cut fish and shrimps in pieces and sauté in oil. Add minced
onions and curry spices. Add water to cover, and salt. Simmer
for 10–15 minutes. Add the coconut milk shortly before serving
with quarters of lemon.

Burmese Soup

500 g (1 lb) fish trimmings such as skin, head and bones
1 litre (1¾ pints) water
2 minced onions
2 cloves garlic
Oil or *ghee* (see page 38)
2 chopped carrots
250 g (8 oz) chopped cabbage

Salt
Coriander

Bring the fish trimmings and water to a boil. Add one onion. Reduce the heat and simmer for ½ hour. Reduce to thicken. Put through a strainer or food mill.

Chop the garlic, brown it in a little oil or *ghee*, and add the strained fish stock. Add the other ingredients and simmer for 5–10 minutes.

Thai Shrimp and Courgette Soup

Dried shrimps can be bought at oriental markets.

> 75 g (3 oz) dried shrimps
> 1 tablespoon star anise or Szechuan pepper (see page 42)
> 3–4 shallots or spring onions
> 1 small, fresh hot chili, chopped, or ½ tablespoon crushed chili
> Salt
> 500 g (1 lb) courgettes
> 4–6 cups (1 litre) water

Grind the shrimps and star anise or Szechuan pepper very finely in a pestle and mortar. Put some of the shrimp powder in each person's bowl, along with finely chopped shallots and chili, and about ¼ teaspoon of salt.

Peel the courgettes and cut into 6-mm (¼-in) slices. Bring the water to the boil; add the courgettes. As soon as the water boils again, pour it into the serving bowls. Stir up the seasonings and serve.

VARIATION   Replace the courgettes with yam bean or bitter melon.

Mango Soup

>   1 tablespoon curry spices such as turmeric, cardamom, cloves,
>   fenugreek, cayenne
>   *Ghee* (see page 38) or vegetable oil
>   3 chopped mangoes
>   1 litre (1¾ pints) water
>   Salt
>   1 tablespoon grated fresh ginger

Fry the curry spices in *ghee* or vegetable oil. Add 3 chopped
mangoes, sauté briefly and then add the water, salt, and ginger.
Simmer for 40–50 minutes. Strain if desired, or serve as it is.

Wakame no suimono
Japanese Clear Soup with Seaweed

Japanese soups, both clear and flavoured with *miso* (see page 134),
are based on a stock made from dried bonito (*katsuobushi*) or
sardines and kelp (*kombu* seaweed). The clear soups in particular
are some of the most delicious and original of all the world's
soups. In making stock for *suimono* you must be careful not to
leave the seaweed too long in the boiling water or the broth will
turn bitter. The briefly boiled kelp can be reused to make the
coarser stock used for *miso* soup.

Japanese food shops stock *katsuobushi*, *miso* and varieties of
seaweeds, including *kombu* and *wakame*. Health food shops stock
miso and seaweeds.

>   1 sheet about 10 g (⅓ oz) dried *kombu* (kelp) seaweed
>   1 litre (2 pints) water
>   10 g (⅓ oz) flaked dried bonito (*katsuobushi*)
>   15 g (½ oz) dried *wakame* seaweed

Soy sauce
Salt
1 bean curd pad, cut into 1-cm cubes

Rinse the *kombu* seaweed. To prepare a soup stock bring the water to a boil, add the seaweed and stir it in the water for 30–60 seconds. Then remove the seaweed (save it for *miso* soup stock) and add the dried flaked bonito. Remove the pan from heat and leave for 1–2 minutes. Strain the broth and reserve the bonito for *miso* soup.

Soak the *wakame* seaweed in cold water for 10 minutes. Drain and cut into 1-cm (½-in) pieces. Season the clear stock with soy sauce and salt. Add the seaweed and bean curd and bring to a boil. Lower the heat and simmer for 3–4 minutes before serving.

Miso Soup

Miso is a fermented soya bean product which is salty, flavourful and high in protein. It is used in soups and stews and makes even a vegetarian meal taste meaty. *Miso* soups may be drunk at any meal in Japan, including breakfast.

Left over or unused *kombu* and dried bonito (see preceding recipe)
750 ml (1¼ pints) water
1–2 carrots, thinly sliced
100 g (4 oz) thinly sliced *daikon* (see page 177) or radishes
1 spring onion, chopped
175 g (6 oz) finely shredded Chinese celery cabbage
4–5 tablespoons red *miso* paste

Prepare a stock by boiling leftover *kombu* and bonito in the water for 10 minutes. Strain the broth through cheesecloth. Place the carrots, radish, spring onion and cabbage in a large saucepan with the stock; cover and simmer until the vegetables are just tender. Dilute the *miso* with a little of the soup stock, stir until all lumps are removed, and then add to the soup. Keep the soup hot but do not boil again after adding *miso*.

Bitter Melon Soup

Bitter melon is a green, wrinkled and warty vegetable resembling a cucumber in both size and shape. It is sold in Chinese food shops, and should be firm and unblemished. It has an unusual bitter taste, highly prized by the Cantonese.

1–2 bitter melons
1 litre (1¾ pints) water, salted
250 g (8 oz) chicken or pork
1–2 tablespoons soy sauce
1 tablespoon dry sherry

Wash the bitter melon and slice lengthwise. Do not peel. Scoop out the seeds and discard. Cut the shells in half and slice into strips. Blanch in salted boiling water for 2–3 minutes and drain. This reduces the bitterness.

Shred the chicken or pork finely.

Bring the water to a boil. Reduce to a medium heat. Add the melon. Return to the boil. Add the meat. Allow to boil gently;

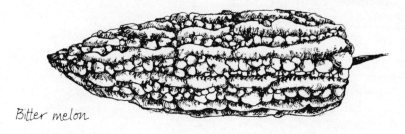

Bitter melon

add the soy sauce and sherry. Simmer for 1–2 minutes until the meat is done and serve hot.

If desired, soak Chinese dried mushrooms for 15–30 minutes, slice and add with the water in which they were soaked to the soup with the melon. Or add garlic shoots or spring onions and cubed bean curd. For a richer soup use stock (any variety) instead of water, or add crushed dried fish or shrimps.

Soup with Chinese Meatballs

> 250 g (8 oz) minced pork
> 1 tablespoon soy sauce
> 1–2 teaspoons fresh ginger
> 1 minced white leek
> 1 tablespoon cornflour
> Pinch of monosodium glutamate
> 1 egg
> Dash of dry white wine or dry sherry
> 1 litre (1¾ pints) meat stock
> Salt

Mix together the minced pork, soy sauce, ginger, leek, cornflour, monosodium glutamate, egg and wine. Shape into small meatballs.
Poach in lightly boiling stock for 10 minutes. Season and serve.

Chinese Cabbage Soup

This soup can be made with any kind of cabbage but is especially good when made with the Chinese variety.

> 250 g (8 oz) pork or chicken
> Peanut oil

250 g (8 oz) chopped cabbage
4 dried mushrooms, soaked (see page 44)
1 litre (1¾pints) meat stock
Dry white wine or dry sherry
Salt and monosodium glutamate
Suggested seasonings: garlic, Szechuan pepper, sesame oil, ginger

Mince the meat and sauté it in peanut oil. Add the cabbage and mushrooms, chopped evenly. Cook for several minutes.

Add the hot stock, wine or sherry, and seasonings. Simmer for 5 minutes until the cabbage is tender but firm.

Soya Soup

Soya, well appreciated in China, is served in many forms (see page 178) but most often as bean curd—cubes of curdled white soya milk.

250 g (8 oz) minced pork
125 g (4 oz) bean curd
5 dried mushrooms, soaked (see page 44)
1 litre (1¾ pints) meat or fish stock
2 tablespoons soy sauce
2 tablespoons vinegar
Salt and pepper
1 tablespoon cornflour

Slice the meat, bean curd and mushrooms. Add the boiling stock and simmer for 5–10 minutes. Add soy sauce, vinegar, salt, pepper, and cornflour pre-mixed with a little cold water. Simmer until thick.

Goimontoi shulyu
Mongolian Lamb Soup

Mongols enjoy this robust soup sitting inside warm felt *yurts* or tents while blizzards sweep the steppe outside. Like many other peoples of central Asia they live a primarily pastoral life, almost purely nomadic, following their herds to greener pastures. Mongolian cooking reflects the fact that meat is readily available—unlike most poor people they eat more meat than vegetable or grain dishes. Their constant wandering accounts for the use of noodles made freshly before each meal, a practice common among all nomads. It is worth remembering that these nomads of north and central Asia are credited with the invention of ravioli, which apparently developed with Siberian Kirghiz *pelmenies*, which became Lithuanian *kolduny*, then *pieroshky* among the Poles, who transmitted the recipe to the Italians during a period of close relations between the two countries in the time of Queen Bona. In China, too, the popularity of ravioli stuffed with meat reveals the culinary influence of this simple but once powerful people. Their influence is also seen in Tibet where *momos* are served at every feast.

In Mongolia the soup is usually made with yak bones, yak meat and yak bacon, and washed down with gulps of *airag*, a strong drink made from fermented mare's milk. Strong beer is an acceptable Western substitute.

SOUP:
1 kg (2 lb) lamb marrow bones
500 g (1 lb) roots and herbs such as parsnip, turnip, parsley, dill
Suggested spices: pepper, coriander seeds, dill seeds
2½ litres (4½ pints) water
500 g (1 lb) lamb meat, cut in chunks
125 g (4 oz) lamb or bacon fat

NOODLES:
125 g (4 oz) flour
Water
Salt

Boil the bones with the roots, herbs, and spices for 2½–3 hours to make about 2¼ litres (4 pints) of good stock.

In the meantime mix the flour with a little water and salt to make firm noodle dough. Leave for a few hours, roll thin and slice into ribbons.

To the highly seasoned stock add pieces of meat and firm pieces of lamb or bacon fat. Simmer the meat for 2½–3 hours.

Add the noodles and simmer for 10–15 minutes more. Serve piping hot.

Serves 6–8.

Lagman po Uyegursky
Lamb and Noodle Soup

This is a very savoury soup from Uzbekistan in the Soviet Union.

NOODLES:
350 g (12 oz) flour
Salt
Butter

SOUP:
1 black radish, small *daikon* (see page 177), or turnip
3–4 sweet peppers
3–4 tomatoes
Clarified butter (see page 40)
450 g (1 lb) chopped lamb or beef
250 ml (½ pint) tomato purée
3–4 cloves garlic

1 ½ litres (2¾ pints) lamb or beef stock
Salt and pepper
4 potatoes
Parsley

NOODLES   Prepare a firm noodle dough from flour, salt and a little water. Roll it into a sausage shape and smear with butter. Leave to rest, covered, for several hours. Roll out thin and fold over. Repeat the rolling and folding 3–4 times. Roll out thin once more and cut into wide noodles.

SOUP   Chop the vegetables, except for the potatoes, and sauté in butter. Add the meat, then the tomato purée and chopped garlic. Add the stock and season. Cut the potatoes into chunks and add to the soup. Simmer for 30–45 minutes.

To serve, cook the noodles in lightly boiling water for 4–5 minutes and drain. Put some noodles on to each person's plate and cover with soup. Sprinkle with parsley.
  Serves 6–8.

Shchi
Cabbage Soup

Served with heavy rye bread and salted cucumber, this soup is a whole meal for many in northern Russia.

  1 small white cabbage
  1 kg (2 lb) stew vegetables such as onion, carrot, leek, turnip, parsnip, swede and celery
  500 g (1 lb) potatoes
  1 ½ litres (2¾ pints) beef stock
  Bay leaf
  Salt, pepper and parsley

Cut up the vegetables. Add to the stock and season. Simmer gently 20–30 minutes until cooked. Stir from time to time.

Serve hot over spoonfuls of hot cooked kasha (see page 100) or with a side dish of dried mushrooms cooked with potatoes or kasha.

Mushroom and Barley Soup

This is very common in Slavic countries.

> Handful dried mushrooms (preferably the Eastern European or Italian variety—see page 44)
> 1 litre (1¾ pints) water
> 4 tablespoons pearl barley
> Salt and pepper
> 2–3 cloves garlic
> 2–3 shallots or small onions
> 4–6 tablespoons double or sour cream

Soak the mushrooms in a small amount of the water for 1 hour. Soak the barley in the rest of the water for at least 1 hour.

Add the mushrooms and the water they soaked in to the barley. Bring to the boil. Add seasoning, garlic, and shallots. Simmer for 30 minutes, until the barley is cooked. Serve with a spoonful of cream in each dish.

VARIATION   Use stock instead of water.

Russian Millet Soup

> 4 tablespoons whole millet
> 1 litre (1¾ pints) water or stock
> 2–3 potatoes, cubed

> 2 minced onions
> 1 stalk fresh dill or fennel, chopped
> 1 tablespoon butter
> Salt

Mix all the ingredients together in a large pan and bring to a boil. Simmer for 20–30 minutes until the millet and potatoes are cooked. Serve with buttered bread.

Borscht
Beetroot Soup

Borscht, the greatest of Ukrainian soups, is a substantial main dish when served with kasha (see page 100) or *pieroshky* (large ravioli stuffed with meat, cabbage or practically anything).

As is usual with such popular dishes, *borscht* has many versions. Besides this basic Ukrainian recipe there are thin *borschts*, green *borschts*, cold and hot *borschts*, Muscovite *borschts*, clear *borschts* etc.

> 450 g (1 lb) beetroot
> 1 white cabbage
> 1 kg (2 lb) stew vegetables such as carrot, onion, potato, turnip, celery, swede and leek
> 4 tomatoes; or 125 g (4 oz) tomato purée
> 2 litres (3½ pints) beef stock
> Bay leaves
> Salt, pepper and parsley
> 1–2 tablespoons sugar
> Juice of ½ lemon
> 500 ml (1 pint) sour cream

Peel the beetroot and other vegetables. Grate some of the beetroot and set aside. Finely chop the remainder and all the vegetables except the tomatoes; add them to boiling stock. Simmer for ½ hour. Add whole tomatoes, herbs and seasoning, sugar and lemon juice; simmer for 5–10 minutes. Ten minutes before serving add the reserved grated beetroots to give the soup to give a deep red colour.

Serve with a big spoonful of sour cream in each dish.

Serves 6–8.

MEAT BORSCHT
All the above ingredients
1 kg (2 lb) stewing beef, cubed

Proceed as above but use water instead of stock. Simmer the beef with the water for 2 hours before adding the vegetables. Then proceed as above. For firmer, textured meat, brown the meat before simmering. In hard times you can make do with a piece of salt pork or bacon.

Serves 6–8.

Okrochka
Beer and Vegetable Soup

It is easy to understand the passion of people in sunny countries like Spain and Greece for cold soups, but it seems surprising in cold countries like Russia. The hot summers of so-called temperate climates explain the apparent contradiction.

The original of this cold summer soup called for *kvass*, a thin rye or barley beer that is practically the national beverage. It is often sold by the glass from kegs on the street corner. *Kvass's* natural companion is heavy rye bread. Note that this soup is *not* cooked.

1 cucumber
2–3 cold cooked potatoes

1 bunch spring onions
2–3 hard-boiled eggs
500 g (1 lb) cold cooked beetroot
250 g (8 oz) soaked dried fruits such as prunes, apricots,
    apples, pears
25 g (1 oz) dried mushrooms, soaked (see page 44)
Chopped fresh parsley or dill
Salt
1 litre (2 pints) kvass or lager
250 ml (¼ pint) sour cream

Peel the vegetables. Dice all the ingredients, mix together and season. Add the kvass or beer and chill for at least 4 hours.

Serve with an ice cube and a big spoonful of sour cream in each dish.

Chicken Soup

In Eastern Europe they used to say that the only time a poor man eats chicken is when he's sick or the chicken was. This soup can be made with just chicken feet and necks.

1 chicken, including feet and neck
1 kg (2–3 lb) stewing vegetables such as onions, celery,
    carrots, parsnip
Fresh dill
3–4 cloves garlic
Salt, peppercorns, bay leaves
Suggested spices: marjoram, thyme, mace, coriander

Cut up the chicken and vegetables. Put them in a large pot with the other ingredients and water to cover. Bring to the boil, skim, cover and simmer for 1½ hours, making sure the water doesn't boil away. Skim off the fat.

Serve as it is or with boiled noodles. Or drain and serve the broth with potato dumplings, boiled potatoes or noodles. Serve the boiled chicken on a separate plate with ground horseradish.

Serves 6–8.

Hungarian Cucumber Soup

    1 small onion, coarsely chopped
    4 leeks (white part only), sliced
    3 tablespoons parsley
    125 g (4 oz) butter
    4 large cucumbers, peeled and chopped
    4 medium potatoes, peeled and cubed
    2 litres (4 pints) chicken stock (see page 56)
    250 ml (½ pint) plain yoghurt

Sauté the onions, leeks and parsley in butter only until the onion is soft but not brown. Meanwhile cook the cucumbers and potatoes in stock until quite soft. Put both mixtures together and pass through a Mouli-légumes or purée in an electric blender. Return to the pan and simmer for 10 minutes. Refrigerate until thoroughly chilled (4–5 hours). Stir in the yoghurt and serve in chilled bowls, topped with chopped chives or finely chopped raw cucumber.

Serves 6–8.

Bulgarian Yoghurt Soup

    600 ml (1 pint) yoghurt
    2 cloves garlic, chopped
    Fresh mint, chopped
    Salt and pepper

250 g (8 oz) leftover cooked rice
250 g (8 oz) chopped, cooked chicken or lamb

Beat the yoghurt in a large bowl until smooth and light; add garlic, mint and seasoning. Heat gently until almost boiling. Add the rice and meat. Simmer for 5–10 minutes and serve hot.

Austrian Leberreis
Liver Dumpling Soup

Meatballs, fishballs, *pelmenies* (Russian ravioli), and other dumplings enrich soups from one end of Europe to the other. These dumplings feature liver.

150 g (5 oz) breadcrumbs moistened with hot milk
100 g (4 oz) finely minced pig's liver
1 finely chopped onion, browned in lard
1 clove garlic, crushed
Salt and pepper
Marjoram to taste
2 eggs, beaten
1 litre (1¾ pints) meat stock

Mix the breadcrumbs, liver, onion, garlic and seasonings. Bind with the egg. Shape into balls the size of walnuts and leave to rest for at least 1 hour.

Poach in abundant lightly boiling salted water. They should be done in about 8–10 minutes. Meanwhile heat the meat stock. Transfer the dumplings to it with a slotted spoon and serve.

Arab Garlic and Tomato Soup

2 chopped onions
3–4 cloves garlic, chopped

Oil
Coriander seeds
4–5 tomatoes, chopped
Salt and pepper
250 g (8 oz) semolina
1 litre (1¾ pints) water or stock

Brown the onion and garlic in oil. Crush the coriander seeds. Add coriander, tomatoes, salt, pepper and semolina to the onion. Remove from the heat and leave to stand for at least 15 minutes for the flavour to develop. Add the water or stock, bring to the boil and simmer for another 15 minutes.

Mast va khiar
Yoghurt, Cucumber and Egg Soup

This Persian cold soup can be prepared in advance and keeps well refrigerated.

¾ litre (1¼ pints) plain yoghurt
125 ml (¼ pint) double cream
1 large, peeled cucumber, finely sliced
4 spring onions, finely chopped
2 chopped hard-boiled eggs
150 g (5 oz) soaked, drained raisins
Salt and pepper
250 ml (½ pint) iced water
Fresh dill or parsley

Mix all the ingredients together and chill thoroughly. Serve sprinkled with chopped fresh dill or parsley.

Chorba
Mutton and Bean Soup

500 g (1 lb) lamb cut into 2.5-cm (1-in) cubes
Oil
2–3 onions
3–4 tomatoes
2–3 courgettes
75 g (3 oz) dried apricots
250 g (8 oz) dried beans, soaked overnight
250 g (8 oz) chickpeas, soaked overnight
175 g (6 oz) noodles
Fresh coriander

Brown the meat in oil. Add the onions, tomatoes and courgettes, chopped evenly. Simmer for ½ hour. Add the apricots, beans, chickpeas and water to cover. Season, cover and simmer for 2–2½ hours.
Fifteen minutes before serving add the noodles and coriander.

Peanut Soup

Peanuts, a staple of Black Africa, find their way into many African recipes, from soups to desserts.

2 tablespoons flour
Mutton or lamb fat (or oil)
1 litre (1¾ pints) chicken stock
125 g (4 oz) roasted, unsalted peanuts
250 g (8 oz) white chicken meat, minced
Suggested seasonings: cayenne, pepper, cumin, salt

Stir the flour into the hot fat to make a brown sauce. Gradually add the stock. Pound the peanuts with the chicken in a pestle and mortar. Mix with the soup and simmer for 10–15 minutes. Season well and serve.

Double cream is sometimes mixed with the chicken and peanuts.

Coconut Soup

Although not a common dish, soup in Black Africa is often surprising and exotic (see also page 157).

> 500 ml (a scant pint) chicken stock
> 500 ml (a scant pint) coconut milk (see page 58)
> 250 ml (½ pint) double cream
> Suggested seasonings: cayenne, cumin, coriander
> Salt
> Roasted peanuts or cashews, chopped

Mix the stock with the coconut milk. Add the cream and season to taste. Simmer gently for 5–10 minutes.

Serve with bits of roasted nuts sprinkled over.

Avgolemono
Egg Lemon Soup

This soup is one of the basic recipes of poor Greeks.

> 50 g (2 oz) rice
> 1 litre (1¾ pints) chicken stock
> 2 eggs
> Juice of 1 lemon
> Salt and pepper

Simmer the rice in the stock for 12–15 minutes. Separate the eggs and beat the whites until stiff. Beat the yolks with the lemon juice in a soup tureen and fold in the beaten egg whites.

Slowly add the hot stock and rice, stirring constantly. Season and serve hot.

Tzatziki
Cucumber Yoghurt Soup

This cold Greek soup is a favourite of the dog days. Yoghurt is a common base for many dishes throughout the Balkans and Middle East. (The Persian version of this is given on page 147).

1 litre (1¾ pints) yoghurt
2–3 cloves garlic, chopped
1 large peeled cucumber, finely chopped or sliced
Juice of ½ lemon
Salt and pepper
Fresh dill or mint, chopped

Mix the yoghurt, garlic, cucumber, and lemon juice. Add salt and pepper. Chill thoroughly.

Serve sprinkled with dill or mint.

The soup tastes better if allowed to stand for a few hours or even overnight before serving.

Andalusian Egg Soup

Quick to prepare, this egg soup is common fare in southern Spain.

500 ml (a scant pint) water
1–2 eggs, separated
2–3 tablespoons olive oil
Salt and pepper
Suggested spices: marjoram, thyme, basil, dill, mustard

Salt the water and bring to the boil. Beat in the egg whites. Remove from the heat for as long as it takes to make a mayonnaise by beating together the egg yolks, oil and seasoning until smooth. Beat egg yolks with a wooden spoon; add the oil a drop at a time at the beginning, beating all the time. Egg yolks should be at room temperature.

Mix the egg bouillon slowly into the mayonnaise. Serve with croutons of fried bread.

Salt Cod Soup

This particular soup comes from the Murcia province of Spain.

    250 g (8 oz) chickpeas, soaked and drained
    1 litre (1¾ pints) water
    2–3 cloves garlic
    Olive oil
    500 g (1 lb) salt cod (*bacalao* see page 38), soaked and drained
        overnight
    Flour
    1 slice of bread
    1 tablespoon vinegar
    A few pistils saffron
    Pepper to taste

Simmer the chickpeas for 45 minutes with water, half of the garlic and a dash of oil.

Shortly before the chickpeas are done dip the cod in flour and sauté in oil. Remove from the frying pan and replace with the slice of bread. Brown the bread on both sides, remove, sprinkle with vinegar, then mash with remaining garlic, saffron mixed in a little warm water, and pepper.

Add fish and spiced bread to the chickpeas and cook for another 5 minutes.

Garlic Soup

Appreciated all over Spain, garlic soup has many regional variants.

3–4 cloves garlic, crushed
1–2 tablespoons olive oil
100 g (4 oz) diced ham
4 tablespoons breadcrumbs
4–5 tomatoes, chopped
Salt and pepper
Tabasco sauce
1 egg, beaten

Brown the garlic in olive oil along with the ham. Add the bread-crumbs and chopped tomatoes. Add enough water to cover. Season and simmer for 20–30 minutes. Shortly before serving mix in a beaten egg to thicken.

Cadiz Soup

3–4 cloves garlic, crushed
100 g (4 oz) diced ham
1–2 tablespoons olive oil
100 g (4 oz) diced fried bread
Salt and pepper
Chopped parsley
2 hard-boiled eggs, sliced
1 egg, beaten
1 litre (1¾ pints) meat stock

Fry the garlic and ham in olive oil. Mix in a tureen with the bread, seasoning, parsley and hard-boiled eggs. Add the beaten egg and mix well, then stir in the hot stock and serve at once.

Gazpacho

This popular cold Spanish soup is called *gazpacho colorado* (red gazpacho) when served hot.

    4 large ripe tomatoes, peeled
    1 large cucumber, peeled
    1 small onion, peeled
    1 small green pepper, seeded
    125 ml (¼ pint) red wine vinegar
    125 ml (¼ pint) olive oil
    1 teaspoon chili sauce (or Tabasco)
    1 teaspoon salt
    ½ teaspoon black pepper
    500 ml (1 pint) chopped, cooked tomatoes or tomato juice
    3–4 cloves garlic

Chop all the vegetables finely. Add the remaining ingredients and pass through a Mouli-légumes or blend in an electric blender. Serve chilled with cucumber and tomato chunks floating in the bowls.

Mint Soup

A delicacy from Portugal.

    1 small chicken, cut into 8 pieces
    750 g (1½ lb) stew vegetables such as onion, carrot, celery
    1½ litres (2¾ pints) water
    100 g (4 oz) rice
    Salt and pepper
    1 lemon
    Fresh or dried mint

Simmer the chicken and vegetables together in the water for 1½ hours to make stock. Skim off the fat and discard. Drain the chicken and vegetables. Simmer the broth for another 20–30 minutes in order to concentrate the flavour. Add rice to the broth and simmer for about 12 minutes. Purée the vegetables and mix into the soup. Season. Add a dash of lemon juice.

To serve pour over crumpled mint: 1 tablespoon of fresh or ½ tablespoon of dried for each serving. Garnish with lemon slices. Serve the boiled chicken separately.

Portuguese Garlic and Egg Soup

In Western as in Eastern Europe, soup is often the whole meal for a family. If there is bread or raw onion too, the family is eating well. In Portugal the bread is often *broa*, a heavy bread which, with slices of smoked ham and mouthfuls of sharp green wine, makes for a fine country lunch.

4 tablespoons fresh herbs: coriander, rosemary, basil, parsley
4 cloves garlic
Salt and pepper
1–2 tablespoons olive oil
Slices of toasted bread
4–6 eggs
1 litre (1¾ pints) water
Black olives

Crush the herbs in a mortar with the garlic, salt, pepper, and oil. Spoon into a soup tureen and cover with slices of toast.

Poach the eggs in the water; remove. Pour the hot water into the tureen. Stir up the seasoning. Lay the eggs on the bread floating on top of the soup. Serve with olives on the side.

VARIATION   Replace the eggs with shellfish such as mussels.

Bulbura
Italian Pumpkin Soup

A light soup such as the poor typically eat in Italy. It originates from Ticino, the Italian-speaking canton of Switzerland.

    500 g (1 lb) pumpkin or custard marrow
    1 onion, finely chopped
    Optional: 1–2 tablespoons sugar
    250 ml (½ pint) milk
    Butter
    250 g (8 oz) cooked broad beans
    Salt and pepper
    Buttered Italian or French bread

Skin the pumpkin and chop the flesh finely. Add the onion. Pour on just enough water to cover and add sugar if desired. Bring to the boil and simmer for 20–30 minutes. Strain or put through a Mouli-légumes to make a creamy purée. Thin with milk, lace with butter and add the cooked, drained beans. Simmer 5–10 minutes more. Season and serve with Italian or French bread and butter.

Bussega
Tripe Soup

This solid Lombardy soup is a whole meal in itself. Tripe can be bought from most butchers.

    250 g (8 oz) dried beans, soaked overnight
    125 g (4 oz) diced smoked bacon
    2 minced onions
    750 g (1½ lb) cabbage, carrot, celery, onions, and turnip
    3–4 tomatoes

500 g (1 lb) cooked tripe
Suggested seasonings : 2–3 cloves garlic, sage, salt, pepper
2 hard-boiled eggs
Grated Parmesan cheese

Simmer the beans in plenty of unsalted water for 40–60 minutes or until tender. Drain.

Brown the bacon. Add the onions, then the vegetables, cut up evenly. Sauté for a few minutes, then add the beans. Add water to cover, then the tomatoes. Simmer for 40–50 minutes.

Add the tripe, finely sliced. Season. Simmer for 30 minutes more. Add more water if necessary.

Serve with quartered hard-boiled eggs and grated Parmesan.

Italian Egg Soup

1 litre (1¾ pints) meat stock
2–3 eggs
40 g (1½ oz) breadcrumbs
Salt and pepper
Grated Parmesan cheese

Heat the stock. Beat the eggs together with the breadcrumbs and season.

Stir the egg mixture into the stock. Simmer for 5 minutes and serve sprinkled with Parmesan.

Gul Artsoppa
Swedish Pork and Pea Soup

This thick pea soup is served with crisp bread and cheese as a whole meal. At Christmas it is traditional to serve light pancakes after the soup.

500 g (1 lb) split peas
3 litres (5¼ pints) water
500 g (1 lb) fresh pork, preferably shoulder
Cooked hambone with some shreds of meat left on it
2 chopped onions
Salt, pepper, thyme
Bread and strong Cheddar cheese

Soak the peas overnight. Drain off the soaking water; add the
water and boil. Skim and simmer for 1 hour.

Add the meat, hambone and onions. Simmer for 2 hours.
Remove the pork and hambone. Cut the cooked pork into cubes
and scrape the shreds of ham from the bone. Return meats to
the soup. Season well.

Serve with bread and cheese.

The hambone may be replaced with a salted pig's knuckle.

Serves 6–8.

Coconut Soup II

This is a common Latin-American version of coconut soup (see
also page 149).

1 coconut
1 litre (1¾ pints) beef stock
1 tablespoon cornflour
2–3 tablespoons double cream
Salt and pepper
Suggested spices: coriander, cumin
Nutmeg or mace

Break open the coconut shell, saving the sap. Grate the coconut
flesh as you would for making coconut milk (see page 58). Add

sap and grated coconut to the beef stock and simmer for 45 minutes.

Thicken with cornflour and a little cream. Season and sprinkle with nutmeg or mace.

Before serving beat the soup to make it light.

Colombian Almond and Onion Soup

> 2 onions
> Lard or oil
> 1 litre (1¾ pints) meat stock
> 150 g (5 oz) almonds, sliced or chopped
> Salt and pepper
> Croutons
> Grated mature Cheddar cheese

Brown the onions in lard or oil. Add the stock and almonds. (If desired, brown the almonds with the onions first.) Season with salt and pepper.

Serve with croutons and grated cheese.

Chupe

This thick soup is found in different versions in many Latin American countries. The best known, and supposedly the original, is Peruvian *chupe*. This basic recipe can be varied by mixing in different ingredients such as other meats, shellfish or eggs.

> 1–2 chopped onions
> Oil
> 1–2 cloves garlic
> 250 ml (½ pint) tomato sauce (see page 55)
> 250 g (8 oz) rice or breadcrumbs

Salt
Powdered chili
1 litre (1¾ pints) water, stock or milk or a mixture of these
500 g (1 lb) diced chicken or shelled shrimps
3–4 potatoes
Goat's cheese

Brown the onions in a little oil. Add garlic and tomato sauce, then rice or breadcrumbs, salt and a pinch of powdered chili. Add about a quarter of the water, stock or milk. Cover and simmer for 20–30 minutes. Mash to make a thick sauce. Add chicken or shrimps and simmer for 3–5 minutes more. Strain, reserving the meat.

Mix with the remaining liquid. Add the potatoes and simmer until they are cooked; about 30 minutes.

Serve, putting a piece of goat's cheese and some of the meat on each plate. Cover with soup.

Poor Indians make this soup with dried mutton and corn.

Aguada
Mexican Tomato Soup

This is called *aguada* because it is very liquid.

500 g (1 lb) fresh noodles (or parboiled dried noodles)
Lard
250 ml (½ pint) tomato sauce (see page 55)
1 litre (1¾ pints) meat stock
Suggested spices: pepper, cumin, coriander, powdered chili, basil, salt

Sauté the noodles in lard. Add the tomato sauce. Simmer for a few minutes before adding the stock. Season and cook for 4–8 minutes until the noodles swell.

n Vegetable Soup

Another popular Mexican dish.

> 1 kg (2 lb) vegetables in season such as peas, marrow, broccoli,
>   green beans
> 1 litre (1¾ pints) meat stock
> 2 onions, chopped
> Oil
> 3–4 tomatoes, chopped
> Salt and pepper
> Suggested spices: bay leaf, basil, powdered chili

Chop the vegetables and simmer in the stock until tender; about 15 minutes. Brown the onions in some oil, add the tomatoes, seasoning and spices. Simmer for 10–15 minutes to make a sauce, then add it to the soup.

Mexican Pumpkin Soup

This soup is good served hot in the winter and cool in the summer.

> 2 onions, chopped
> Lard or margarine
> 1 litre (1¾ pints) chicken stock
> Salt, mace, coriander, pepper
> 500 g (1 lb) cooked pumpkin purée (see page 290)
> 125 ml (¼ pint) cream or milk
> 4 tomatoes, peeled and chopped
> 1 bunch spring onions, chopped

Brown the onions in the fat. Add stock, salt, pepper, spices and pumpkin. Simmer for 10–15 minutes. Add the cream or milk when the soup is almost cooked.

Immediately before serving mix in the tomatoes and spring onions. Reheat gently and serve.

Indonesian Tripe Soup

Tripe is prepared in similar ways all over the world, perhaps because tripe varies less in character and taste than do people. In Indonesia the variation includes coconut milk. Parboiled tripe can be bought at many butchers.

> 500 g (1 lb) cooked tripe, cut up finely
> Oil or clarified butter (see page 40)
> Suggested spices: coriander, cardamom
> 1 teaspoon grated fresh ginger
> 2–3 minced leek whites
> 1 minced onion
> 250 ml (½ pint) coconut milk (see page 58)
> 1 lemon, sliced
> Salt and pepper

Brown the pieces of cooked tripe in oil or clarified butter. Add spices, crushed finely. Add all other ingredients except the coconut milk and lemon. Add water to cover and simmer for 15–20 minutes.

Add the coconut milk and lemon just before serving. Season well.

Mayeritsa

A traditional Greek Easter soup. When the fortnight of fasting preceding the Holy Saturday is energetically broken after midnight Mass, *mayeritsa*, made from the offal of the Pascal lamb, is served and greeted with general joy.

Liver, lungs, heart and kidneys of a lamb
Salt and pepper
Butter
1 bunch spring onions
Dill or fennel
Mint
100 g (4 oz) rice
3 eggs
Juice of 2 lemons

Wash the meat. Cover with water and cook for ½ hour. Season with salt. Drain, reserving the stock. Cut the meat into small pieces and brown in butter with spring onions and herbs. Return to the stock. Season and simmer for 1 hour, adding the rice 20 minutes before serving.

To serve, beat the eggs with lemon juice and mix gradually into the soup. Do not boil again.

Lentil Soup

250 g (8 oz) lentils
1 litre (1¾ pints) water or stock
1 medium onion, chopped
1 teaspoon salt
¼ teaspoon pepper

Soak the lentils in the water or stock overnight. The next day bring the lentils and onion to the boil, add seasoning, cover and cook slowly until tender; about 1½ hours. If you want the soup to be very smooth you can put it in a blender or through a food mill. Lentil soup is also good with the addition of bits of ham or pork.

Nettle Soup

Nettles, when picked young and tender, are a wholesome and tasty green and can easily be gathered wild in the spring and summer. They must be cooked to take away the sting, either steamed like spinach and served with butter, or parboiled, drained and mixed with bits of bacon and baked *au gratin*. Here is an appetizing nettle soup:

500 g (1 lb) fresh nettles
125 g (4 oz) bacon or pork belly
1 litre (1¾ pints) water or stock

Wash the nettles. Cut them up and simmer them with the diced bacon in the stock for 20–30 minutes. Serve hot. You can also use half nettles and half lettuce leaves.

VEGETABLES

Vegetable Cutlets

>1 kg (2 lb) vegetables, such as carrots, turnips, potatoes, celery
>Curry spices: coriander, cumin, turmeric, clove, cinnamon, fenugreek
>1–2 onions, finely chopped
>100 g (4 oz) grated almonds or coconut
>2 eggs
>Breadcrumbs

Boil or steam the vegetables. Drain and mash.

Brown the minced onions and curry, grated almonds or coconut. Add the vegetables and sauté briefly. Mix in an egg to bind. Shape into balls or patties, then dip in beaten egg and breadcrumbs.

Fry in oil, or dry fry like *chapatis* (see page 64). Serve crisp. If the only vegetable used is potato, add some chopped fresh mint.

Indian Stuffed Vegetables

Meat is a luxury for most in India, so vegetables that can be stuffed, such as marrow, peppers, aubergine and tomatoes, are often stuffed with the following mixture:

>2 onions, finely chopped
>Curry spices: turmeric, clove, cumin, cayenne
>2 mashed potatoes
>4 tablespoons grated coconut
>500 g (1 lb) minced vegetables such as peppers, carrots, peas

Brown the onions and curry spices. Add the other ingredients, mix well together and simmer for 5–10 minutes.

Indian Greens

This is not solely a vegetable dish, as it often includes lamb or mutton. It is made with the tender leaves of almost any vegetable, even leaves we would ordinarily throw away: radish, turnip, cauliflower, carrots, beets, marrow, pumpkin.

    1–2 onions, finely chopped
    Ghee (see page 38) or vegetable oil
    Curry spices: cumin, cardamom, clove, turmeric, anis, fenu-
        greek
    2–3 cloves garlic
    1–2 teaspoons fresh grated ginger
    1–2 hot fresh chilis, or cayenne
    500 g (1 lb) lamb, minced
    1½ kg (3 lb) greens, shredded
    Salt and pepper

Brown the onions in the oil. Add curry spices, garlic, ginger and chilis. Add the meat and cook until brown. Then add the greens and a little water. Add salt and pepper and simmer for 20–30 minutes until the meat is cooked.

Indian Banana Foogath

An unusual vegetable curry, this is made with banana peels.

    500 g (1 lb) banana peels (from 6–8 bananas)
    Curry spices: turmeric, fenugreek, cardamom, cloves, cumin,
        anise
    Ghee (see page 38) or vegetable oil
    1 onion, finely chopped
    2 cloves garlic
    2 fresh hot chilis, or cayenne

Cut the banana peels into medium-sized pieces, wash and soak in water for 1 hour.

Fry the curry in *ghee* or oil with the onion, garlic and chilis. Add the drained pieces of banana peel and cook for 15–20 minutes.

This can be made equally well with green bananas.

If desired, add grated coconut, tamarind paste (mix 1 teaspoon of paste with 1–2 teaspoons of water) or sliced fresh ginger.

Gado-gado
Indonesian Vegetable Salad with Peanut and Coconut Sauce

This Indonesian salad, made with a mixture of raw and cooked vegetables, varies greatly from region to region.

DRESSING:
2–3 onions, chopped
2–3 cloves garlic, crushed
Ghee (see page 38) or vegetable oil
2–6 fresh or soaked dried chilis with seeds and stems removed, chopped; or 2–5 teaspoons powdered chilis
750 ml (1¼ pints) coconut milk (see page 58)
500 g (1 lb) freshly crushed or ground roasted peanuts or peanut butter
2–4 teaspoons grated fresh ginger
2 tablespoons brown sugar
Salt
Juice of 1 lemon

SALAD:
2 large bean curd cakes (see page 181), cut into cubes and fried in peanut oil
250 g (8 oz) boiled new potatoes, sliced
500 g (1 lb) green beans, lightly cooked

250 g (8 oz) carrots, sliced lengthwise and lightly cooked
2 cucumbers, partially peeled, cut in half and sliced length-
    wise
500 g (1 lb) bean sprouts, blanched
1 Chinese cabbage, finely shredded and blanched
2 hard-boiled eggs, sliced

Prepare the dressing first by lightly sautéing the onions and garlic
in the *ghee* or oil for a few minutes, then adding the chopped
chilis. Sauté for a few more minutes, mashing the chilis as well
as you can. Now add the coconut milk, crushed roasted peanuts
or peanut butter, ginger, brown sugar, and salt. (You can also
grind the roasted peanuts together with the coconut milk, fried
onions, chilis and other ingredients using a blender, returning the
mixture to the heat only to thicken it.) Simmer, stirring, for about
10 minutes until the sauce is fairly thick but will pour without
difficulty. You may need to add as much as 250 ml (½ pint) water
to get the proper thickness. When the sauce is done remove from
the heat, add lemon juice, and allow to cool to room temperature.

SALAD   Layer the salad ingredients in a large bowl (or place side
by side on a platter), topping with bean sprouts, cabbage and
sliced hard-boiled eggs. Pour the sauce over the salad and serve.
Serves 8–10.

Vegetable Curry

Curry spices: cardamom, turmeric, fenugreek, coriander,
    cumin
Ghee (see page 38) or butter
2 chopped onions
2–3 cloves garlic
1–2 fresh hot chilis, or cayenne

1–2 teaspoons grated fresh ginger
1 kg (2 lb) diced vegetables such as cauliflower, okra, celery, aubergine
125 ml (¼ pint) coconut milk (see page 58)
125 ml (¼ pint) yoghurt or curds (see page 37)

Fry the curry spices in the *ghee* or butter with onions, garlic, chilis and ginger. Blanch and then add the vegetables. Add a little water, the coconut milk and the yoghurt or curds. Cover and simmer for 30 minutes.

Pe t'sai
Celery Cabbage

Do not confuse *pe t'sai* with *bok choy* (Chinese chard), even though both are often sold as 'Chinese cabbage' and are often interchangeable—in fact, this dish could be easily made with *bok choy*.

500 g (1 lb) chopped celery cabbage
Pinch of bicarbonate of soda
5 dried mushrooms, soaked for at least ½ hour
1 tablespoon cornflour
250 ml (½ pint) chicken stock
2 tablespoons milk
Monosodium glutamate and pepper
100 g (4 oz) diced cooked ham

Blanch the cabbage by simmering it for 2–3 minutes with a pinch of bicarbonate of soda added to the water. Drain.

Drain and mince the mushrooms. Stir the cornflour into the stock and add the milk and seasonings.

Heat a little oil in a wok or frying pan and pour in the liquid. Simmer the sauce for a few minutes to thicken before adding the cabbage and mushrooms. Cook for 3 minutes. Serve sprinkled with diced ham.

Chinese Sweet and Sour Cabbage

  1 Chinese cabbage or Chinese chard, chopped
  1–2 teaspoons sliced fresh ginger
  Peanut oil
  1 tablespoon cornflour
  2 tablespoons soy sauce
  2 tablespoons sugar
  Dash of vinegar
  Salt

Soak the cabbage in cold water for 20 minutes. Drain. Sauté with the ginger in oil in a wok or frying pan. Mix the cornflour with the soy sauce, and add this mixture together with the other ingredients.

Finish cooking quickly as the cabbage must remain firm, as always in Chinese cooking.

Bok Choy

An important Chinese variety of cabbage, bok choy has thick, crisp white stems with dark green leaves. Remove the leaves, which are good for soups, and slice the stems evenly. The slices can be steamed and served plain, with a little soy sauce, but are best in soups or stir-fried. Heat peanut oil or lard very hot, then stir in finely sliced meats or vegetables. Bok choy retains its crispness well but should be added not long before cooking is done.

Mix bok choy with shredded beef, chicken or pork, spring onions, Chinese mushrooms etc., and season with soy sauce, sesame oil, garlic and ginger as desired.

Kimchi
Korean Pickled Cabbage

> 500 g (1 lb) chopped Chinese cabbage with some coarsely
>   grated black radish
> 2–3 fresh or dried hot chili peppers
> 1 clove garlic
> 1–2 teaspoons grated fresh ginger
> 2 spring onions, chopped
> 6 tablespoons salt

Salt the cabbage well, add water to cover, and soak for at least
2 hours. Rinse and drain.

Chop the seasonings together and mix with the cabbage. Add
the salt. Put in a glass or porcelain container and add just enough
water to cover. Keep covered and marinate in a cool place for at
least 3 days.

Serve with Chinese-style rice or millet porridge (see page 88).

Kimchi can also be bought prepared in Japanese or Chinese
food shops.

Water Chestnuts

Water chestnuts are eaten daily in many countries, but they have
passed out of most Western cooking. They are the same colour
as chestnuts but smaller and covered by a soft shell ending in
four crossed horns. The flesh also resembles that of chestnuts but
is crisper. Stored under water they can keep through the winter.
Cultivating them is easy: simply throw some water chestnuts in
shallow water and they should take root.

Water chestnuts can be eaten raw, boiled, or baked on coals, just
like chestnuts. They must be peeled. (Once peeled, they will dis-
colour unless placed in water to cover.)

China cultivates the plant seriously, as it is very nourishing and easy to produce. Its crisp texture, unaffected by cooking, is highly prized in many dishes. Much of the harvest comes from Chekiang, a region of very pure lakes with especially fertile bottoms. These water chestnuts are smooth, tender, and succulent, with fine skins, and rich in sugar, starch, vitamins and minerals. They can be eaten fresh but are often dried in the open air for storage. The Chinese also use them to make sugar, vinegar and many liqueurs.

Canned water chestnuts are available, but do not have the sweetness of fresh water chestnuts, which can be bought at many Chinese groceries.

Rumaki
Chicken Livers and Water Chestnuts

Despite the apparently Japanese name, this is originally a Chinese dish. Most of the ingredients, except for the water chestnuts which define the recipe, can be replaced by what is available.

    250 g (8 oz) water chestnuts
    250 ml (½ pint) chicken stock
    500 ml (1 pint) soy sauce

1–2 tablespoons sugar
Cinnamon, bay leaves
1–2 teaspoons grated fresh ginger
2 cloves garlic
Star anise or Szechuan pepper (see page 42)
500 g (1 lb) chicken livers
500 g (1 lb) sliced bacon
Vegetable oil

Peel the fresh water chestnuts and steam or parboil them for 5–10 minutes. Drain. (Canned water chestnuts need no parboiling.)

Mix the stock, soy sauce, sugar and spices. Bring to a boil and simmer for 5 minutes. Add the livers and simmer for 15 minutes. Drain the livers and allow to cool. (The marinade can be set aside and saved for future use.)

Cut each water chestnut in halves or thirds. Wrap a piece of liver and water chestnut in a strip of bacon and tie with thread.

Put a tiny bit of oil in a frying pan and fry the *rumaki* so that the bacon is crisp. Drain and serve hot.

Water Chestnuts with Giblets

This is a common dish in southern China.

350 g (12 oz) fresh (or a handful dried) water chestnuts
750 ml (1¼ pints) water
500 g (1 lb) chicken giblets
2 tablespoons soy sauce
1–2 teaspoons sugar

Canned water chestnuts should not be used in this recipe.

Pare and slice the water chestnuts. Simmer them gently in the water, along with the giblets, for 10–15 minutes. Add soy sauce and sugar.

If desired add some chopped onions or spring onions and fresh
ginger when serving.

Chinese Meat Roll

DOUGH:
250 g (8 oz) flour
125 g (4 oz) lard or margarine
1 egg

STUFFING:
250 g (8 oz) minced pork
125 g (4 oz) flaked crab meat or minced shrimp
250 g (8 oz) cooked water chestnuts, chopped
1 bunch spring onions, finely sliced
2 tablespoons soy sauce
Salt
2 pinches powdered ginger
2–3 cloves garlic, crushed
1 egg
Breadcrumbs

DOUGH   Knead the flour, lard and egg together to make a supple
dough. Add a little water if necessary.

STUFFING   Sauté the pork briefly in a wok or frying pan. (The
wok makes it possible to cook with very little grease or water,
which accounts for the crispness of Chinese cooking.) Add the
other ingredients, except the dough. Leave to cool.

Roll out the dough and divide into 4 rectangles. Lay some of
the stuffing on each piece of dough and roll up into long cylinders.
Seal the edges and lay out on a baking sheet. Bake for ½ hour at
175°C (350°F) or Gas 4. Cut in slices and serve. It is as good cold
as hot.

Dried Vegetables

In China, especially in the north where the severe winter prevents year-round cultivation of any vegetables, the need to preserve vegetables has led to the development of strange techniques. For instance, vegetables gathered at the onset of winter are piled in the courtyard and covered with earth. The pile is drenched with water, which freezes quickly. The vegetables thus stored will keep fresh until spring. When a cook needs a cabbage, a well-aimed pick can knock one out, protected by a shell of dirt and ice. This method, which works well for green vegetables, is varied for roots, which are buried 4 metres deep and dug up when needed.

A more useful technique for modern kitchens is drying vegetables; until recently it was one of the talents expected of a Chinese girl aspiring to marriage.

Vegetables delicately sliced, washed and salted, are strung on cotton thread and set to dry in the sun for a day. The needle used for stringing is always bamboo, and the method is used mainly in the south.

Dried Chinese vegetables are commonly available in oriental food shops and can be used to substitute for fresh vegetables in soups and some other dishes, though the flavour is often quite different. Dried water chestnuts and dried bitter melon strips are particularly recommended.

Daikon
Oriental Radish

A long thick white radish, often weighing over 1 kg (2 lb), *daikon* is one of the most commonly used vegetables in China and Japan.

    1 small *daikon*
    2–3 tablespoons sesame seeds
    1–2 tablespoons soy sauce
    1 tablespoon vinegar

Scrub the *daikon* and grate or slice finely. Toast the sesame seeds in a dry pan. Mix the ingredients together and serve.

If desired replace the sesame seed with 1–2 tablespoons of sesame oil.

Daikon can also be sliced and stir-fried with shredded chicken or bean curd, like water chestnuts or *bok choy* (see page 172).

Sautéed Pancake Strips and Vegetables

> 125 g (4 oz) flour
> Salt
> About 250 ml (½ pint) water
> 1 kg (2 lb) fresh vegetables such as broccoli, onions, peas, cabbage
> Peanut oil
> 2–3 tablespoons soy sauce
> Fresh coriander, watercress, parsley, sesame oil, hot peppers

Make a batter from the flour, salt and water and cook like pancakes. Roll out, leave to rest and then slice into ribbons. In a wok or frying pan sauté the mixed vegetables quickly in a very little peanut oil. Add the pancake ribbons. Season with soy sauce, sesame oil, spices and herbs.

Soya Beans

This common Asian bean was practically unknown in Europe and America until very recently, being known only as a health or exotic food and a commodity future, although we have now awakened to the value of soya beans as a substitute for meat.

The daily food of the Chinese peasant, soya balances an otherwise protein and vitamin-deficient diet. Soya lends itself for use in many recipes in many different forms, from flour to bean curd. Its hardiness as a plant is no small advantage: it is not attacked by insects and grows even in arid lands. Cultivated in China for at least 6,000 years, it did not reach Japan until the sixth century AD. Europe never heard the name until the seventeenth century. Now, although the human consumption of soya products is relatively low there, the United States is the leading producer of soya beans in the world. In the U.K. experiments are continuing to breed a strain of soya bean which will grow ̱atisfactorily in the colder climate.

There are many varieties of soya bean: yellow and red for salads, black—almost sweet—for soups, green for soups too. Sprouted soya beans, if less economical, are prized as green vegetables. Ground to a fine flour in the family mill, soya can be kneaded into noodles that keep through the winter. The simplest use of the flour is to boil it into porridge, often all there is to eat through lean periods. Serve soya porridge with bowls of hot water, without even a tea leaf for flavour, and hunger and thirst are officially relieved. Northern Chinese peasants make two kinds of 'butter', called *chiang*, from soya—one red, one black. Bean curd, bought from a grocer when means permit, though it can also be prepared at home, has a firm, smooth texture and can be fried or boiled in soups for simple meals or used in more elaborate recipes.

Although similar to other beans in appearance, soya's composition is different. Its proteins have the same balance of nutrients as animal proteins. Soya is also very digestible, due to low starch content and the presence in its oil of enzymes that break down proteins, sugars, and fats. But it needs longer cooking than any other bean—at least 2 hours simmering, longer if not tender by then. However long the cooking takes the beans will remain whole and firm, unlike some other types which start to disintegrate.

Soya flour can be used anywhere in place of wheat flour; for instance, in soya noodles. It also is used to make *shoyu* (soy sauce) and *miso*. Shoyu is a brown liquid obtained by the fermentation of soya mash mixed with barley and sea salt. The fermentation proceeds for 2 years before the mash is pressed to yield *shoyu*, the oriental seasoning *par excellence*.

Soy sauce is used carefully in soups and sauces, generally when the cooking is almost done.

Soya Salad

250 g (8 oz) soya beans, soaked overnight
750 ml (1½ pints) water
1–2 tablespoons soy sauce
2 tablespoons oil
2 tablespoons vinegar
700 g (1½ lb) diced or sliced fresh vegetables such as cucumber, radish, cabbage

Bring the soya beans and unsalted water to a boil. Cover and simmer for at least 2 hours. The beans will keep their texture no matter how long you cook them. Drain.

Season the beans with soy sauce, oil and vinegar. Mix in the vegetables.

Soup with Soya

2 onions
1 kg (2 lb) celery, cabbage, carrot, *bok choy* (see page 172)
Oil
1 litre (2 pints) water or stock
2 tablespoons soya flour
1–2 tablespoons soy sauce
3–4 tomatoes, diced

Coarsely chop the onions and vegetables, then brown in oil. Add the water or stock and simmer for 5–10 minutes. Thicken with soya flour previously mixed with a little cold water and simmer for 5 minutes. Add soy sauce and serve with the diced tomatoes.

Soya Milk

Thirty per cent sugars, thirty-five per cent proteins and fourteen per cent fat, soya beans can be made into a wonderfully rich vegetable milk which can be used by itself or further processed to make bean curd.

>   250 g (8 oz) soya beans
>   1.5 litres (2½ pints) water

Soak the soya beans for at least 10 hours. Purée in a food mill or blender and return to the water in which they soaked. Let the puréed soya soak for 24 hours, then squeeze out the milk by pressing through muslin. Or boil the mixture gently for 5–10 minutes, squeeze out the milk through muslin, return the remaining pulp to heat with a little more water, boil and press again, then mix the two filtrations. The milk has a fine aroma of malt and resembles condensed milk in texture. Consisting of 3 per cent vegetable casein and nearly 10 per cent fat, soya milk can be used to enrich soups and sauces, and in place of milk when baking cakes, pastry, etc.

The dry pulp left over, known as *okaru*, can be used like bran in baking.

Tofu
Soya Bean Curd

>   500 g (1 lb) soya beans
>   2½ litres (4½ pints) water

Curdling agent: 1¼ teaspoons *nigari* (Japanese sea salt);
   or 2½ tablespoons lemon or lime juice;
   or 1¼ teaspoons Epsom salts

Soak the beans, purée, and press as above to make soya milk.
Boil the soya milk over a medium heat for 5–7 minutes. Mix the
curdling agent in a cup of water and stir one-third of the solution
thoroughly into the milk. Sprinkle another one-third over the
surface and leave to stand for 3 minutes. Sprinkle the last third of
the solution over the soya milk and stir gently, barely dipping
the stirrer below the surface. Wait 4–6 minutes, then again stir
gently on the surface for 20–30 seconds. Try to avoid breaking up
the curds.

The curds should by now be suspended in almost clear whey.
Gently ladle the curds, breaking them up as little as possible, into
a fine strainer lined with cheesecloth and dampened with a little
of the whey. Fold the cloth over the curds and cover with a lid that
will fit directly on the curds. Put a weight on the lid and leave to
drain. After 10–15 minutes there should be no more whey dripping.

Carefully lift the curds in the cheesecloth out of the strainer
and place in a bowl of cold water. Remove the cheesecloth.

Keep bean curd cool under water until you are ready to use it.

The whole operation takes less than an hour if you have the
utensils to hand.

Bean Curd with Mushrooms

250 g (8 oz) mushrooms
Peanut oil
1 large bean curd pad
2 tablespoons soy sauce
Salt
1 tablespoon cornflour

Sauté the mushrooms in peanut oil. Add fine slices of bean curd, soy sauce and salt. Sauté for 2 minutes more, then thicken with the cornflour previously mixed with a little cold water. If desired, add sesame oil, grated fresh ginger or spring onions to taste.

Serves 2.

Fried Bean Curd

    500 g (1 lb) bean curd
    50 g (2 oz) flour
    1 egg
    100 ml (a scant ¼ pint) milk or beer
    Peanut oil

Cut the bean curd into cubes or slices. Mix the flour, egg and milk to make a thick frying batter. If desired, separate the egg first and beat the white before mixing into the batter. Dip the bean curd in the batter and deep fry in peanut oil. Serve with sautéed onion rings and shrimp.

Sautéed Bean Curd

    1 large bean curd pad
    Peanut oil
    2 tablespoons soy sauce
    1 tablespoon cornflour
    2 cloves garlic
    2 shallots

Cut the bean curd into 1-cm (½-in) cubes. Sauté quickly in a little peanut oil in a wok or frying pan stirring constantly. Add soy sauce, cornflour (mixed first with a little water), crushed garlic and shallots. Salt and serve.

Hiya Yakko
Japanese Bean Curd with Shrimps

>   1 handful dried shrimps or tuna
>   1 large bean curd pad
>   1 small onion, chopped
>   1 tablespoon soy sauce
>   1 pinch monosodium glutamate
>   Fresh ginger (optional)

Soak the shrimps or tuna in a little warm water for 15 minutes. Cut the bean curd in thick slices and arrange on a serving plate. Cover with shrimps and raw onion. Sprinkle with soy sauce and monosodium glutamate. Add grated fresh ginger if desired.
    Serve cool just as it is.

Soup with Bean Curd and Water Chestnuts

>   250 g (8 oz) water chestnuts
>   1 litre (2 pints) stock
>   250 g (8 oz) finely minced pork
>   250 g (8 oz) chopped Chinese cabbage
>   500 g (1 lb) bean curd, cut into (½-in) cubes
>   2 tablespoons soy sauce

Pare and slice the water chestnuts; heat the stock. Add the pork and simmer for 3 minutes before adding the cabbage, water chestnuts and bean curd. Simmer for 5 minutes more, add the soy sauce and serve.

Sautéed Soya Beans

>   500 g (1 lb) soya beans, soaked overnight
>   250 g (8 oz) pork or fish

1 tablespoon oil
1 leek, finely sliced
1–2 teaspoons grated or sliced fresh ginger
2 tablespoons dry white wine or dry sherry
3 tablespoons soy sauce
1 tablespoon sugar

Simmer the soya beans for 2 hours in unsalted water. Drain.

Sauté 1-cm (½-in) cubes of pork or slices of fish in the oil. Add the leek, ginger, wine, soy sauce and sugar. Mix in the beans and cover tightly. Simmer gently for ½ hour.

Serve hot or cold.

Ful medames
Arab Beans

Ful is eaten with flat, braided Egyptian bread.

500 g (1 lb) dry red beans, soaked overnight
250 g (8 oz) red lentils, soaked overnight
2 litres (4 pints) water
Salt
150 ml (¼ pint) olive oil
Juice of 2 lemons

Put beans and lentils into a large saucepan, add the water and cook for about 2 hours. Make sure to keep up the water level. Avoid lifting the pot cover often or the beans will blacken.

When cooked, add salt and sprinkle them with olive oil and lemon juice.

Serve with hard-boiled eggs, onions or fresh herbs such as mint, parsley or coriander.

Ta'amia
Bean Croquettes

These Arab croquettes are very good with aperitifs.

> 250 g (8 oz) dried beans, soaked overnight
> Chopped fresh parsley
> 150 g (5 oz) moistened breadcrumbs
> Salt
> Coriander
> 2 chopped onions
> Pinch of bicarbonate of soda
> Oil
> 1–2 cloves garlic
> 125 g (4 oz) chopped almonds or walnuts (optional)

Drain the beans and put through a food grinder. Mash together with the other ingredients (except oil) in a mortar, leave for about 2 hours, then shape into croquettes and fry in oil.

If desired, grind in the chopped almonds or walnuts.

Ethiopian Wot
Bean Stew

This very spicy concoction complements *indjera* (see page 73), wide grey pancakes made from millet flour. Wot is cooked in a clay pot over a fire of dried cow dung. It is served to a circle of gathered guests, who convivially dip *indjera* in the common pot to soak up the sauce. The Ethiopians wash it down with gulps of *talla*, a tart barley beer. Women eat after the men have finished. The meal is rounded off with some dental hygiene—chewing on a twig—then some spiced coffee sweetened with honey. Wot can be made from any available protein; eggs and chicken are often used.

2 chopped onions
Butter
250 g (8 oz) dried haricot beans, soaked overnight, or 500 g
    (1 lb) fresh beans in season
Cayenne
Salt

Brown the onions in butter. Add the beans and lots of cayenne; this dish should be hot. Add plenty of water and simmer for 1½–2 hours. Add salt when cooked.

On flush days add a chicken or pieces of lamb or beef to stew with the beans. Otherwise serve with hard-boiled eggs.

Boston Baked Beans

The New England classic.

500 g (1 lb) haricot beans, washed and soaked overnight in
    water 3 to 4 times their volume
1 small onion
1 clove garlic
125 ml (¼ pint) molasses or black treacle
4 tablespoons beer or bean water
1 tablespoon dry mustard
4 tablespoons ketchup
1 tablespoon salt

Stir together all ingredients except the beans and leave to stand. Cook the beans in the soaking water until tender; about 1 hour. Drain, reserving the liquid. Mix together the sauce and drained beans and turn into a well-greased baking dish (or bean pot). Bake, covered, for 8–10 hours at 120°C (250°F) or Gas ½. Stir once an hour for the first 3 hours; add reserved liquid as needed to keep them from drying out. Remove the cover for the last ½ hour of cooking.

Cassoulet

This simple French bean stew is best known in the following version from Toulouse, but there are many regional variations. Cassoulet owes its name to a kind of clay pot once used to cook the stew slowly throughout the day as it sat near the warm hearth. The dish is still best prepared in an earthenware dish in a low oven.

> 500 g (1 lb) dried white beans (navy or haricot beans)
> 1½ litres (3 pints) cold water
> Bay leaves, sage, rosemary, parsley
> 1 onion stuck with 3 or 4 cloves
> 600 g (1–1½ lb) chopped bacon, rind, ham and salt pork, mixed
> 1½ kg (3–4 lb) lamb, whole or cut up coarsely
> 500 g (1 lb) smoked garlic sausage, such as *cervelas*
> 75 g (3 oz) breadcrumbs

Pick over the beans carefully and rinse twice. Add the cold water. Soak overnight or bring to a boil, remove from heat and soak for 40 minutes. Drain.

Tie the herbs and spices up in a piece of cheesecloth and put into a large clay pot with the beans, the onion, the pork and enough water to cover the beans by at least 1 cm. Bring to a boil slowly and simmer for 1 hour. Be sure to use very low heat or an asbestos pad to prevent cracking. During that hour cook the lamb partially by baking at 110°C (225°F) or Gas ¼.

Drain the meat and beans, reserving the liquid. Discard herbs and onion. Return about ⅓ of the beans to the pot, cover with a layer of sliced sausage, then a layer of beans, then the lamb, then the rest of the beans. Cover with a thin layer of breadcrumbs and sprinkle with about half the liquid. Bake in a low oven 130°C (250°F) or Gas ½ for 1 hour, checking to be sure the beans do not dry out. The breadcrumbs should brown.

Stir the mixture, top with another layer of breadcrumbs, then add the rest of the liquid. Add water or stock if the beans are too dry. Cook for another hour until the breadcrumbs brown and form a crust.

Serve in earthenware bowls.

Serves 6–8.

Feijoada
Brazilian Black Bean Stew

Feijoada is the Brazilian national dish, made with black beans and as many different kinds of meat as possible. The various parts of the pig—ears, snout, knuckles, trotters, tongue, jowls, organs, and rind—usually relegated to sausages in this country—in addition to the more familiar fatback and salt pork, are particularly important in giving a fine richness to the black beans. It is sad to note that Brazil's 'economic miracle', its fast industrial growth and entry into the world market, has caused neglect of its black bean crop in favour of dramatic increases in export cash crops such as soya beans and coffee. As a result this popular staple has had to be rationed.

1 kg (2 lb) salt pork, ears, tail, skin, knuckles, snout etc.
1 kg (2 lb) black beans
500 g (1 lb) *linguiça* (Brazilian sausage), *chorizo* or other sharp, smoked sausage.
1 large fresh or smoked beef tongue, or a large joint of meat such as lamb shoulder
Bay leaves, mace
2–3 onions, chopped
500 g (1 lb) tomatoes, chopped
2–3 cloves garlic
Parsley

Oranges
250 g (8 oz) bacon

Soak the pork in cold water overnight, rinse and drain.

Pick over the beans carefully—there are often stones among the beans even when they come in a plastic package. Rinse twice and soak in 3 litres (6 pints) water overnight. Or rinse twice, cover with cold water, bring to the boil, remove from heat and leave for 40–60 minutes. Drain.

Put the drained beans, bacon, sausage, pork, and tongue in a big pan. If using a salted or pickled tongue, soak for several hours, rinse and drain before cooking. Also, if the tongue weighs over 2½ kg (5 lb), simmer it for 30–60 minutes before adding the beans and pork. Add fresh water to cover. Add bay leaves and mace. Bring to the boil and simmer gently for about 2 hours.

Sauté the onions, tomatoes, garlic and parsley in fat skimmed from the beans or in butter. Add a ladle or two of the cooked beans from the pot, sauté and mash to make a thick, smooth sauce. Use a blender if desired.

Remove the tongue or joint from the pot. Mix in the sauce with the beans. Season to taste. Skin the tongue and slice or carve the joint. Serve on a platter together with bowls of beans, rice, *farofa* (see below) and sliced oranges. If desired, take unwanted pieces of pork out of the beans before serving.

Serves 8–10.

Farofa
Manioc Garnish

A Brazilian dish served with *feijoada*. The *mandioca* meal is available at delicatessens.

150 g (5 oz) manioc (*mandioca*) meal
30 g (2–3 tablespoons) fat or butter

Brown the *mandioca* meal in the hot fat. It should be crisp. Sprinkle over the *feijoada*.

Frijoles
Mexican Beans

A Mexican favourite, also called refried beans.

> 500 g (1 lb) black beans, soaked overnight
> 2–3 hot dried or fresh chilis, or 1 teaspoon chili powder
> 100 g (4 oz) diced ham
> Lard
> 2–3 onions, finely chopped
> 2—3 sliced sweet peppers
> 2–3 cloves garlic
> Salt and pepper

Cook the beans for 1½ hours in the water they soaked in. Drain, saving the water. Remove seeds and stems from the chilis. If using dried chilis soak for 20–30 minutes in warm water. Drain, saving the liquid to add to the beans, and chop.

Sauté the ham in lard. Add the onions, chilis, sweet peppers and garlic and sauté a few minutes longer.

Add the beans and seasoning. Cook, stirring and mashing, occasionally adding a little of the water saved from cooking the beans so that the mixture forms a smooth cream.

Serve piping hot. Like tortillas, this is often a complete meal.

Dhal

> 375 g (12 oz) *moong dhal* (small yellow grains similar to split peas), or other *dhal* (see pages 65, 310)

    1 litre (2 pints) water
    Salt
    2 cloves garlic, chopped
    3–5 whole cardamoms
    1 tablespoon cumin seeds
    Ghee (see page 38) or oil
    The juice of 1 lime

Bring the *dhal* and water to a boil, cover and simmer for 1 hour. The result should be a moist but thick porridge. Season with salt when cooked.

Fry the garlic, cardamom, and cumin for 5 minutes in *ghee*. If you prefer not to have whole spices in this dish, grind them in a pestle and mortar before frying. Mix with the *dhal*. Sprinkle with the lime juice and serve with rice.

VARIATION Boil the *dhal* with whole cardamoms and cumin for 1 hour. Mix with lime juice and serve with rice.

Creole Lentils

    700 g (1½ lb) lentils, soaked overnight
    3 onions, finely chopped
    3 sliced sweet peppers
    500 g (1 lb) tomatoes, chopped
    Salt, pepper, sugar

Cook the lentils in plenty of *unsalted* boiling water for about 30 minutes. Drain.

Brown the onions and peppers and add the tomatoes. Season, add the lentils and simmer for ½ hour or so.

Serve with rice.

Mexican Lentils

This dish is also commonly made with black beans.

250 g (8 oz) lentils, soaked overnight
250 ml (½ pint) tomato sauce (see page 55) with chilis and
   epazote (see page 41)
2 onions, finely sliced
2 sweet potatoes, minced

Simmer the lentils in plenty of *unsalted* water for about 30 minutes. Drain. Add to a thick, highly seasoned tomato sauce and simmer for 5–10 minutes.

Brown the onions and sweet potatoes (called *camotes* in Mexico, often available as *batatas*). Add to the lentils, simmer gently another few minutes and serve.

Serves 2–3

Black-eyed Peas

A standard vegetable from the American Deep South, black-eyed peas are usually bought dried and prepared like other dried legumes. Cooking time is greatly reduced if they are soaked overnight before cooking.

250 g (8 oz) black-eyed peas
750 ml (1½ pints) water
250 g (8 oz) salt pork or 3 strips bacon
1 large onion
Salt, pepper, basil to taste

Soak the peas overnight, then bring to a boil in the soaking water, reducing the heat to a simmer. Cook until tender; about 2 hours. Add the onion and salt pork at the beginning of the cooking time; seasonings at the end.

Stewed Greens and Pot Likker

Greens are the most common element of all 'soul food'—the typical food of black (and white) Americans from the rural South. They can be collard greens, mustard greens, turnip or beet tops, kale, dandelion, cress or pokeweed, but they are all cooked in about the same manner. If meat is added to the dish, it can be served as the main course; if meat isn't added, put in a little bacon fat or salt pork for flavour.

> 1½ kg (3 lb) fresh greens
> 500 g (1 lb) ham or 250 g (8 oz) salt pork or bacon
> 1½ litre (3 pints) water
> ¼ teaspoon red pepper
> Salt and black pepper

Wash and drain the greens; if they are old, place them in ice water to help draw away the bitterness. Chop coarsely. Chop the meat into small chunks and cook in water for about an hour. Add the greens, season and simmer for another 30 minutes. Drain off the greens and ham, spoon them over corn bread or potatoes and spoon the cooking juice—pot likker—over all.

Baked Lettuce

Any of the soft varieties of lettuce with a strong taste—such as chicory, escarole, or endive—is good cooked as well as in salads. Ordinary salad lettuce, grown for its crispness, does not have enough taste to be used in cooking. Curly endive, escarole, and common chicory (not to be mistaken for the expensive Belgian chicory) can be washed and steamed for 5–10 minutes and served like spinach with lemon or butter.

A popular French way to serve wilted lettuce, and for that matter any greens (turnip, carrot, beet tops or nettles) is *au gratin*, that is, baked until it has a crust.

  1 head escarole, lettuce, curly endive or common chicory
  1 thick slice bacon, chopped
  Thyme and pepper (optional)

Wash the lettuce and discard the core. Parboil in salted water for 2–3 minutes to reduce the bitterness and drain. Dry thoroughly. Chop and mix with chopped bacon (and some thyme and pepper) and put in a baking dish. Bake at 190°C (375°F) or Gas 5 for 30–40 minutes until crisp on top. Serve hot.

   You can sprinkle grated hard cheese, such as Gruyère, over the lettuce before baking.

Antilles Sweet Corn

  6 ears fresh sweet corn
  2 onions, finely chopped
  2 sliced green peppers, deseeded
  250 ml (½ pint) thick tomato sauce (see page 55)
  Salt and pepper
  Suggested spices : cayenne, cumin
  Breadcrumbs
  Grated cheese

Cut the grains of corn from the cob.

   Brown the onions and peppers; add tomato sauce and seasoning. Simmer for 2–3 minutes before adding the corn. Cover and simmer for 5–8 minutes until tender.

   Pour into a baking tin and sprinkle with breadcrumbs and grated cheese. Bake for 20 minutes at 175°C (350°F) or Gas 4.

Succotash

This fresh corn and bean stew, adapted by American colonists from the American Indian dish *m'sick-quotash*, has innumerable 'authentic' versions, not the least interesting of which is a Pennsylvania Dutch variation which adds potatoes and tomatoes.

4–5 rashers bacon, finely chopped
2 onions, chopped
1 green pepper, cut into strips
450 g (1 lb) sweet corn kernels, fresh or canned
450 g (1 lb) fresh broad beans or canned butter beans
4 tablespoons water
1 tablespoon chopped parsley
1 tablespoon butter
Salt and pepper

Render the bacon over medium heat, add the onions and pepper, and sauté until onions are golden. Add the corn, the beans and water; cover and simmer until vegetables are tender. Mix in the finely chopped parsley, butter, salt and pepper (be liberal with the pepper). Adjust seasoning to taste and serve.

Turkish Carrots

750 g (1½ lb) carrots
1 egg, beaten
100 g (4 oz) breadcrumbs
Oil
250 ml (½ pint) yoghurt
1–2 cloves garlic, crushed
Salt
Fresh mint, crumpled

Cook the carrots in water for 10–15 minutes. Do not overcook as they should be firm. Drain, dip in egg and breadcrumbs and fry in oil.

Beat the yoghurt with the garlic, salt and mint. Pour over the hot carrots and serve. This is also good cold.

Central European Potatoes

Potatoes are central Europe's standard fare, and are used there in innumerable recipes, though simple boiled potatoes are still favourites from the Atlantic to the Urals, whether served plain, with soup or with sour cream.

For variety, potatoes are often made into dumplings or *gnocchi*, and poached. Recipes of that type are numerous, from *knödels* to *kluskis* (see page 294). Stuffed dumplings akin to *pieroshki* and ravioli can be found in the meat chapter of this book—they are really ways to stretch a little meat to feed a lot of people.

Hutspot
Dutch Potatoes and Carrots

Eaten every 3 October in Leyden in honour of the raising of a year-long siege by the Spanish in 1573. The starving Dutch broke the siege so suddenly that the Spanish left their dinners cooking behind them. This may have been the first time the Dutch saw potatoes, which had only recently arrived in Europe from Peru.

700 g (1½ lb) potatoes
2–3 carrots
2–3 onions
2–3 cloves
Salt and pepper

Peel the potatoes, carrots, and onions. Cover with water along with the cloves, salt and pepper and boil for 30 minutes. Drain and mash. Serve with boiled beef.

Bubble and Squeak (Colcannon)
Refried Potatoes and Cabbage

Known in Yorkshire as 'bubble and squeak' on account of the sounds it makes when cooking, is leftover mashed potatoes fried with some leftover green vegetable, usually cabbage. Stir the cold vegetables together with the potatoes and fry them lightly in butter, stirring occasionally. They should be moist and hot but not particularly crisp on the bottom. Scoop the bubble and squeak on to plates, making a depression in the centre for 1 tablespoon of butter. The dish is called Colcannon in Ireland and is traditionally made with kale, not cabbage.

Stuffed Cabbage

Throughout much of Eastern Europe Jews and Christians shared villages and a taste for stuffed cabbage. The Christians made theirs with pork and a spicy meat gravy. The Jews made theirs with beef and a sweet and sour sauce. This is a Jewish recipe.

    1 large green cabbage
    1 onion, chopped
    500 g (1 lb) minced beef or lamb
    125 g (4 oz) rice
    1 carrot, grated
    50 g (2 oz) raisins
    Salt and pepper
    250 ml (½ pint) tomato sauce (see page 55)

75 g (3 oz) honey or brown sugar
Juice of 2 lemons or 4 tablespoons vinegar

Simmer the cabbage in salted water for 10–15 minutes. Remove from the water and carefully peel off the outer leaves. Repeat, simmering 5–10 minutes more and removing another few layers of leaves. Cut away any tough ribs that will make it difficult to roll the leaves.

Brown the onion in oil, mix in the meat, rice, carrot and some of the raisins. Cook for 2–3 minutes, add salt and pepper. Put one or two spoonfuls of meat on each leaf, fold the edges over the stuffing and roll closed. Set in a casserole with the seam down.

Mix the tomato sauce with honey, lemon juice and the rest of the raisins. Pour over the stuffed cabbage, cover and bake for 40–50 minutes at 175°C (350°F) or Gas 4. Serve hot.

Celeriac

The knobby root of a scraggly variety of celery, celeriac has a stronger but perhaps more complex taste and a denser texture. It can be peeled and grated coarsely or sliced finely to be served raw

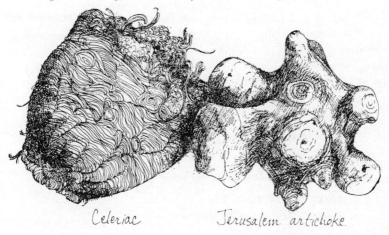

Celeriac   Jerusalem artichoke.

as a salad with some lemon juice or mayonnaise. Or, scrub it, cover with salted water and boil gently, whole, for 20–30 minutes. Drain, peel and cut up. Serve hot with butter or lemon.

It is good grated in stews and salads.

Jerusalem Artichokes

The Jerusalem artichoke is the root of a common sunflower and the name may be a corruption of the Italian word for that plant, *girasole*. Once a staple of the American Indians, it resembles a ginger root in appearance. Although often available in green-grocers here it is not as popular as it is in France and Italy, where it is prized as a delicacy.

Peel and grate for a salad. Or, scrub and boil for 15 minutes and serve like celeriac (see above). It gets mushy if overcooked, so check frequently while cooking to see if it is getting tender.

A popular way to prepare it is *au gratin*:

> 500 g (1 lb) Jerusalem artichokes
> 2 tablespoons butter
> Grated Parmesan or other hard cheese

Scrub the roots and put into lightly boiling salted water. Simmer for 5–10 minutes until they begin to get tender. Drain, slice evenly and lay out in a baking dish. Dot with butter and sprinkle with cheese. Bake for 30–40 minutes at 190°C (375°F) or Gas 5 until a crust forms. Serve hot.

Spinach with Sesame

This dish is of Japanese origin.

> 2 tablespoons sesame seeds
> 2 tablespoons soy sauce

2 tablespoons rice vinegar
1 tablespoon sugar
750 g (1½ lb) cooked, drained spinach

Grill the sesame seeds gently in a frying pan. Crush and mix with
soy sauce and vinegar. Add the sugar.
  Mix with spinach and serve cold.

Spinach Cocas
Spinach Turnovers

From Majorca.

  BREAD DOUGH:
  15 g (½ oz) dried yeast
  ½ teaspoon sugar
  About 350 ml (12 fl oz) lukewarm water
  500 g (1 lb) flour
  ½ teaspoon salt
  Oil

  FILLING:
  500 g (1 lb) cooked spinach
  Fresh, chopped parsley
  1–2 cloves garlic, minced
  Salt, pepper, cayenne
  250 g (8 oz) Cheddar cheese
  Milk

Mix the yeast and sugar with ⅓ of the water and leave to stand
until frothy, 10–15 minutes. Add to the flour and salt gradually
with enough of the remaining water to make a firm dough. Knead
for 8–10 minutes on a floured board. Cover and let rise for 1–2
hours in a warm place.

Reknead the dough, working in a little oil to make it softer. Leave under a cloth for 20–30 minutes to rise.

Roll out the dough and cut into saucer-like discs.

Stuff each disc with some spinach mixed with parsley, garlic, seasonings and a piece of cheese. Fold over and seal the sides like a turnover. Brush with milk and bake for ½ hour at 175°C (350°F) or Gas 4.

Kombu Seaweed Salad

A Japanese delicacy, dried *kombu* or kelp is available at Japanese or health food shops.

> 250 g (8 oz) dried *kombu*
> 3 tablespoons soy sauce
> Juice of 1 lemon

Soak the *kombu* in water to cover for at least 30 minutes. Drain, reserving the liquid. Mix the *kombu* with soy sauce, lemon juice and about half the liquid. Marinate for 20–30 minutes and serve.

Fresh Seaweed Salad

To find fresh seaweed you'll probably have to forage it yourself. If you live near the sea you will discover that edible seaweed is easy to identify and pick. If not familiar with the different kinds consult Richard Mabey's *Food for Free* (Fontana/Collins.)

> 500 g (1 lb) fresh seaweed (kelp or laver)
> 450 ml (¾ pint) coconut milk (see page 58)
> Juice of 1 lemon
> ½–1 teaspoon cayenne

Wash the seaweed thoroughly and marinate in coconut milk, lemon juice and cayenne for at least 20 minutes.

Samphire or Glasswort

Often confused with seaweed, marsh samphire (*Salicornia europaea* or glasswort)grows along the coast on tidal flats.Samphirewas once very popular along the shores of both France and England, usually preserved in vinegar, like gherkins. In France it is still commercially cultivated. Elsewhere you may have to gather it yourself—not such a difficult task if you live near the sea, since the plants are common and easily identifiable. Glasswort can be served fresh in salad or cooked as a vegetable. Only the fleshy parts of the leaves are good to eat and only when very fresh.

   1½ kg (3 lb) fresh samphire
   Butter

Wash well and trim, cutting away sticky and withered parts. Boil for approximately 30 minutes. Drain carefully and serve with butter.

   Eat by biting down on the stems and pulling out the edible pulp with your teeth.

Panisses
Chickpea Polenta

All around the Mediterranean chickpeas are not only used as a vegetable indispensable in many recipes, but also ground for flour. The flour is used in this Provençale recipe for *panisses*, which are known as *panizze* in Portugal. Chickpea flour can be produced at home in a blender or coffee grinder (see page 48), if you can't find it in any stores.

250 g (8 oz) chickpea flour
1 litre (2 pints) water
Bay leaves
Olive oil
Salt

Mix the flour with the water to make a smooth cream. Add a few bay leaves, a dash of oil and simmer the mixture in a pot, stirring steadily for 20–30 minutes until it thickens. Remove and season with salt.

Pour into a wide-rimmed plate or into saucers or moulds. Leave to cool, turn the *polenta* out of the moulds and fry gently.

NOTE   *Panisses* can also be made with maize flour.

Italian *farinada* is similar to *panisses* but is made with white pea flour.

Calentica
Chickpea Bread

Use the same ingredients as for *panisses*, except for the bay leaves.

Mix the chickpea flour with the water. Add salt, pepper and a dash of oil. Leave to stand for several hours.

Beat for a short time, then pour into an oiled baking tin. Bake for 20 minutes at 230°C (450°F) or Gas 8. Serve hot.

Like *panisses*, *calentica* is often sold by street vendors.

Hummus
Chickpea Paste

125 ml (¼ pint) *tahina* (sesame paste or powder)
250 g (8 oz) chickpeas, soaked overnight

125 ml (¼ pint) olive oil
Juice of 1 lemon
Salt and pepper
3–4 cloves garlic, crushed
Crushed mint

Simmer the chickpeas in *unsalted* water to cover for 2 hours or until tender. Drain, saving the liquid.

Mash the chickpeas in a pestle and mortar to make a thick, dry purée. Add the *tahina*, oil, lemon juice, salt, pepper, garlic and crushed mint. Or mix chickpeas with other ingredients and purée in a blender, adding chickpea liquid if the mixture is too dry.

Let cool in a serving plate or individual bowls. It should be firm.

Serve with salted cucumbers, raw vegetables, and the famous Arab round, flat bread, *pita*. Use pieces of *pita* or raw onion as scoops to eat the hummus. If desired, sprinkle with additional olive oil and chopped parsley, and serve together with *ful medames* (see page 185).

Hummus may be prepared with *tahina* or oil, or with smaller quantities than given here.

Bollitos

250 g (8 oz) chickpeas, soaked overnight
2 eggs
2–3 cloves garlic, crushed
Salt and pepper
Oil or fat

Simmer the chickpeas in *unsalted* water to cover for 2 hours or until tender. Drain. Crush with garlic in a pestle and mortar or put through a Mouli-légumes. Mix with eggs and seasoning to make a thick paste. Leave for an hour or more, then drop spoonfuls into very hot fat and fry on both sides. Drain and serve burning hot.

Israeli Falafel

> 250 g (8 oz) chickpea purée
> 3–4 cloves garlic, crushed
> Salt and pepper
> 2 eggs
> About 4 tablespoons water
> Flour

Mash all the ingredients together or purée in a blender to make a stiff paste. Place in the refrigerator for a few hours.

Shape into sausages or balls and dip in flour.

Lay out on an oiled, floured baking sheet. Bake for 15–20 minutes at 200°C (400°F) or Gas 6 until brown. They may also be browned in a pan or deep fried.

Serve falafel hot by itself or with salad. It is commonly served in *pita* bread with salad, *tahina* (sesame paste) and *harif* (hot sauce).

If desired, add spices and herbs such as mint, basil, cumin and fresh coriander to the paste.

Nahit
Roasted Chickpeas

A traditional Israeli treat.

> 250 g (8 oz) chickpeas, soaked overnight
> Salt

Simmer the chickpeas for 1–2 hours until just tender; drain. Spread on a large oiled baking sheet and sprinkle with salt.

Bake for 20 minutes at 175°C (350°F) or Gas 4.

Serve like salted nuts.

Tuono e lampo
Chickpeas with Pasta

The Italians call this *tuono e lampo*, 'thunder and lightning'. It is made from broken pasta sold cheaply.

> 250 g (8 oz) chickpeas, soaked overnight
> 500 ml (1 pint) water
> Bay leaves
> 250 g (8 oz) broken pasta
> 250 ml (½ pint) tomato sauce (see page 55)
> Salt and pepper
> Chopped fresh basil and parsley
> Oil or butter
> Grated Parmesan cheese

Cook the soaked chickpeas in the water with bay leaves for 2 hours or until tender. Cook the broken pasta separately in abundant salted water; drain. Drain the chickpeas, reserving the water in which they were cooked. Reduce this water to about 150 ml (¼ pint) and add to the tomato sauce. Mix sauce, seasonings, chickpeas and pasta.

Serve sprinkled with oil and plenty of Parmesan.

Romanian Chickpeas

> 500 g (1 lb) cooked chickpeas
> 125 g (4 oz) rice
> 500 ml (1 pint) water
> 175 ml (6 oz) honey
> Salt

Mix all the ingredients in a casserole and simmer for 20 minutes, adding water as necessary.

Bake for 15 minutes at 175°C (350°F) or Gas 4 to brown the top.

Garbanzos and Rice
Spanish Chickpeas

> 2 onions, finely chopped
> Olive oil
> 1½ kg (2–3 lb) chicken or rabbit, cut up
> 125 g (4 oz) ham
> 2–3 cloves garlic, chopped
> Salt and pepper
> 500 ml (1 pint) water
> 250 g (8 oz) chickpeas, soaked overnight
> 250 g (8 oz) rice
> 125 g (4 oz) *chorizo* (Spanish sausage)
> 4 eggs, beaten

Brown the onions in oil. Add the chicken, ham and garlic and brown. Season and add water to cover. Simmer for 40 minutes.

Add the chickpeas, rice, sliced *chorizo* and more water to cover. Simmer for 50 minutes. Pour over the beaten eggs and bake for 5–10 minutes at 175°C (350°F) or Gas 4 until the eggs are just cooked.

Serve hot.

Bagna Cauda
Raw Vegetables in Hot Anchovy Dip

This classic peasant dish from the Piedmont region of Italy is usually consumed with plenty of coarse red wine and bread. The sauce should be prepared in an earthenware pot and kept warm over very low heat while the dipping goes on. To finish off the meal (when you run out of vegetables and a little sauce is still left in the pot), break a couple of eggs into the pot, turn up the flame (or put on a very low flame over a gas burner) and scramble the mixture together.

4 tablespoons butter
250 ml (½ pint) olive oil
2–4 cloves garlic, chopped
250 g (8 oz) anchovies, chopped (1 small can)
Assorted raw vegetables, washed and peeled: sweet peppers, spinach, carrots, cardoons (if possible, or celery), courgettes, fennel, radishes, sliced cabbage, broccoli (especially the stalks)
Salt to taste

Melt the butter and oil in a pot over a low heat. Add the garlic and sauté for a minute or two; then add the chopped anchovies. The anchovies will gradually dissolve and you can help the process by mashing with a wooden spoon as you stir. Simmer for about 10 minutes stirring occasionally. Transfer the pot to sit above a candle or spirit warmer on the table. Give the vegetables a good dip in the sauce, stirring up the anchovy paste from time to time to keep it mixed in with the oil. A chunk of bread held under the dipped vegetable will keep the oil from dripping on the table.

Stuffed Squash Flowers

The Greek peasants who developed this recipe get their fresh-picked marrow or pumpkin flowers from their own garden plots.

1–2 cloves garlic
1 bunch spring onions
Olive oil

250 g (8 oz) rice
4 tablespoons tomato purée
Fennel and mint
Fresh parsley
Salt, sugar, cinnamon
2 dozen marrow flowers in full bloom
1 egg, beaten
Lemon juice

Finely chop the garlic and spring onions and brown in oil. Add the rice, tomato purée, herbs and seasonings.

Carefully stuff each flower and turn the petals in over the stuffing. Arrange out in a frying pan and cover with water. Cook for 25 minutes over a low flame. Thicken the gravy with a beaten egg and add a dash of lemon juice.

VARIATION   The water in which the stuffed flowers are cooked may be replaced with tomato sauce. Sometimes minced lamb is added to the stuffing, replacing some of the rice.

Male blossom (on stem)

Female blossom (on young squash)

Radikya
Greek Dandelion Leaves

Young dandelion leaves or *radikya* are well appreciated in Greece, especially as a cooked salad.

   1 kg (2 lb) dandelion leaves
   Olive oil
   Lemon juice
   Salt and pepper

Wash the dandelion leaves well and blanch (boil briefly) in salted water. Drain completely.

   Serve sprinkled with oil, lemon juice, salt and pepper. Radikya often accompanies fish and meat.

Bamias
Greek Okra and Tomatoes

These plump green vegetables are often found in Mediterranean cooking.

   1 kg (2 lb) okra
   Salt
   2 minced onions
   Olive oil
   500 g (1 lb) chopped tomatoes
   Sugar, salt, pepper
   Dash of vinegar

Trim the ends of the okra. Salt and let them 'sweat'—lose some of their moisture—preferably in the sun.

   Brown the onions in oil and add the chopped tomatoes. Add the rinsed and drained okra and seasonings. Simmer for about 1 hour.

   Serve hot or cold.

Egyptian Bamias
Okra and Lamb

Dried *bamias* (dried okra) are available at some Middle Eastern shops.

> 1 kg (2 lb) fresh *bamias* or 200 g (7 oz) dried *bamias*
> 2–3 chopped onions
> 2–3 cloves garlic, chopped
> Oil or lamb fat
> 350 g (12 oz) diced lamb
> 400 ml (¾ pint) boiling water
> Salt and pepper
> Ground coriander, cumin

Soak fresh *bamias* for ½ hour in salted water. Drain. (If using dried *bamias* soak in fresh water for at least 1 hour. Drain.)

Brown the onions and garlic in oil or lamb fat, add the *bamias* and then the meat. Season and add the boiling water.

Simmer gently until the meat is tender; about 1 hour. (If you use minced lamb, you only need cook it for 30–45 minutes.)

Dolmas
Stuffed Vine Leaves

Stuffed vine leaves are another of the dishes common all around the Mediterranean. The stuffing is not rich, being composed mainly of rice, but on flush days it may include some mutton, the local cheap meat. Gather fresh young leaves off a grape vine; or use tinned vine leaves (from delicatessen or Greek food shops); or white and tender inner cabbage leaves.·

> 10–20 tender grape vine leaves
> 150 g (5 oz) rice

1 bunch spring onions
Fennel and mint
Salt and pepper
Olive oil
250 ml (½ pint) water

Blanch the leaves gently for 2 minutes and drain in cheesecloth.

Mix the rice, spring onions, herbs and seasoning with a little oil. Brown and then cook for 10–12 minutes in the water.

Stuff each leaf with a spoonful of stuffing. Close by rolling the leaves and folding in the ends.

Arrange in a frying pan and cover with water. Simmer for 20–30 minutes. It is advisable to lay a flat plate over the *dolmas* as they are cooking to prevent them from bursting.

Serve hot or cold with whipped yoghurt or a sauce made by reducing the cooking juice, thickening it with egg and adding a dash of lemon.

VARIATION   Use ground lamb and an equal volume of rice in the stuffing. Add some chopped lamb fat. Season and follow the above recipe.

Marinated Aubergine

This relish keeps well and is used to accompany meats and starches.

1 kg (2 lb) aubergine
250 ml (½ pint) vinegar
500 ml (1 pint) oil
Fennel seeds
Peppercorns

Cut the aubergines in two; do not peel. Soak in heavily salted water. Drain and fry lightly.

Put in glass jars and cover with oil and vinegar. Add fennel seeds and peppercorns to taste. Cover and leave for the flavours to penetrate the aubergine before using.

Fassolia
Beans in Tomato Sauce

> 250 g (8 oz) kidney beans, soaked overnight
> Olive oil
> 2 cloves garlic
> Thyme
> Bay leaf
> 4 tablespoons tomato purée
> Salt and pepper

Dry the beans on kitchen paper, then brown them in oil. Add the garlic, tomato purée and herbs. Add hot water to cover and season. Simmer for $1\frac{1}{2}$–2 hours, reducing the liquid to gravy.

Serve as in Greece with a dash of lemon and chopped raw onions either hot or cold.

Courgette Rissoles

This is another favourite Mediterranean dish.

> 500 ml (1 pint) cooked courgette purée
> 500 ml (1 pint) mashed potato
> 3–4 chopped onions
> 125 g (4 oz) grated cheese
> Salt, pepper, parsley, mint
> 1 egg
> 125 g (4 oz) breadcrumbs

Mix together all the ingredients except the breadcrumbs and egg. Bind with the egg, shape into patties and roll in the breadcrumbs. Fry on both sides and serve hot.

Sweet Acorns

From central Europe to Japan, from North America to the Mediterranean where Castille, Greek and *ballote* oaks thrive, and to south-west France where the holm-oak acorns prized by ancestors are now neglected, the poor have gratefully gathered nature's largesse of acorns. Acorns can be eaten boiled or roasted like chestnuts. They may also be roasted, ground, and brewed like coffee. In Portugal, North Africa, the Middle East and Corsica, acorns still fill bellies that need to be filled.

The celebrated *racahout* of the Arabs is a sort of fine porridge, mainly for children, made from acorn flour, cocoa, sugar, starch and *salep*, a milky drink made from ground-up orchid roots.

Here is how North American Indians made bread from acorns: first they broke the shells on a stone and crushed the meats into fine flour. The flour then had to be washed, mashed, dried, and precooked to extract the tannin before it was ready to be kneaded to make dough. (Acorns must always be soaked before use.) The dough was then worked down with a smooth rock roller on a flat rock to a thin flat cake that could be quickly cooked on hot hearth stones.

Chestnut Polenta

Chestnut flour, although almost unknown now in Europe where it more than once supported the people through famine, is still a staple for some. It lends itself to many savoury preparations, giving even simple porridge an exciting flavour. Chestnut flour is available, irregularly, at Italian food shops and can be made in the home by grinding dried sweet chestnuts in a grain mill or blender.

> 250 g (8 oz) chestnut flour
> 1 ¼ litres (2 ¼ pints) water
> Salt

Slowly stir the chestnut flour into boiling salted water. Simmer for 20 minutes. Press into a bowl and turn out on to a plate while still hot. Slice and serve.

Cold chestnut *polenta* is good sliced and fried.

Indonesian Sweet Potatoes

> 1 kg (2 lb) sweet potatoes, cooked and sliced
> 1 peeled orange, cubed
> 1 tablespoon sugar
> 3 tablespoons melted butter
> 125 ml (¼ pint) honey or brown roux (flour cooked in oil or butter)
> 50 g (2 oz) grated coconut
> 250 ml (½ pint) coconut milk (see page 58)

Mix together the sweet potato slices and orange cubes in a baking dish. Mix together the other ingredients and pour over the mixture.

Bake at 175°C (350°F) or Gas 4 for about ¾ hour.

Jicama or Yam Bean

This is a bulbous, smooth-skinned, off-white root sometimes found in Asian food shops. It should be tender but not soft. Its crisp white flesh has a delicate fine taste like cucumber or water chestnut, and it can be used like cucumber or water chestnut in salads or to provide contrasting textures in soups or stir-fried dishes.

Peel and slice into thin julienne strips. Serve plain or sprinkled with lemon or lime juice, or vinegar. Or add to a soup shortly before serving.

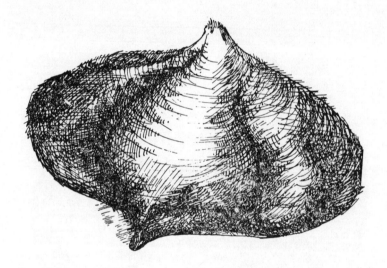

Stuffed Calabaza

The *calabaza*, a large squash or gourd like a pumpkin, is well appreciated in Latin America. Any kind of large marrow can be stuffed, but the round types are easier to prepare, and look more attractive on the table, than the usual long type.

    1 large *calabaza* or round marrow
    250 g (8 oz) ground beef or pork
    125 g (4 oz) diced ham
    2 chopped onions
    2 sliced green peppers

1–2 cloves garlic
Salt, pepper, oregano
1 tablespoon vinegar
75 g (3 oz) raisins
75 g (3 oz) olives, stoned
250 ml (½ pint) tomato sauce (see page 55)
2 eggs, beaten

Cut off the top of the marrow and set aside. Scoop out the pulp
with a spoon. Steam the pulp gently for 10–15 minutes. Drain.
(You can also leave the pulp in and gently cook the entire gourd,
taking care not to break the skin. Once cooked you can cut off the
top, remove the pulp, and stuff it.)

Brown the meat and ham separately. Add all the remaining ingredients except the eggs.

Simmer 5 minutes or so, then thicken with the eggs. Mix in the worked pulp. Stuff the marrow and put the top back on.

Bake for 1 hour at 175°C (350°F) or Gas 4. Allow to cool for 15 minutes before cutting and serving.

If there is no beef or pork, use chicken; if no chicken, use simple mashed potatoes or corn porridge.

Serves 6.

Chayote

This smooth, clear green fruit, popular in the Caribbean and parts of Latin America and known as *xuxu* in Brazil, is shaped like a pear but eaten like courgette. It has a mild, fresh taste, best when set off with lemon or cheese. Get young fruits with firm un-wrinkled skins. The skin and seed are tender enough to eat. Chayote is only found in shops specializing in tropical foods.

Chayote
Lemon

Cut the *chayote*—lengthwise through the seed—into quarters. Steam gently for 10–15 minutes. Serve hot sprinkled with lemon juice.

STUFFED CHAYOTE
3–4 chayotes
1 small onion, chopped
Butter
125 g (4 oz) grated Cheddar cheese
Breadcrumbs
Salt and pepper

Cut the *chayotes* in half. Steam gently for 10 minutes and cool slightly. Scoop out some pulp and the seed, leaving a 1-cm (½-in) thick shell.

Brown the onion in butter. Mash with the *chayote* pulp and seed, mix with cheese and fill the *chayote* pulp and seed, mix with cheese and fill the *chayote* shells. Sprinkle with breadcrumbs, dot with butter and season to taste. Set in a pan with about a half inch of water. Bake at 175°C (350°F) or Gas 4 for 20–30 minutes until the crust is browned.

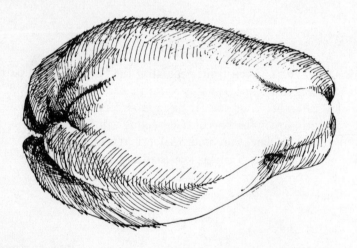

Cactus Salad

The young pads of the Opuntia cactus or prickly pear have long been appreciated by the American Indians and Mexicans. The Mexicans, who call these vegetables *nopales* or *nopalios*, use the plant with great versatility. The red, seedy insides vaguely resemble pomegranates. Everything but the skin is edible.

2–4 prickly pears
1–2 tomatoes, chopped

1 Spanish onion, chopped
1 fresh or soaked dried hot chili, with seeds and stem
  removed
Fresh coriander to taste (or substitute parsley)
Oil and vinegar dressing
Salt and pepper

Dig out the pointy black eyes of the prickly pears with the tip of
a vegetable peeler; then peel and cut into 1-cm (½-in) cubes. (It's
best to wear gloves while doing this, to avoid being pricked.)
Cook in boiling salted water for about 5 minutes until tender.
Rinse and dry. Mix together all the ingredients and leave to stand
for a few minutes before serving.

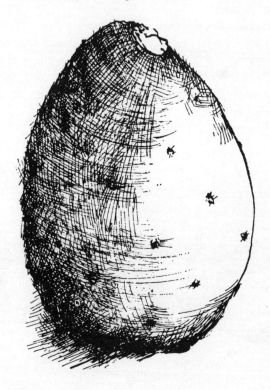

Tropical Roots

Dasheen, *yautia*, *malanga*, *ñame*, *yuca*, and *batata* are names and varieties of tropical roots commonly available in Latin-American markets. They take the place of potatoes and even of bread in the Caribbean, Africa, South America, south-east Asia, and Polynesia. There are cultivated versions of the roots that pre-agricultural and post-famine man turn to, along with berries, for sustenance in the last resort. They are almost pure starch, with little other food value. An important variety, bitter cassava (or bitter manioc) requires boiling to remove a poison, but the roots that can generally be bought fresh need only be boiled and served plain.

Dasheen and *yautia*, each of which is sometimes sold as *malanga*, are varieties of taro.

Dasheen, sold also in oriental food shops and sometimes called Chinese potato, is a fat, regularly shaped ellipsoid root with rings of rootlets giving it a banded appearance. It should be thoroughly scrubbed. Bake it whole until tender all the way through—40–90 minutes depending on size—and serve it sliced; or cut it up and boil for 10–15 minutes.

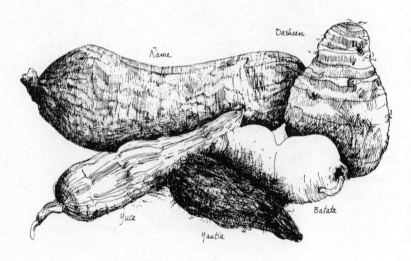

Yautia is an irregularly shaped hairy root, somewhat thinner, darker, and more pointed than potatoes. Peel, cut up and boil for 10–15 minutes. It is usually served plain, though without seasoning it tends to be very bland.

Yuca—also known as sweet manioc, or cassava, or as *aipim* in Brazil where it is particularly popular—is a long, hairy, cylindrical root, tapering at one end, that can be boiled and eaten like potatoes. It is often reduced to a pulp and dried for meal, called manioc or *mandioca* meal, and used for *farofa* in Brazil (see page 190) and *gari foto* in West Africa. Its close relative, bitter manioc or cassava, is poisonous until heated. It is most often used processed into manioc meal or tapioca. In its various forms manioc is one of the most important foods of Africa and Latin America.

Certain kinds of manioc have sweet and tender leaves. In Black Africa the leaves are cooked like spinach, with palm nut oil or karité butter (see page 19) and liberally sprinkled with hot pepper. The dish is very savoury and delicate when prepared by the Congolese, who are capable cooks.

Ñame is the most common kind of true yam, another important tropical staple. A brown, hairy, unpointed cylindrical root, it can be prepared by peeling, washing, cutting up and boiling in salted water for 10–15 minutes. Drain and serve plain or in any recipe in place of potatoes.

Batatas, known in Mexico as *camotes* (see page 281), are a kind of sweet potato, generally pear-shaped, with a smooth, tender, purplish flesh. Peeled and boiled they become almost transparent and have a singularly fine and delicate sweetness, somewhat different from orange yams (not true yams like *ñame*) or sweet potatoes. They can also be baked or boiled whole.

Breadfruit

This fruit, although sometimes eaten when fully ripe, is at its best when harvested slightly green and its flesh is white and firm.

This texture and appearance, together with a high starch content and a fresh taste with a hint of artichoke, are what earned this fruit its name. Breadfruit may be found at greengrocers catering for West Indian communities.

Peel, slice thickly, and roast breadfruit for 5–10 minutes. Or bake whole in the oven at 200°C (400°F) or Gas 6 for 30–60 minutes, depending on size, until tender all the way through. Serve like potatoes.

Breadfruit may also be boiled or cut up and steamed.

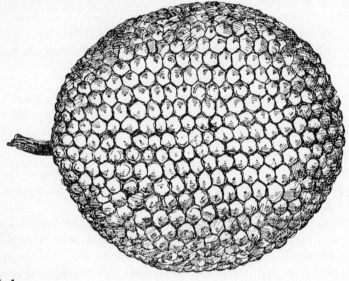

Kaku
Breadfruit Mash

> 2 breadfruits
> 250 ml (½ pint) coconut milk (see page 58)

Bake whole breadfruit in a 200°C (400°F) or Gas 6 oven for 30–45 minutes until tender all the way through. Peel, cut up, and mash in a mortar. Mix with coconut milk to make a thick creamy paste. Eat like *popoi* (see below), either plain or with fish or vegetables.

Popoi
Polynesian Breadfruit Paste

Popoi is one of the most common ways that Polynesians prepare breadfruit, it is a thick, cool, yellowish cream eaten with cupped fingers. The dish has two virtues: coolness and a light acidity that makes it very digestible. It is also called *poi*, in Hawaii for instance, and can be made with taro.

Polynesians roast almost ripe breadfruits over coals and then peel them with a sharpened shell—metal knives may affect the taste. The pulp obtained—which is tender, white and spongy with a faint taste of artichoke or chestnut—is put into wooden tubs, sprinkled with water and mashed with stone pestles to reduce it to a fine smooth paste. The tubs are buried in trenches lined with large *ti* leaves and allowed to ferment. After a few days the fermented paste is watered and mashed again. The *popoi* is ready. They eat the *popoi* as it is, or as a sauce for small, uncooked fish.

To prepare *popoi* or *poi* at home, bake breadfruit at 200°C (400°F) or Gas 6 for 30–40 minutes until tender all the way through. Peel and mash in a non-metallic bowl, sprinkling with water to make a thick paste. Cover and leave in a cool place for 1–3 days. It will ferment naturally, and the taste will get pleasantly sour.

Several other vegetables can be used to make *popoi*: taro and sweet potatoes. Bananas, almonds and coconut are sometimes mashed with the breadfruit, taro or sweet potatoes before fermentation, or more often served separately, together with plain *popoi*.

Nursing infants begin to eat *popoi* shortly after birth. *Popoi* sweetened with mashed tropical fruits is known as *keikai*.

Plantains
Green Bananas

A fruit of the tropics, bananas are known there in many forms generally unknown in northern countries. Plantains for instance are hard, starchy bananas which are an important part of tropical diet.

Since plantains are tough, they should be pounded to prepare them for eating. They can be cooked with soup, chicken or meat, or take the place of bread in the same way as yams. Different varieties, such as light *platanos* and dark *maduros* have different textures and tastes.

To prepare simply, pound with a wooden mallet or a rolling pin for a minute or two, peel and slice, then fry in lard, oil or butter.

Bananas Baked in Sugar

This banana, or plantain, dish is served as a vegetable with chicken in Africa and India, as well as in Latin America. Bananas are an important source of protein.

    1 kg (2 lb) bananas or plantains
    125 g (4 oz) sugar
    125 g (4 oz) butter
    Mace, pepper, cinnamon, salt

If using plantains, pound with a wooden mallet or rolling pin for a minute. Peel. Arrange in a baking tin, cover with a layer of sugar and pieces of butter. Sprinkle with spices and bake for 20–25 minutes at 175°C (350°F) or Gas 4.

Poe
Polynesian Fruit Balls

Taro or breadfruit
Banana, pineapple, or papaya
Palm leaves or banana leaves
Sugar syrup or coconut milk (see page 58)

Bake the taro or breadfruit for 30–40 minutes at 200C° (400°F) or Gas 6. Peel and mash with the fruit. Shape into balls. Wrap each ball in a palm leaf and bake for 15–20 minutes at 200°C (400°F) or Gas 6. Serve with sugar syrup or coconut milk.

If you cannot obtain palm or banana leaves substitute dried corn husks. Soak the dried leaves for at least 1 hour before using.

EGG AND CHEESE DISHES

Saganaki
Greek Fried Cheese

One of the popular snacks served in local taverns, called *bouzoukias*. The Greek cheeses called for below are usually available in delicatessens.

> 500 g (1 lb) *kasseri* or *kefalotiri* cheese; or any hard, strong cheese
> Flour or fine breadcrumbs
> Olive oil
> Lemon juice

Cut the cheese in thick slices. Dip in flour and fry in olive oil. Serve with a dash of lemon juice.

Kajmak
Yugoslavian Sheep Cheese

This accompanies corn bread in country meals. Raw sheep's milk is generally available only on farms, but you can substitute raw milk of any kind—health food stores often carry raw cow's milk. Pasteurized or homogenized milk will not curdle naturally.

> Sheep's milk
> Salt

Boil the sheep's milk and leave to cool in an earthenware pot. The cream will rise. Skim and set aside in a wooden pot. Add salt. Repeat the same procedure with 2 or 3 fresh batches of milk, adding the cream to the wooden pot and salting each time. After a few days you get a real cheese, yellow, with a somewhat strong smell. Keep it in a cool place.

When fresh this cheese is baked in delicious little cakes.

Yugoslavian Cheese and Maize Pie

700 g (1 ½ lb) *mamaliga* (see page 105)
Lard
250 g (8 oz) sheep cheese e.g. *feta*; or *kasseri* or other strong
    cheese
3 eggs
Salt and pepper

Press the hot *mamaliga* into a greased baking tin and cover with
a layer of grated or crumbled cheese. Lightly scramble then
season the eggs; pour over the cheese. Cover with another layer
of cheese and serve.

VARIATION   Save some of the *mamaliga* and spread it over the
layer of eggs. Cover with cheese.

VARIATION   Bake for 10 minutes at 200°C (400°F) or Gas 6
to melt the cheese. For this version beat the eggs but do not
scramble them first.

Yugoslavian Paski
Fried Goat Cheese

500 g (1 lb) goat cheese, e.g. *kasseri*; or other strong goat or
    sheep cheese
1 egg
Breadcrumbs
Corn or olive oil

Cube the goat cheese. Dip in beaten egg and then in breadcrumbs.
Fry lightly in oil. Serve crisp.

Indian Cheese Curry

Curds are a basic ingredient of Indian cooking, used both in liquid form and drained and solidified.

250–500 g (½–1 lb) dry curds or Cheddar cheese (see page 36)
500 g (1 lb) fresh peas
Ghee (see page 38) or margarine
2 onions, chopped
½ tablespoon crushed coriander
1–2 cloves garlic
1–2 hot fresh chilis, or cayenne
1 teaspoon grated fresh ginger
2 large tomatoes, chopped

Drain the curds well in cheesecloth. Press flat and cut into cubes. Boil or steam the peas and set aside.

Fry the cheese in *ghee*. In a separate pan, brown the onions and spices. Add the chopped tomatoes and simmer for 5–10 minutes (they should not be completely cooked). Add water to cover and top with the fried cheese and peas. Bring to the boil and serve.

Spanish Pisto

2 onions, finely chopped
2 peppers de-seeded and finely chopped
4 courgettes, finely chopped
6 tomatoes, chopped
Olive oil
500 g (1 lb) diced potatoes
Salt, pepper
4 eggs, beaten
Fried croutons

Sauté all the vegetables except the potatoes in oil.

Sauté the potatoes separately for 5–10 minutes. Add to the other vegetables, season to taste and mix well. Add the beaten eggs and stir continuously until they set.

Serve immediately over fried croutons.

M'guena
African Omelet

>   2 potatoes, cooked and mashed
>   2 chopped onions
>   2–3 cloves garlic, crushed
>   500 g (1 lb) cooked carrots or peas
>   4–5 beaten eggs
>   Salt, pepper, all spice
>   Nutmeg
>   2–3 chopped hard-boiled eggs

Mix all the ingredients except the oil together and pour into a greased mould or pan. Bake for 20 minutes at 175°C (350°F) or Gas 4.

Serve hot or cold.

Tchakchuka
North African Eggs and Vegetables

>   2–3 onions, chopped
>   2–3 sweet peppers, de-seeded and sliced
>   3–4 tomatoes, chopped
>   Salt and pepper
>   Suggested spices : thyme, oregano, cumin
>   3–5 eggs

Brown the onions and peppers. Add the tomatoes, seasoning and spices to taste. Simmer for 15–20 minutes.

Break the eggs into the pan with the vegetables, cover and simmer for another 5–10 minutes until the eggs are done. Serve.

VARIATION   Add leftover minced meat to cook with the onions and peppers before adding the tomatoes.

Chu pa pa
Stuffed Egg Pancakes

The batter for these *chu pa pa* is halfway between omelet and pancake batter. These egg pancakes are served with almost all meals in the parts of China where wheat and millet replace rice. They are also served rolled and cut into ribbons, sautéed with vegetables (see page 178) or cooked in soup.

PANCAKES:
3 eggs
125 g (4 oz) flour
About 125 ml (¼ pint) water
Salt

STUFFING:
2 onions, finely chopped
2 peppers sweet, de-seeded and sliced
500 g (1 lb) chopped vegetables such as cabbage, broccoli, celery
Peanut oil
2 tablespoons soy sauce

Mix the eggs, flour, water and salt to make a smooth, liquid batter. Cook as thin pancakes on one side only and pile on a cloth, cooked side up.

Sauté the onions, peppers and vegetables in peanut oil. Add soy sauce. Spread the pancakes with the mixture, then roll up and fold closed with the uncooked side outside. Brown in oil.

If desired add a little sesame oil to the stuffing for taste.

Egg fu yung
Chinese Omelet

> 125 g (4 oz) shredded chicken, beef, pork or shrimps
> 2–3 spring onions
> 1 small stalk celery or 4 sprigs watercress
> 2 tablespoons lard or peanut oil
> 1 tablespoon soy sauce
> 1 teaspoon sesame oil (optional)
> 4 eggs

Shred the meat, spring onions and celery finely. Stir-fry (sauté quickly) the meat in half the lard or oil for 1 minute in a hot wok or frying pan. Add the spring onions and celery and stir-fry another minute. Add soy sauce and sesame oil. Remove from the pan and set aside in a warm place.

Heat the rest of the lard or oil in the pan. Beat the eggs lightly and pour into the pan over medium heat. After about a minute, when the eggs are about half-cooked, add the meat and vegetables, reserving the juice. Fold over on itself and serve hot, using the juice as sauce.

To make more sauce, add some stock to the juice and thicken with cornflour.

MEAT
AND
FISH

Although it may seem strange to put meat and fish together in a cookbook they share the character of being occasional luxuries for most of the world's people. The exotic delicacies we associate with Third World cooking are rare delights. Peking duck, however delicious, never finds its way to a poor man's table, which is more likely to be graced with a garlic shoot wrapped in a pancake. That is not to say you will not find some true delicacies in the pages that follow, but remember that these are the feasts of the common man, not their usual daily fare.

Papuan Pork and Potatoes

Pork, like chicken, is important in the diets of all poor peoples. Pigs are so prized in some areas as to be treated almost like children. Papuan women in New Guinea do not hesitate to nurse a suckling pig deprived of its mother. The pig was brought to Papua by white men. Before, the Papuans raised dogs resembling foxes and fattened them like pigs. They cook pork with sweet potatoes and sometimes fish from streams and rivers.

Sweet and Sour Pork

Poor Chinese usually buy pork from a butcher in infinitesimal portions—a tiny parcel wrapped in a dried lotus leaf.

    500 g (1 lb) pork finely diced
    1 egg, beaten
    Flour or cornflour
    Peanut oil
    2 onions, finely chopped
    2 sweet peppers, de-seeded and finely chopped
    4 tablespoons sugar

    3 tablespoons soy sauce
    3 tablespoons rice vinegar and 1 tablespoon dry white wine
      or dry sherry; or use 4 tablespoons cider vinegar
    1 tablespoon cornflour

Coat the meat in egg, then in flour. Fry in oil in a wok or frying pan, drain and set aside.

Sauté the vegetables in the wok. Mix the sugar, soy sauce, vinegar and wine and pour over the vegetables. Mix the cornflour in a little water and add to the sauce. Bring to a boil, then add the meat. Mix completely before serving.

Roast Pork with Daikon

This feast dish employs the common oriental white radish.

    3–4 *daikon*, oriental radishes
    3 kg (6–8 lb) pork roast
    Salt and pepper

Blanch the radishes, then arrange around the seasoned pork, ready to go into the oven. Roast at 170°C (325°F) or Gas 3 for about 35 minutes per pound.

    Serves 8-10.

Mexican Pork

    1 kg (2 lb) shoulder of pork, cut up
    Lard
    4 onions, finely chopped
    Salt and pepper

1 teaspoon powdered chili
Bay leaf
Oregano
500 ml (1 pint) water
1–2 tablespoons maize meal

Brown the meat in lard, add the onions, and work gently until softened. Add the seasonings and the water, cover and simmer for 1½ hours until the meat is tender.

Skim off the fat and add the maize meal mixed with a little cold water. Simmer for 15 minutes more.

If possible serve in a wooden bowl.

Ameijoas na cataplana
Portuguese Pork and Clam Stew

This pork stew with clams or cockles is cooked in a primitive pressure cooker, called *cataplana*. Any pressure cooker will do the job.

4 onions, chopped
750 g (1½ lb) pork, cut into small cubes
125 ml (¼ pint) tomato purée
250 ml (½ pint) dry white wine or meat stock
Salt and pepper
30 clams or 40 cockles

Brown the onions in oil, then add the meat. Mix in the tomato purée and the wine; season with salt and pepper. Seal in a pressure cooker and simmer for 20 minutes (or simmer for 1½ hours in a covered pot). Wash the shellfish carefully to remove all sand and add to the stew. Simmer for 15 minutes more without bringing back to pressure.

Kari
Réunion Island Yams and Pork Chops

    4–6 pork chops
    Lard or fat
    3 onions, chopped
    2–3 cloves garlic, crushed
    4 tomatoes, chopped
    Salt and pepper
    750 g (1½ lb) yams

Sauté the chops in lard or oil. Add the onions, tomatoes, salt and pepper. Peel the yams, known as *kari*, cut into thick slices and add to the meat. Cover and simmer for 25–30 minutes.

Before serving crush some of the yam into the juice to thicken it.

Chiao-tzu
Chinese Ravioli

Poor relations of a culture of great culinary finesse, less-favoured Chinese make artful dishes from meagre resources. With art even simple dishes are very tasty, like these Chinese ravioli.

Chiao-tzu are a central feature of New Year celebrations in the Gobi Desert. A peasant cook shapes them into little ears in the hope that by eating many of them, he will not lose his own ears to frost in the cold winter ahead. Tibetan *momos* is a close cousin.

    375 g (13 oz) flour
    250 ml (½ pint) hot water
    250 g (8 oz) chopped Chinese (celery) cabbage
    250 g (8 oz) minced fresh pork
    1 white leek, finely chopped
    Soy sauce

Salt
1–2 teaspoons fresh, grated ginger
Dash of sesame oil
Water or stock

Knead the flour and water into a supple dough. Leave to rest for several hours, then roll out on a floured board and, using a cup, cut into discs.

While the dough is resting soak the cabbage in salted water to draw out some of the moisture. Drain and mix with all the remaining ingredients.

Fill each disc of dough with a spoonful of stuffing. Fold over to form ear-shaped ravioli and seal the edges.

Poach gently in water or stock for about 20 minutes. Serve in stock, or plain.

Steamed Chicken

Cheaper to raise than even the most economical pig, chicken is the most easily available meat all over the world. The Chinese have even mastered techniques of drying, salting and smoking it just as they have pork—they gut and stuff the chicken with salt and hang it to dry unplucked.

> 1 oven-ready chicken, giblets removed
> 1 tablespoon sugar
> Salt
> 1–2 teaspoons fresh, grated ginger
> Fresh coriander, parsley, watercress
> 1 tablespoon dry wine
> 3 tablespoons soy sauce
> 1 tablespoon cornflour

Brown the chicken thoroughly by sautéing. Drain well. Place in a large pot with the herbs, seasonings, and just a little water. Add the wine and soy sauce. Cover very tightly and steam gently for about ¾ hour. The skin should remain intact and the flesh should be tender enough to be eaten with chopsticks.

Thicken the sauce with a little cornflour and pour over the chicken when serving.

Chicken with Peanuts

This is a Congolese feast dish.

> 1 chicken, cut up
> Coconut or peanut oil
> 100 g (4 oz) grilled or roasted peanuts
> Salt and pepper
> 1 teaspoon cayenne

Brown the chicken all over in oil.

Crush the peanuts in a mortar, then heat in a few tablespoons of water to make a smooth cream. Pour over the chicken and seasonings. Cover and simmer for 30–45 minutes.

Chicken and Coconut

This is a central African recipe, where chicken is the easiest meat to get but still generally too expensive to be used except on festive occasions.

    1 coconut
    1 chicken
    500 g (1 lb) tomatoes, chopped
    1 onion
    Garlic to taste
    ½–1 teaspoon cayenne

Boil the coconut for 20 minutes; drain and remove shell. Mash in a pestle and mortar to make a pulp.

   Roast the chicken in your usual way. While it is cooking prepare a tomato sauce by browning the onion and garlic and simmering for 30 minutes with the tomatoes. Season with the cayenne. Thicken the sauce with the coconut pulp and simmer for 10–15 minutes longer. Meanwhile remove the chicken from the oven and cut into pieces.

Chicken Paprikás

As the name indicates this is chicken with paprika. No feast among gypsies or Hungarians is complete without hot paprika.

    1.8 kg (3½–4 lb) chicken, cut into pieces
    Flour
    Salt
    Oil
    2–3 onions, chopped
    3–4 cloves garlic, chopped

250 ml (½ pint) yoghurt or sour cream
2–3 teaspoons paprika

Dredge the pieces of chicken in flour. Sprinkle with salt and sauté in oil. Allow to brown deeply, remove and drain.

Put the onions and garlic in the pan used for the chicken while it is still hot. Cook for a few minutes, then add the chicken and yoghurt and sprinkle with paprika. Cover and simmer for about ½ hour.

(It is also common to cook the chicken in a tomato sauce, saving the yoghurt for the last minute.)

Serve sprinkled with herbs such as dill, mint, or parsley accompanied by noodles or *knödels* (potato dumplings).

Indian Chicken

This 'chicken sausage' should be wrapped in banana leaves, but these can be replaced by sweet corn husks or cheesecloth.

1 boiled chicken
Juice of 1 lemon
½ coconut or 4 tablespoons dried coconut, puréed
1–2 cloves garlic
1–2 teaspoons fresh, grated ginger
2 teaspoons ground coriander
1 tablespoon sugar
3–4 tablespoons vinegar
½ teaspoon cayenne
Banana leaves, sweetcorn husks or cheesecloth

Bone the boiled chicken. Sprinkle the meat with lemon juice and pour the puréed coconut pulp over. Add the seasonings and chop and mash the meat and seasonings together.

Wrap the chicken mixture in an oiled or buttered leaf and tie.

Place the roll in a greased casserole and moisten with a little vinegar. Cook for 15 minutes over a low flame, covered but turning often. When the vinegar is absorbed remove the cover and cook for 2–3 minutes longer.

Unwrap the leaf and serve.

Chicken with Curds

Curds, a common ingredient in Indian cooking, are used here as a marinade for chicken—as always the poor man's meat.

> 2 cloves garlic, minced
> 2 teaspoons grated fresh ginger
> Salt
> 250 ml (½ pint) curds (see page 36) or yoghurt
> 1 chicken, cut up

Mix the garlic, ginger and a little salt with the curds or yoghurt. Marinate the chicken in the seasoned curds for a few hours, then bake at 230°C (450°F) or Gas 8, or simmer on top of the store, until the chicken is cooked—about 45 minutes.

Molé poblano
Chicken or Turkey with Chili and Chocolate Sauce

This is a Mexican speciality.

> 1 large chicken, or 2 kg (4–5 lb) turkey, cut up
> Salt
> 6–8 dried *ancho* chilis (mild. sweet chilis)
> 2–3 dried hot chilis (4–5 *pequins*)
> 50 g (2 oz) raisins
> 75 g (3 oz) shelled almonds

2 sprigs fresh coriander
6–8 coriander seeds
1 tablespoon sesame seeds
1 toasted tortilla, crushed; or 50 g (2 oz) breadcrumbs
2 cloves garlic
1 onion
1 clove
Pinch of anise
250 g (8 oz) tomatoes, chopped
Lard, oil or chicken fat for frying
25 g (1 oz) unsweetened chocolate
Flour

Put the chicken or turkey pieces in a pot or casserole, add salted water to cover, bring to a boil and simmer for 1 hour. Drain, reserving the broth.

Remove the stems, seeds, and membranes from the chilis and soak for 20–30 minutes in hot water to cover. If using a *molcajete* or pestle and mortar, drain the chilis, reserving the liquid, and grind together with the raisins, almonds, fresh coriander, coriander seeds, sesame seeds, tortilla or breadcrumbs, garlic, onion, clove, and anise. Mix with the chopped tomatoes, the liquid from soaking the chilis, and 1 cup of the broth to make a thick, smooth sauce. If using a blender : coarsely purée the soaked chilis in their water with the other seasonings, raisins, almonds, tomatoes and 1 cup of broth to make a thick, smooth sauce. Season with salt.

Fry the sauce in the lard, oil, or chicken fat in a heavy frying pan for 5 minutes, stirring often. Remove from the heat and stir in the chocolate, chopped or grated to make it melt faster.

Dry the cooked, drained turkey or chicken pieces, dip in flour and brown in oil, lard or chicken fat. Drain, put in a casserole and spread with the sauce. Cover and bake at 120°C (250°F) or Gas ½ for 30 minutes.

Serve sprinkled with freshly ground black pepper and sesame seeds. Accompany with Mexican rice and beans (see page 120).

Pulao
Lamb or Chicken with Rice

As is common in India, curds are used here as a sauce and flavouring.

> 1.2 kg (2½ lb) chicken, cut up into small pieces : or lamb, cubed
> 250 g (8 oz) curds (see page 36) or yoghurt
> 1 tablespoon curry spices : turmeric, cumin, anise, fenugreek, cinnamon, clove, and coriander
> 3 onions, finely chopped
> *Ghee* (see page 38) or vegetable oil
> About 400 ml (¾ pint) water
> 250 g (8 oz) rice

Soak the meat in curds and curry spices for a few hours. Sauté the onions in *ghee*, add to the meat, cover and cook gently for 1 hour. Add water and rice, cover and simmer for 20 minutes more. The juice should be completely absorbed.

Afghani Pancakes
Lamb Patties

In Afghanistan these patties are made with *dumba*, the fat from the tails of certain oriental species of sheep. Some tails can yield up to 3½ kg (7 lb) of fine fat. Use ordinary lamb fat cut from stewing meat or chops.

> 500 g (1 lb) minced lamb
> 200 g (7 oz) fat, minced or finely chopped
> 1–2 cloves garlic
> 2 onions, chopped
> Salt and pepper
> Juice of 1 lemon
> 2 eggs, separated

Simmer the lamb in a little water for about 10–15 minutes. Grind, together with the fat, garlic and onions, in a mortar. Season with salt and pepper, moisten with lemon juice and bind with the egg yolks. The mixture should be a thick paste. Shape into patties and roll in lightly beaten egg whites.

Fry on both sides until done; about 5 minutes a side.

Pakistani Lamb

> 500 g (1 lb) minced lamb
> 125 g (4 oz) lentils, soaked overnight
> 500 ml (1 pint) water
> 2 eggs
> 125 g (¼ pint) curds (see page 36) or yoghurt
> 1 onion, chopped
> Salt
> 1–2 cloves garlic, crushed
> 2 sprigs fresh coriander
> 1–2 teaspoons fresh, grated ginger
> ½ teaspoon cayenne

Simmer the meat and lentils in the water for about 45 minutes. Mash and thicken with eggs and curds. Leave to cool.

Mix together the onion, a little salt, the garlic, fresh coriander, ginger and cayenne. Take tablespoonfuls of this onion stuffing and shape meat/lentil patties around them. Fry in fat or oil, or grill on both sides.

Leben immou
Meat with Curds

Recipes based on curds and yoghurt are well known from North Africa to India, especially in countries formerly dominated by the Turks, such as Rumania, Bulgaria and Greece.

500 g (1 lb) lamb, cut into cubes
Lamb fat cut from stewing meat or chops
1 litre (2 pints) curds (see page 36) or yoghurt
Salt, ground coriander, cumin

Sauté the meat in lamb fat. Add water to cover and simmer for 1½–2 hours or until cooked. When done add curds and seasonings and simmer for 5–10 minutes more. The sauce should be thick.
  Serve with rice.

Afghani Lamb

Afghanis use herbs such as madder, castor bean, and manna that are not easily available in this country. They also use rhubarb, which is in season here in the spring. Fresh coriander can replace the exotic herbs.

500 g (1 lb) minced lamb
1 stalk rhubarb, sliced
250 ml (½ pint) tomato sauce (see page 55)
2–3 sprigs fresh coriander
Crushed fresh mint
Cayenne and black pepper
3–4 leeks
1 bunch spring onions
250 ml (½ pint) yoghurt

Sauté the meat with the rhubarb until it turns pale. Add the tomato sauce, coriander, mint, cayenne and pepper. Cook for 5–10 minutes. Then add the minced leeks and spring onions. Cook for 3–5 more minutes. Add yoghurt and serve with rice pilaf (see page 123).

Kobbe
Lamb Loaf

A recipe from the Near East.

>500 g (1 lb) chopped or minced lamb
>2 onions, chopped
>Salt and pepper
>500 g (1 lb) *bulgur* (see page 95)
>50 g (2 oz) pine nuts or sliced almonds
>100 g (4 oz) chopped lamb fat cut from stewing meat or chops

Mix the lamb together with one of the chopped onions, salt and pepper. Mash together with the *bulgur* to make a smooth paste.

Brown the remaining chopped onion with the pine nuts in lamb fat.

Spread half the meat on a large greased plate. Spread the browned nuts and onions over the meat then cover with the rest of the meat. Press with your hands or a plate to make a firm loaf. Cut into squares and rectangles and sprinkle with melted lamb fat. Bake at 175°C (350°F) or Gas 4 for 30–40 minutes or fry on both sides.

VARIATION To make *Kobbe samak* or fish loaf. Prepare as above, replacing the meat with fish, and the lamb fat with olive oil.

Brunswick Stew

There are countless variations of this American 'soul food' dish; only purists insist on squirrel meat.

>2 chickens, 2 rabbits or 4 squirrels
>500 g (1 lb) cooked butter beans

1 kg (2 lb) stewed tomatoes
750 g (1½ lb) sweet corn kernels
Salt, pepper and red pepper to taste
125 g (4 oz) butter

Boil the meat in plenty of water until very tender—3–4 hours.
Take out, cut into small pieces and put back into pot. Add the
beans, tomatoes, and sweet corn; cook together for 30 minutes.
Season to taste and stir in the butter just before serving.
  Serves 8.

Rabbit in Cider

Rabbit is both a poor man's meat and a luxury. It is not uncommon for a poor man in Europe or Latin America to raise a few
rabbits behind his house as an additional source of protein. The
firm but tender pink flesh of rabbit has earned it a secure place in
fine cookery.

1–2 kg (2–4 lb) rabbit (including head), cut up
150 ml (¼ pint) cider vinegar
425 ml (¾ pint) cider or dry white wine
1–2 onions, chopped
Bay leaves, sage, thyme, crushed peppercorns
Flour
Salt
Lard or butter

Soak the rabbit for 1 hour in salted water to clean out the blood.
Rinse and drain. Marinate in a non-metallic casserole in the
vinegar, cider, onions and spices for at least 4 hours. Drain and
pat dry, reserving the marinade. Set aside the kidneys, liver, and
heart; discard the head.
  Dip the rabbit pieces in flour and fry quickly in lard or butter

in a large heavy frying pan until brown. Add the marinade and salt. Cover and simmer for 1 hour. Slice the organs, and fry in butter or lard.

Serve the rabbit with its offal alongside, accompanied by boiled potatoes and kale.

Serves 6.

Retfo
Ethiopian Beef Sauté

> 1 onion, chopped
> 1 sweet pepper with seeds removed, chopped
> Oil
> 500 g (1 lb) minced beef or lamb
> Salt and pepper
> ½ teaspoon cayenne

Brown the vegetables in oil. Add the meat and seasoning; simmer a few minutes.

To serve, mix with rice pilaf (see page 123).

Gehakte leber
Chopped Liver

> 1 large onion, chopped
> 1 tablespoon chicken fat or corn oil
> 250 g (8 oz) liver, preferably chicken or turkey, but also calves' or ox
> Salt and pepper
> 1 carrot

Brown the onion in fat or oil. Add the liver, season with salt and pepper, and simmer for 5–10 minutes until cooked through. Chop in a wooden bowl with the raw carrot until it is all more or less finely minced, according to your preference for texture.

Serve on celery sticks or crackers, either warm or cold.

Serves 4 as an appetizer.

Mexican Meatballs

    250 g (8 oz) minced beef
    250 g (8 oz) minced pork
    1 egg
    1–2 sprigs fresh coriander
    Oregano and salt
    Breadcrumbs
    1–2 cloves garlic, chopped
    Lard
    500 g (1 lb) peeled, chopped tomatoes
    Parsley, ground chilis, cumin, *epazote* (see page 41), salt

Mix together the beef and pork. Bind with an egg. Add chopped fresh coriander, oregano and salt, and thicken with breadcrumbs. Shape into meatballs.

Brown the garlic in lard then add the tomatoes and other seasonings. Simmer for 20–30 minutes.

Brown the meatballs in lard, then cover with the hot and spicy tomato sauce and simmer for 45 minutes.

Chili con carne

Real chili, so say the Texans, is made only with chunks of beef, not minced beef. Chili peppers come in many varieties, some hotter than others, so caution is advisable. (For fuller discussion of chilis see page 42.) The different varieties of peppers have, of course, different tastes.

500 g (1 lb) red kidney beans
1.5 kg (3 lb) beef, cut into small cubes
Salt
6–8 large dried mild chilis (such as *ancho* chilis)
2–4 dried hot chilis (4–8 *pequin* chilis)
2 onions
4–6 cloves garlic
Oregano, cumin, salt

Soak the beans overnight. Drain, add water to cover, cover and simmer for 2 hours or until tender. Add more water as necessary.

Simmer the beef in water to cover for 1½–2 hours. Add salt.

Remove stems and seed from the chili peppers. Soak the chilis for 30 minutes in warm water. Grind the chilis, garlic, onion and spices together in a *molcajete* (stone pestle and mortar), adding the water in which the chilis soaked to make a liquid sauce. You can also purée the ingredients in a blender. Fry the sauce in a tablespoonful of oil or fat for about 5 minutes.

Add the beans to the beef and broth, then the chili sauce. Simmer gently for 30 minutes and serve hot.

This is one of those dishes that often tastes even better the next day, when the flavours have developed.

Serves 6–8.

Pigs in Blankets

500 g (1 lb) minced beef, or beef and pork
400 g (14 oz) cooked rice
Suggested seasoning: marjoram, oregano, mace, pepper
1 cooked white cabbage, whole or quartered
Tomato sauce (see page 55)

Fry together the beef, rice and seasonings, chopped onion, peppers or celery may be added if desired. Place a tablespoonful of this mixture on a cabbage leaf and wrap into a package; tie with a piece of thin string. Place in a casserole. Repeat until the casserole is layered tightly with these 'pigs'. Cover with tomato sauce and bake for 30–40 minutes at 175°C (350°F) or Gas 4 or until most of the liquid is absorbed. This dish is better the second or third day. Just keep adding a little liquid and warming up, but make sure it is properly heated through.

Scrapple

This Pennsylvania Dutch creation has had a glorious history in mid-Atlantic American kitchens for over two centuries. It is generally served at breakfast.

> 500 g (1 lb) ox or pig's liver
> 500 g (1 lb) pork or bacon scraps, lamb or beef pieces without bones
> 3–4 litres (6–8 pints) water
> 1 teaspoon thyme
> 1 teaspoon sage
> 1 teaspoon black pepper
> 350 g (12 oz) maize meal
> 500 ml (1 pint) water

Cook the meat slowly in the water for about 2 hours until quite tender. (Add more water to cover if necessary.) Cool, reserving the broth, and chop or mince the meat finely. Measure off 1½ litres (3 pints) of broth and add seasonings. Mix the maizemeal with the cold water. Add the meat to the seasoned broth and bring to a boil, then add the maize meal gradually, stirring constantly until the mixture is thick and bubbling. (Add more meal if the mixture doesn't thicken well.) Pour into a greased pan (or 2 bread tins) and chill overnight. To serve, slice scrapple 1 cm (½ in) thick, dredge with flour, and brown quickly on both sides in a hot buttered frying pan. Serve with maple syrup and pancakes.

Meat and Grain Stew

75 g (3 oz) whole wheat or cracked wheat
75 g (3 oz) sorghum (see page 89)
50 g (2 oz) whole oats, rice or barley
2 litres (4 pints) water or meat stock
500 g (1 lb) cooked meat: beef, pork, lamb, and any available bones
750 g (1½ lb) coarsely chopped vegetables (onion, carrot, celery, turnip, swede, beans, beetroot, sweet corn)
250 ml (½ pint) milk
1 tablespoon salt
1 teaspoon black pepper
¼ teaspoon chili powder or cayenne, or crushed fresh chilis

Clean and soak the grains overnight in water or stock. Boil them in the liquid they were soaked in for about an hour. (If bones are to be used, add them to the liquid for this cooking.) Add the cooked meat, vegetables, milk and seasoning. Cook, covered, until tender; about 15–20 minutes.

Earth Cooking

Earth or pit cooking is a common way of preparing meat all over the world.

A Papuan oven is a hole about one metre deep, carpeted with live coals, then a layer of glowing hot stones, covered in turn by a thick layer of leaves. Meat and vegetables are laid on top, covered with leaves and then earth to seal the primitive oven. Meats are seasoned with salt before cooking. Snake cooked this way is exceptionally succulent, not unlike smoked eel. Fires must be kept burning night and day to feed these ovens.

In Madagascar a fire is built in a hole lined with stones. When the fire burns down, pieces of meat wrapped in banana leaves are laid on the hot stones and embers. The hole is sealed with earth. Then the wait begins.

In Hawaii a big hole is dug and lined with stones. The varied foods to be cooked are laid in concentric circles: suckling pigs in the centre, then chickens and fish wrapped in banana leaves, and outside that, another circle of balls of vegetables and banana and papaya *poe* (see page 227), also wrapped in banana leaves. All this is covered by thick mats of braided leaves and branches and cooked for at least 3 hours.

A Mexican *barbacoa* pit is dug 150 cm deep by 60 cm wide. The sides are daubed with mud and the bottom carpeted with *tezontles*, porous volcanic rocks that hold in heat. A fire built in the pit heats the rocks. Most of the live coals are dug out and the bottom is covered with a layer of maguey leaves. A rack is then placed in the pit; on the rack is placed a pot filled with beans, rice, soup, etc. to be served with the meat. On top of that is placed a sheep, quartered or cut into smaller pieces, with the shoulders, legs, shins and head on top; no salt. Maguey leaves are then laid over the meat. The pile is held down by a metal sheet covered

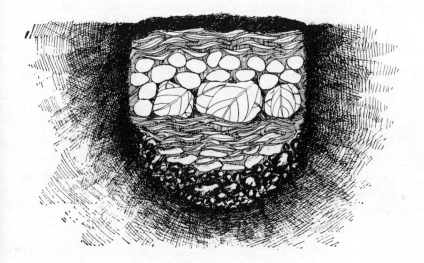

with leaves, a mat, and then mud for a hermetic seal. On top a fire is kept burning steadily for around 6 hours.

Pit cooking is readily adaptable to temperate climates, and particularly appropriate for outdoor expeditions. Be sure to line the pit well with big stones that hold heat, such as granite, and to make the pit large enough to hold the meat. Heat the pit well by keeping a big fire burning in it for several hours. The meat, a small pig or turkey, should be wrapped in burlap soaked in salad oil. When ready to cook, dig out the coals and ashes, leaving some covering the bottom of the pit. Put in the meat and fill in the pit with more live coals. Seal carefully with soil—if there is any steam escaping, the oven will cool off rapidly. Allow 6 to 7 hours for a 5–6 kilogram (10–12 lb) turkey.

The major difficulty in cooking in earth ovens is knowing when the meal is cooked. Once the oven is opened it cannot be sealed again.

Another variety of earth cooking, common in Africa, uses *pot-pot*, or laterite, a common component of central African soil. The *pot-pot* is thinned with water and used to coat an unplucked chicken. A termite hill, heated by burning a fire around it and partly filling it with hot stones, often serves as an oven. The chicken is placed in the termite hill and sealed shut; the fire continues roaring around it. After several hours when the chicken is cooked it is removed from the termite hill. Natives break away the clay shell with a machete and serve the chicken with tomato sauce spiced with cayenne or wild peppers.

Meat Barbecued with Ground Peanuts

In Africa elephant, buffalo or monkey is often cooked with ground-up peanuts. Beef, pork and chicken are also excellent this way.

250 g (8 oz) raw, shelled peanuts
500 g (1 lb) tomatoes, chopped

2 onions, chopped
3–4 cloves garlic, chopped
1–2 teaspoons cayenne pepper
1 tablespoon flour
1 tablespoon butter
1 kg (2 lb) meat, barbecued

Put the peanuts on a baking sheet in a 200°C (400°F) or Gas 6 oven for 20 minutes. Crush in a stone mortar to make a thick, smooth purée.

Sauté the tomatoes with onions and garlic, adding a good dose of cayenne pepper. Mix together flour and butter over heat and add to the tomato sauce. Add the barbecued meat and simmer for 10 minutes, thickening the sauce with the ground peanuts.

Pressed Tongue

A fresh ox or calf tongue, 1 kg (2–3 lb)
1 small onion, quartered
1 teaspoon salt
¼ teaspoon pepper (or 6 peppercorns)

Cover the tongue with boiling water. Add all the other ingredients and simmer uncovered until it is fork-tender; 2½–3½ hours (or 30 minutes in a pressure cooker). Drain, preserving the cooking liquid, and soak for 3–5 minutes in cold water so you can handle it. Using a fork to help you hold the tongue, skin it and remove any gristle and bones from the base (don't delay; the skin is difficult to remove once the tongue has cooled). Place the tongue sideways in a small deep bowl, curled around itself. Pour the cooking liquid around it to the level of the tongue and weight it with a plate. Refrigerate. When cold, the tongue is sliced and served with mustard or horseradish.

Brawn

The poor are by necessity less choosy, more daring, or, if you wish, more refined in eating a greater variety of the meats of an animal—the 'corners of the cow'. Oxtail stew, calf's head, tripe and chitterlings are delicacies made from parts of the animal too often disdained. Fine French cooking, which sometimes calls for meats like coxcombs and pig's trotters, owes a large debt to the culinary adventures of the hungry man. The quality of the protein is consistent and the taste more varied. Brawn, usually made with a pig's head, is a prime example of the best offal cuisine. Calf's head can be ordered from some butchers although not generally kept in stock.

1 calf's or pig's head
3 small onions
125 g (4 oz) butter
125 ml (¼ pint) red wine
Salt, pepper, nutmeg and cloves to taste

Split the calf's head into 3 or 4 pieces. Take out the brains and eyes, cut off the ears and snout, and trim off as much fat as you can. Cover with cold water, add the onions and boil for 2–3 hours until the meat falls from the bones. Meanwhile boil the brains in salted water until firm; about 20 minutes. Trim the meat from the head and cut into small pieces. Combine meat and brains (which have been chopped up), butter, wine and seasoning. Place in a baking dish and bake for 30–40 minutes. This can be covered with a pastry before baking, or served with a gravy made from the reserved stock. It can also be chilled with a weighted cover and sliced before serving.

Chitterlings

Chitterlings are the small intestines of a pig and are a great delicacy of the American South. They are mostly used to make sausage skins in this country nowadays, but you may sometimes find them in a pork butcher's, when they will have been cleaned and boiled ready for use.

    4 kg (8–10 lb) prepared chitterlings
    1 large onion, chopped
    1 clove garlic, sliced
    1 tablespoon salt
    Several whole peppercorns
    4 tablespoons vinegar, white wine, or apple cider
    1 bay leaf
    1 teaspoon crushed hot chilis, or 3 dried hot chilis

Cover the chitterlings with cold water and add the rest of the ingredients. Bring to the boil slowly and then simmer until tender —about ½ hour. Drain the chitterlings, cut into 5-cm (2-in) lengths and return them to the pot. In the American South chitterlings would be served with maize bread and greens.
    Serves 10–12.

Haggis
Stuffed Sheep Stomach

Making haggis is not something to undertake lightly; you will need a friendly butcher to get a sheep's stomach specially for you, and the courage to clean it. If lacking both these requirements, cheat and cook it in foil.

    1 sheep's stomach
    Sheep's liver, kidneys and heart

250 g (8 oz) suet
500 g (1 lb) rolled oats
2–3 onions, chopped
1 tablespoon salt
1 teaspoon pepper
Mashed potatoes with mashed turnips stirred in

Clean the stomach bag and soak overnight in salted water. Cook the sheep parts for 1–2 hours, or until tender. Put this cooked meat through a food grinder along with the suet. Combine meat and suet mixture with the oats, onion and seasonings. Moisten this mixture with a cup or two of the cooking liquid, then put into the stomach bag, not filling too tightly. Sew up the bag and prick it in several places to keep it from exploding. Place in a large pot of boiling water and simmer for 3 hours. To serve, make a large cross in the top with a sharp knife. Spoon out over a mound of mashed potatoes and turnips.

Serves 6–8.

Kok koretsi
Innards Brochettes

No Greek Easter feast is complete without the roasting of a Pascal lamb accompanied by these curious brochettes. The feast is prepared outside as the celebrants dance by the fire to the sound of the *santouri* and clarinet.

Lamb heart, liver, lungs, kidneys and brain, cut into 3-cm
 (1½-in) cubes
Chopped parsley, basil and mint
Lemon juice
Lamb intestine, cleaned and washed

Skewer the cubed meats and sprinkle with herbs and lemon. Wrap the intestines around the skewers in coils. Grill slowly.

Paella
Chicken or Shellfish in Rice

Paella is a familiar dish to tourists and patrons of Spanish restaurants. It is found in Spain in many variations, enriched with whatever ingredients are at hand.

      1 chicken, cut-up
      Olive oil
      2 onions, chopped
      4 cloves garlic
      Salt and pepper
      3–4 pistils saffron, crushed and soaked in a little water
      125 g (4 oz) *chorizo* (Spanish sausage), sliced
      500 ml (1 pint) chicken stock or water
      250 g (8 oz) rice

Brown the chicken in oil. Add the onions, garlic and seasonings, then the *chorizo*. Transfer to a seasoned clay *paella* dish or large, deep frying pan. Add stock or water, cover and simmer for 40–45 minutes. Add rice and simmer 15 minutes until the rice absorbs all the juice.

VARIATION   *Paella Valenciana*. Replace the chicken with cockles and mussels, both with shells removed. The poorer people of Valencia eat this on Sundays and during local celebrations, both patriotic and religious, such as the festivals in honour of San Vicente Martír and El Cristo del Grao.

Arroz a banda
Rice and Fish

Spanish fisherman's rice.

      4 onions, chopped
      Olive oil

675 g (1½ lb) tomatoes, chopped
2 litres (4 pints) water
Bay leaf, peppercorns, sage
½–1½ kg (1–3 lb) fish heads and trimmings
1 kg (2 lb) fish, cleaned and prepared
1 kg (2 lb) mussels and crayfish, mixed
3–4 pistils saffron
3–4 cloves garlic
500 g (1 lb) rice

Brown the onions in oil. Add the tomatoes, water, seasoning, fish heads and trimmings. Simmer for ½ hour to make a rich fish stock flavoured and coloured with tomato. Strain.

Slice the fish into chunks. Wash the mussels and crayfish. Open the mussels and remove one of the shells. Lay the fish, mussels and crayfish in a big pot and pour in about half the fish stock. Simmer about 8 minutes; season with saffron crushed with the garlic and simmer for another 8 minutes.

Meanwhile cook the rice in the remaining stock (there should be about 1 litre (2 pints). Cook until all liquid is completely absorbed.

Pile the rice on a serving plate and serve the fish and shellfish *a banda*—that is, on the side.

Serves 6.

Indonesian Fish

500 g (1 lb) white fish
3 chili peppers, seeds removed
1–2 cloves garlic
Turmeric, lemongrass, salt
1 teaspoon fresh, grated ginger
1 tablespoon sugar
2 onions, chopped

Juice of 1–2 lemons
Banana leaves (or corn husks or aluminium foil)

Fillet the fish or cut into steaks. Crush the seasonings in a mortar, mix with the onion and lemon juice and spread over the fish. Wrap in banana leaves and cook in the oven for 15–20 minutes at 175°C (350°F) or Gas 4.

Indian Koftas
Fish Balls

> 500 g (1 lb) fillets of white fish
> 1 onion, chopped
> Chopped fresh coriander
> 1 tablespoon cumin
> 1–2 hot chilis, fresh and chopped or dried and crushed
> Salt and pepper
> Egg
> Breadcrumbs
> *Ghee* (see page 38) or oil

Crush the fish together with the onion in a mortar; add herbs and spices. Bind with egg, shape into balls and roll in breadcrumbs. Fry in *ghee* or oil.

In vegetarian regions of India where no eggs are eaten the binder for these balls is a paste made from *gram dhal* (*dhal* flour—see page 34), water, salt and a pinch of baking powder.

Greek Fish

> 1 whole fish weighing 1.7 kg (3–5 lb), cleaned and prepared
> Salt and pepper
> Lemon juice

2 onions, finely chopped
3–4 cloves garlic
Chopped fresh parsley
Olive oil
2–3 tomatoes, peeled
250 ml (½ pint) dry white wine
1 tablespoon sugar
Tomato slices

Wash the fish thoroughly. Sprinkle with salt, pepper and lemon juice. Arrange in a baking dish, slashing the skin in 2 or 3 places.

Brown the onions, garlic, and parsley in olive oil. Add the tomatoes, a little water, the white wine and the sugar.

Pour the sauce over the fish and cover with tomato slices. Bake for 30–40 minutes at 200°C (400°F) or Gas 6. Test with a fork to see if cooked through; do not overcook.

Seafood Gumbo

One of the important ingredients in any gumbo is *filé*, a seasoning made from powdered sassafras, available in herb and spice stores.

1 prepared chicken
4 litres (8 pints) water
125 g (4 oz) flour
125 g (4 oz) bacon fat
1 large onion, chopped
1 stalk celery, chopped
250 g (8 oz) tomatoes
500 g (1 lb) okra
1 kg (2 lb) peeled, deveined shrimps
1½ tablespoons salt and pepper

2–3 chilis with seeds removed, chopped; or 1 teaspoon
powdered chilis

500 ml (1 pint) fresh shelled oysters, including juice

1½ tablespoons *filé*

Simmer the chicken, with the giblets, for 1½ hours in enough
of the water to cover. Drain, reserving the broth. Bone and skin
the chicken.

Stir the flour into hot fat and brown deeply. Add the chicken
broth and remaining water. Stir and boil for 20–30 minutes. Add
the onion and celery and simmer for another 30 minutes. Add the
tomatoes, okra, shrimps, salt, pepper and chilis. Simmer 10–15
minutes until the shrimps are tender. Add the oysters and chicken
meat and simmer for another 5–10 minutes until the oysters curl
at the edges. Remove from the heat and stir in *filé*. Serve with rice.
    Serves 6–8.

Sushi
Japanese Stuffed Seaweed

500 g (1 lb) cooked rice, preferably the sticky, wide-grained
Japanese kind.

125 g (4 oz) raw fish such as tuna, bass, octopus or mackerel

Japanese hot radish paste or hot mustard

Rice vinegar

6–10 sheets *nori* seaweed (purple laver)

All of these ingredients can be tracked down in shops selling
Japanese foodstuffs or, with the exception of radish paste and fresh
fish, at health food stores.

Form the rice into long cylinders with strips of fish running
through or along them. Daub with a little hot radish paste and
sprinkle with vinegar. Roll up in a sheet of laver, moistened with
vinegar. Serve cut into 2.5-cm (1-in) sections.

For a more economical version of sushi replace the fish with vegetables, such as *daikon* or carrot, or a sliced, hard-boiled egg.

Peruvian Ceviche

This method of serving fish in lemon juice is found not only on the Pacific coast of South America but also in the Pacific islands—in fact *ceviche* could just as well be called Tahitian.

500 g (1 lb) raw firm-fleshed white fish such as haddock
6–10 lemons
Salt
2 cloves garlic, chopped
1–2 hot dried chilis, with seeds removed and chopped, or ½ teaspoon powdered chilis
1–2 onions, cut into rings
1–2 sweet peppers, de-seeded and sliced

Skin and fillet the fish and wash well. Dice and cover with lemon juice. Add salt, garlic and chilis. Stir to make sure the pieces are well marinated. Cover with raw onion rings and sliced pepper and leave in a cool place for a few hours.

Serve with boiled sweet potatoes.

VARIATION   Replace the fish with raw shrimps.

Bacalao

Portuguese Cod

Cod used to be the poor man's fish all over the world and Portugal, as a fishing nation, is noted for its large variety of cod recipes.

500 g (1 lb) dried salt cod (*bacalao*, see page 38)
3 onions, chopped
2–3 cloves garlic, chopped
Black pepper
Chopped parsley
500 g (1 lb) potatoes
Olive oil

Soak the cod overnight in plenty of water. Drain.

Spread the onions in a frying pan. Sprinkle with garlic, pepper and chopped parsley. Cover with an even layer of cod, then of sliced potatoes.

Add oil to cover, or sprinkle generously with oil.

Cover and cook for at least 1 hour over a low heat.

African Dried Cod in Tomato Sauce

Dried fish is an important resource at certain times of the year. This dish is served with *chi kuang*, the traditional manioc balls (also known as *fufu* and often made with yam or plantain paste instead of manioc). Leftovers may be shaped into sausages, wrapped in banana leaves, tied with vines, then poached. Cooked this way, they keep for a long time. Fish and manioc are sometimes accompanied by *gombos*, or *okra* mixed into a plate of spinach or young manioc leaves, boiled and crushed to a paste, then thickened with ground-up peanuts and seasoned with hot pepper. Boiled green bananas take the place of bread.

> 2–3 onions, chopped
> 1–2 cloves garlic, chopped
> Vegetable or peanut oil
> 2–3 fresh or soaked dried chilis with seeds and stems removed, chopped, or 2 tablespoons powdered chilis
> 4–6 tomatoes, chopped
> 500 g (1 lb) salt cod (see page 38) soaked overnight in cold water, drained and cut into 5-cm (2-in) pieces

Sauté the onions and garlic in 1–2 tablespoons of oil. Add the chilis and fry for a few minutes. Add the tomatoes and simmer for 10 minutes before adding the salt cod. Serve with manioc balls:

> 125 g (4 oz) manioc meal
> 500 ml (1 pint) water
> Salt

Add the manioc meal gradually to boiling salted water, stirring constantly. Simmer, stirring, for 20 minutes. Leave to cool. Shape into walnut-sized balls and serve.

Squid with Rice

Octopus and squid are eaten fresh or dried in many countries, such as Spain, Portugal, Turkey, Japan, the Windward Isles and France. In the British Isles squid or cuttlefish used to be sold only for fishing bait, but is becoming more popular as more people have eaten it on Continental holidays.

> 500 g (1 lb) small squid
> Flour
> Olive oil
> 2 cloves garlic, crushed
> Chopped fresh parsley
> 250 ml (½ pint) tomato sauce (see page 55)
> 1–2 onions, chopped
> 350 g (12 oz) rice
> 3–4 pistils saffron
> 750 ml (1½ pints) water or stock

Prepare the squid by removing the sepia hood. Young, small squid do not have the cuttle bone that must be removed in larger squid. Blanch for 3–5 minutes in boiling, salted water. Drain. Wipe dry, dip in flour, and fry in oil for 10 minutes. Sprinkle with garlic and parsley and put into an aromatic tomato sauce. Meanwhile make a rice pilaf by frying onions with rice and crushed saffron in olive oil, then adding water or stock and simmering until absorbed. Combine squid, tomato mixture and rice and serve, with mussels on the side if wished.

Preserved Squid

> 1 kg (2lb) small squid
> Shallots or small white onions
> 250 ml (¼ pint) dry white wine
> 250 ml (¼ pint) water

Bay leaf, peppercorns, thyme
Salt and vinegar

Prepare the squid by removing the sepia hood and pounding to tenderize. Simmer for 15–20 minutes in a spicy court bouillon made with shallots, wine, water and herbs. Put in glass jars and cover with a marinade consisting of equal volumes of the court bouillon in which the squid was cooked, vinegar and water. Add more fresh seasonings (bay leaves, thyme, pepper, etc.)

Prepared this way in the early autumn squid will keep throughout the winter. It can be eaten in salads or cooked in stews.

Greek Octopus

1 octopus, weighing about 675 g (1½ lb)
125 ml (¼ pint) wine vinegar
125 ml (¼ pint) olive oil
250 ml (½ pint) water
4 onions
2 cloves garlic
Pepper

Remove head, eyes, beak, and ink sac from the octopus. Cut across the tentacles to make 6-mm (¼-in) slices and pound with a wooden mallet or rolling pin to tenderize.

Put all the ingredients in a pot. *Do not salt.* Close tightly and simmer for 2 hours.

Make sure the octopus is entirely covered by liquid and close tightly—otherwise the octopus will be tough and uneatable.

Spanish Octopus

1 octopus, weighing about 675 g (1½ lb)
2 onions, chopped

Olive oil
250 ml (½ pint) dry white wine
2–3 tomatoes
2–3 cloves garlic
Chopped fresh parsley and basil
Salt, pepper, thyme
½ teaspoon cayenne

Remove head, eyes, beak and ink sac from the octopus. Cut across
the tentacles to make 6-mm (¼-in) slices and pound with a wooden
mallet or rolling pin to tenderize.

Brown the onions in oil. Add the white wine, tomato, garlic,
herbs and seasonings. Put in the pieces of octopus, cover tightly
and simmer for 2 hours.

Serve, adding butter to the sauce.

DESSERTS AND DRINKS

Korean Melon

    1 melon
    250 ml (½ pint) water
    250 g (8 oz) sugar
    1 orange or lemon

Cube an oval melon. Prepare a syrup by simmering the water, sugar, grated orange or lemon peel and orange or lemon juice together for 10–15 minutes. Mix the cubes with the syrup and bring to the boil. Cover and simmer for 10–15 minutes.

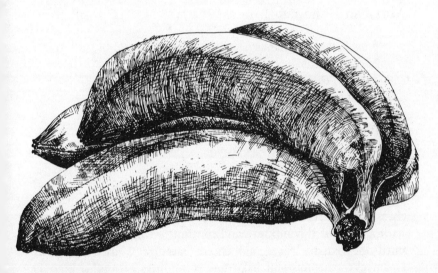

Candied Maduros

Maduros are a variety of plantains, tougher in texture than ordinary bananas, with a dark skin.

    6 *maduros* or bananas
    Lard or butter

250 ml (½ pint) dry white wine
125 g (4 oz) sugar
½ teaspoon cinnamon
½ teaspoon vanilla essence

Slice the ripe *maduros* or bananas and soak for 20–30 minutes in salted water to remove excess moisture. Drain.

Sauté them in fat and pour over the white wine, sugar, cinnamon and vanilla.

Simmer for 15 minutes or so.

Mexican Bananas

6 *maduros* or bananas
Lard or butter
250 g (8 oz) cream cheese
125 g (4 oz) sugar
125 ml (¼ pint) rum
Cinnamon
125 ml (¼ pint) double cream

Peel and slice the bananas; brown in lard or butter. Place a layer of slices on the bottom of a greased baking tin. Beat together the cheese, sugar, rum and cinnamon. Cover the bananas in the tin with a layer of this mixture and continue with alternating layers until the banana slices and cheese mixture is used up. Pour cream over the top and bake for 25 minutes at 175°C (350°F) or Gas 4. The cream should be almost entirely absorbed. Serve hot.

Oriental Oranges

12 mandarin oranges, tangerines or small thin-skinned oranges
500 g (1 lb) sugar

1 litre (2 pints) water
½ teaspoon vanilla essence

Scrape the oranges but do not peel. Mix the sugar and water together and add the vanilla. Add the oranges and simmer for at least 1 hour. Cool and serve in the syrup.

If refrigerated these oranges will keep for a month.

Camotes in Syrup
Latin-American Sweet Potatoes

Camote is the Mexican name for a variety of sweet potato which is also known as *batata* and *boniato*.

1 kg (2 lb) *camotes* (sweet potatoes)
125 g (4 oz) sugar
Water

Peel and simmer the *camotes* in a very little water for 10 minutes until half-cooked. Drain.

Put in a pan with the sugar and enough water to cover. Simmer for 20 minutes or so. The sweet potatoes should look glazed and almost transparent.

Serve cold in the syrup.

El mistouf
Sweet Couscous

500 g (1 lb) *couscous* (see page 103)
250 g (8 oz) dates, stoned
75 g (3 oz) almonds
75 g (3 oz) raisins
75 g (3 oz) sugar

75 g (3 oz) shelled, unsalted pistachio nuts
Grated orange peel
Butter

Prepare couscous according to recipe on page 103 os use leftover couscous. Cover with halved dates before the last steaming (or resteam leftovers).

Meanwhile crush the almonds, raisins, sugar, pistachio nuts, and orange peel together in a mortar (you can grate the nuts first if that's easier). Mix with the couscous and sprinkle with melted butter.

Peanut Caramel

500 g (1 lb) raw, unshelled peanuts
750 g (1½ lb) sugar
250 ml (½ pint) water

Roast the peanuts for 10–15 minutes in a 200°C (400°F) or Gas 6 oven, and shell them by rubbing between your hands. Mix the sugar and water and boil for 10–15 minutes until you have a thick syrup. Add the peanuts and continue boiling, stirring until the caramel thickens and takes on colour. Spread on a buttered plate or marble slab, like nougat. Cut when cooled.

Russian Candied Milk

500 ml (1 pint) rich fresh or raw milk (see page 36)
500 g (1 lb) sugar

Heat sugar and milk gently and simmer 2–3 hours, stirring frequently : the mixture will get very thick and take on a golden colour. Pour into little pots or spread on to a cold slab and cut into 3-cm (1½-in) squares when cool. This dessert will keep for a long time.

Sarikauja
Malaysian Custard

250 g (8 oz) sugar
4 eggs
500 ml (1 pint) coconut milk (see page 58)
1 teaspoon rose water (from chemists)

Beat the sugar and eggs together. Add coconut milk and flavour with rose water. Pour into greased individual moulds. Set in a pan half-full of hot water, cover and cook for 45 minutes in the oven at 175°C (350°F) or Gas 4.

Turn out of the moulds when cooled.

Tamina el bejauia
Semolina Pudding

Serve with mint tea, as in North Africa

500 g (1 lb) couscous (coarse semolina)
500 ml (1 pint) honey
250 g (8 oz) butter
Chopped dates (optional)

Dry-fry couscous over a moderate heat in a heavy ungreased frying pan for 3 minutes. Shake constantly so it will not stick.

Melt the honey and butter together to make a smooth cream. Mix quickly with the hot couscous. If desired, add chopped dates. Pour on to a buttered plate or into a shallow pan, and smooth with a palette knife. When cool cut into squares.

Mazamorra
Uruguayan Maize Pudding

250 g (8 oz) whole dried sweetcorn kernels (maize)
1 teaspoon bicarbonate of soda
Milk
Sugar

Soak the kernels overnight. Bring to a boil and simmer for 45 minutes or until tender. Add the bicarbonate of soda dissolved in some cold water, boil a few moments then remove from heat. Pour into a bowl and leave to cool.

Serve with milk and sugar.

Indian Pudding

The key to making this classic American dessert is to cook it very slowly for a long time. If possible use a stone or clay pot.

125 g (4 oz) maize meal
125 g (4 oz) black treacle
125 g (4 oz) sugar
50 g (2 oz) lard or butter
¼ teaspoon salt
¼ teaspoon bicarbonate of soda
2 eggs
1.5 litres (3 pints) hot milk

Mix together the maize meal, molasses, sugar, fat, salt, eggs, half the bicarbonate of soda and the milk in a saucepan. Bring to the boil over a high flame on top of the stove. Pour the mixture into a well-greased stoneware or clay pot, mix in the remaining milk and bake in the bottom of the lowest possible oven for 5–7 hours.

The temperature in the oven should be so low that the pudding is just barely bubbling without actually boiling. Bake until the pudding browns slightly and comes away from the edges.

Billila
Whole Wheat Pudding

This Greek dessert is a speciality on the feast of Saint Barbara. In Yugoslavia a similar dish called *jito* is prepared in honour of the household's patron saint's day. A priest traditionally comes to bless the *jito* as well as the *kolach*, a festive cake.

> 250 g (8 oz) whole wheat grains
> 75 g (3 oz) sugar
> 125 g (4 oz) chopped almonds or walnuts
> Anise or orange water

Boil the wheat grains until they burst. as if preparing *bulgur* (see page 95), but do not grind. Simmer for 20–30 minutes more.

Mix in the sugar and chopped almonds or walnuts. Flavour to taste with anise or orange water. Pour into a bowl, chill and serve.

Bean Pudding

There is nothing unusual about multiple uses for beans, but one Indian tribe of North and Central America uses beans so much they earned the name Papagos—the bean people.

> 250 g (8 oz) white or red beans, soaked overnight
> 750 ml (1¼ pints) water
> 150 g (5 oz) dried figs

175 g (6 oz) sugar
½ teaspoon vanilla essence

Drain the beans, add plenty of unsalted water and simmer for about 2½ hours. Drain and purée in a Mouli-légumes, or mash. Meanwhile simmer the figs for ½ hour in a little water, drain and chop. Add to the beans along with two-thirds of the sugar and the vanilla essence. Heat gently and stir so that it thickens evenly.

Melt the remaining sugar over a medium heat in a dry, heavy frying pan. Add 2 tablespoons of water and stir until the caramelized sugar is dissolved. Pour into a mould. Then add the bean purée and chill. Turn out of the mould and serve.

Squash Pudding

A favourite in Latin America, this is made with *calabaza*, a large, round pumpkin-like vegetable. Suitable alternatives are the American winter squashes such as Butternut or Hubbard; or the British pumpkin.

500 g (1 lb) calabaza, squash or pumpkin
150 g (5 oz) cornflour
750 ml (1¼ pints) milk
275 g (10 oz) sugar
Juice and peel from 5 oranges
1 egg, beaten
2 tablespoons water

Peel and cut up the squash or pumpkin. Steam for 5–10 minutes, then purée in a Mouli-légumes or blender. Mix the cornflour with the milk and heat gently until it starts to thicken. Add the purée, most of the sugar, orange juice, grated peel and the egg. Heat gently, stirring steadily.

Meanwhile melt the remaining sugar over moderate heat in a

dry, heavy pan. Add the water and stir to dissolve the caramelized sugar. Pour into a mould.

Pour the pudding into the mould and chill. Turn out to serve.

Sago Pudding

Sago is starch from the pith of the Sago palm of south-east Asia.

> 125 g (4 oz) sago
> 1 litre (2 pints) milk
> Sugar to taste
> 1 kg (2 lb) peeled, sliced apples
> 125 ml (¼ pint) water

Stir the sago into the milk in a medium-sized saucepan; bring just to a boil and simmer slowly, stirring occasionally, until the mixture thickens; about ½ hour. Sweeten to taste. Meanwhile stew the apples in the water (cover pan tightly and they will make their own juice) until tender. Sweeten to taste and sprinkle with a little cinnamon, then place in a baking dish and pour the sago over them. Bake at 160°C (325°F) or Gas 3 for ½ hour.

Scottish Carrageen Pudding

Carrageen, a seaweed also known as Irish moss, is available in many health food stores. It is a vegetable substitute for gelatine, which is made from animal protein.

> 15 g (½ oz) dried carrageen
> Lemon peel
> 750 ml (1¼ pints) milk
> 75 g (3 oz) sugar

Soak the carrageen in water for 15 minutes and drain. Heat the lemon peel with the milk and stir in the sugar. Add the soaked carrageen. Return to the heat and boil gently for 20 minutes. Pour into a chilled, wet mould. Take out of the mould when cold and set.

Beetroot Halva

> 5 large beetroots
> 275 g (10 oz) sugar
> 6–7 tablespoons *ghee* (see page 38) or butter
> 75 g (3 oz) chopped raisins
> 75 g (3 oz) chopped cashew nuts

Wash and steam the beetroot for 15–20 minutes until tender all the way through. Purée in a Mouli-légumes or blender and add the sugar. Simmer gently for 20–30 minutes, stirring frequently. Gradually mix in the *ghee*, raisins and nuts. Pour into a wide plate and smooth the top. Serve cold.

VARIATION   Replace the beetroot with potato.

Egg Halva

In the strict vegetarian districts of India this dish is made with cooked, puréed carrots or marrow instead of scrambled eggs.

> 4 eggs
> 250 ml (½ pint) coconut milk (see page 58)
> 125 g (4 oz) sugar
> 75 g (3 oz) raisins
> ½–1 teaspoon cinnamon
> 75 g (3 oz) chopped almonds or diced fruit

Scramble the eggs. Meanwhile gently heat the coconut milk with the sugar and raisins and cook for 5–8 minutes, to thicken. Add to the eggs and simmer gently for 5 minutes. Stir in the cinnamon, grated almonds or diced fruit and remove from the heat.

Bunuelos
Mexican Sweet Fritters

All over the world fritters are the easiest and quickest pastry to prepare.

    2 eggs
    250 g (8 oz) flour
    150 g (5 oz) sugar
    Oil
    2 tablespoons aniseeds or 3 cinnamon sticks
    150 ml (¼ pint) water

Beat the eggs with 2 tablespoons of sugar then mix thoroughly with the flour to get a loose dough. Leave to rest for 20 minutes. Divide into walnut-sized balls and flatten by slapping them between your hands. Deep fry in oil and drain. Bring the anise or cinnamon and water to a boil and simmer for 20–30 minutes. Remove cinnamon or anise. Stir in the remaining sugar, turn up the heat and boil for 5–10 minutes. Pour over the fritters and serve.

Filhos
Portuguese Pumpkin Fritters

These fritters are treats at every *carnaval*.

    250 g (8 oz) pumpkin flesh
    250 g (8 oz) flour

3 eggs, separated
2 orange peels, grated
250 ml (½ pint) ruby port wine
Oil for deep frying
250 g (8 oz) sugar

Cut the pumpkin flesh into a few large chunks and steam for 30 minutes until tender. Purée in a Mouli-légumes or blender. Pour off any excess liquid or drain in cheesecloth, if necessary. Add the flour, yolks and orange peel. Mix together and moisten with a little wine. The result should be a thick, smooth paste. Leave to stand.

Add stiffly beaten egg whites. The mixture should now have the consistency of normal fritter batter; if it is too thick add a little more wine.

Drop by tablespoons into hot deep frying oil. Cook quickly and drain well.

Stir the sugar into the remaining wine and bring to the boil. Boil for about 5 minutes to make a syrup and pour over the fritters. Serve.

Jallabis
Indian Fritters

In India desserts are numerous and often very fine, but they are not generally served at the end of a meal. Instead they are eaten like other sweets all through the day. The poorer people, of course, taste these sweets only on special occasions.

250 g (8 oz) flour
½ teaspoon dried yeast
750 ml (1¼ pints) lukewarm water
400 g (14 oz) sugar

Ghee (see page 38) or oil
Pistachio nuts, grated or crushed

Mix the flour and yeast with 400 ml (¾ pint) of the water to the consistency of thick cream. Leave, covered, for 6–12 hours.

Stir the sugar into the remaining water, bring to the boil for 5–10 minutes. Keep warm.

Heat the *ghee* or oil in a frying pan. Dribble the batter by tablespoonfuls through a funnel into the oil. Fry until golden brown; drain. Soak in the syrup for 10 minutes, drain and serve sprinkled with crushed pistachio nuts.

Brazilian Beer Biscuits

500 g (1 lb) flour
125 g (4 oz) sugar
125 g (4 oz) butter
4 tablespoons beer
Pinch of bicarbonate of soda
½–1 teaspoon cinnamon

Knead all the ingredients to make a thick dough. Divide into balls and flatten between your palms. Arrange on a buttered baking sheet and bake for 15 minutes at 175°C (350°F) or Gas 4. Leave to cool on a rack.

Slavic Kolaches

125 ml (¼ pint) milk
2 teaspoons dried yeast
125 ml (¼ pint) warm water
175 g (6 oz) butter
125 g (4 oz) granulated sugar

1 teaspoon salt
4 egg yolks
500 g (1 lb) sifted white flour
2 tablespoons melted butter
2 tablespoons icing sugar

Scald the milk (bring just to boiling point). Remove from heat and cool to lukewarm. Sprinkle the yeast on the water and stir to dissolve. Cream the butter, sugar, salt and egg yolks together until light and fluffy. Add the yeast, milk and one-third of the flour. Beat well until the batter is very smooth; scrape the bowl frequently. Stir in the remaining flour, a little at a time, making a soft dough that comes away from the sides of the bowl. Place in a lightly greased bowl, turning the dough over to grease the top. Cover and leave to rise in a warm place free from draughts until doubled; 1–1½ hours.

Turn on to a lightly floured board, knead for a minute or two, and divide into 24 pieces of equal size. Shape each piece into a ball. Cover and leave to rest for 10–15 minutes. Place 5 cm (2 in) apart on greased baking sheets; press each piece of dough down in the centre to make a hollow with a 1 cm (½ in) rim around the edge. Fill each hollow with a tablespoon of prune or apricot filling (see below). Cover and leave to rise in a warm place until doubled; 30–40 minutes. Bake at 175°C (350°F) or Gas 4 for 15–20 minutes or until brown. Brush the tops of the rolls lightly with melted butter and sift over the icing sugar. Remove from the baking sheets to wire cooling racks.

Makes 24 kolaches.

PRUNE FILLING:

30 dried prunes
4 tablespoons granulated sugar
½ teaspoon allspice

Cook the prunes in water to cover until tender. Drain, mash with a fork, removing stones and stir in the sugar and allspice. The filling should be very thick, and sufficient to fill 14 kolaches.

APRICOT FILLING:

25 dried apricot halves
4 tablespoons granulated sugar

Cook the apricots in water to cover until tender. Drain and pass through a Mouli-légumes, or put briefly in a blender. Stir in the sugar. The filling should be thick and sufficient to fill 10 kolaches.

Hamantashen
Prune Biscuits

On the holiday of Purim, Jews celebrate the downfall of the villain Haman. They eat these delicious biscuits filled in memory of Haman's pockets (i.e., *hamantashen*), which he no longer needed after the Persian king hanged him.

DOUGH:

500 g (1 lb) flour
200 g (7 oz) sugar
4 eggs, beaten
125 ml (¼ pint) oil
Juice and grated peel of 1 orange, if desired (if you do not
   use juice replace with 2–3 tablespoons cold water)

LEVKAR (Prune filling):

500 g (1 lb) prunes
1 orange, sliced
Cinnamon and allspice

DOUGH   Sift the flour and mix with the other ingredients. Knead into a sticky but firm dough and chill for 1 hour.

LEKVAR   Stew the prunes with the sliced oranges and spices for 15 minutes. Cool, remove stones and chop. If desired add raisins or chopped nuts.

Roll out the dough on a floured board and cut into discs about 10 cm (4 in) in diameter. Or divide the dough into 24 balls and roll each one to make the discs. Place a spoonful of *lekvar* on each disc and fold in at 3 places to form the shape of a three-cornered hat, or perhaps old Persian pockets. Bake at 175°C (350°F) or Gas 4 for 30 minutes. If desired brush with egg white or milk before baking.

For a lighter crust sift 2–3 teaspoons of baking powder with the flour.

Polish Kluskis
Poached Cakes

> 250 g (8 oz) flour
> 1 teaspoon dried yeast
> 2 eggs
> 125 g (4 oz) sugar
> 6–7 tablespoons melted butter

Make a pile of flour and scoop a hole in the middle. Mix the yeast with a little lukewarm water. Place the eggs, sugar and yeast mixture in the hole and stir into the flour. Knead together well. Leave for 3–4 hours to rise.

Divide into 1-cm (½-in) balls, cover with a cloth, and leave to rise for 20–30 minutes.

Poach for 5 minutes in salted water and serve with melted butter.

Molinetes
Chilean Chocolate Roll

> 250 g (8 oz) butter
> 250 g (8 oz) sugar
> 375 g (13 oz) flour
> Orange peel, grated
> 1 teaspoon bicarbonate of soda
> 2 tablespoons cocoa

Beat the butter and sugar together until smooth. Add the flour, orange peel and soda. Mix well and divide the dough into two. Work the cocoa into one of the halves.

Roll out each piece of dough carefully with a buttered, floured rolling pin. Lay the plain dough on top of the chocolate dough and roll up together to make a long cylinder. Leave in a cool place for at least 1 hour.

Cut into thick slices. Lay on a buttered baking sheet and bake for 10 minutes at 175°C (350°F) or Gas 4. Cool on a rack.

Parkin

This moist sweet bread is a favourite teatime snack in the north of England and is usually served on Guy Fawkes Day.

> 100 g (4 oz) brown sugar
> 150 g (6 oz) butter or margarine
> 150 g (6 oz) black treacle
> 1 egg
> 125 ml (¼ pint) milk
> 250 g (8 oz) medium oatmeal
> 250 g (8 oz) plain flour
> 2 teaspoons ground ginger
> 1 teaspoon bicarbonate of soda

Melt the sugar, butter and treacle together over low heat. Beat the egg well, blend with a little of the milk, and add to the first mixture. Combine the oats, flour and ginger in a large bowl and stir in the treacle mixture. Beat well, then add the remaining milk in which the soda has been dissolved. Stir until blended, then pour into a well-buttered 23 cm (9 in) square cake tin. Bake for 1–1¼ hours at 175°C (350°F) or Gas 4. Cool slightly before turning out.

Store in an airtight tin for a week before eating, cut into squares, on its own or spread with butter.

Creole Cake

2 eggs, separated
125 g (4 oz) brown sugar
125 g (4 oz) grated fresh coconut
50 g (2 oz) flour
3 tablespoons butter, melted
Pinch of cinnamon
1 teaspoon bicarbonate of soda

Beat the egg yolks with the sugar. Add coconut, flour, melted butter, cinnamon and soda. Mix in stiffly beaten egg whites at the last moment.

Pour the mixture into a shallow buttered baking pan or mould and bake for 25 minutes at 175°C (350°F) or Gas 4.

Creole Maize Cake

2 eggs, separated
150 g (5 oz) sugar
125 g (4 oz) melted butter

125 g (4 oz) maize meal
50 g (2 oz) white or whole wheat flour
1 tablespoon bicarbonate of soda
2 tablespoons boiling milk

Beat together the egg yolks and sugar and the melted butter. Mix in the flours and soda gradually, then the milk.

Fold in the stiffly beaten egg whites and pour into a buttered baking pan or mould. Bake for 30 minutes at 175°C (350°F) or Gas 4.

Kalva
Greek Semolina Cake

In Greece and every country where a long Turkish occupation has left its mark, semolina cake is a popular dish.

4–5 tablespoons butter
200 g (7 oz) semolina
500 ml (1 pint) milk
125 g (4 oz) sugar

Melt the butter in a saucepan and add the semolina. Brown, stirring constantly. Then pour in the hot milk mixed with sugar. Cover and simmer for 10–15 minutes or so. The semolina should absorb all the liquid.

Spread on to a large plate. When cool cut into squares.

Greek Yoghurt Cake

125 g (4 oz) butter
750 g (1½ lb) sugar
4 eggs, separated

250 ml (½ pint) yoghurt
350 g (12 oz) flour
1 tablespoon bicarbonate of soda
1 lemon
Breadcrumbs

Cream together the butter and sugar. Add the egg yolks, then the yoghurt. Mix in the flour and bicarbonate of soda and add the juice and grated peel of the lemon. Lastly mix in the stiffly beaten egg whites.

Pour into a buttered baking tin or mould lined with breadcrumbs. Bake for 45 minutes at 175°C (350°F) or Gas 4. Make sure it is cooked all the way through. Cool on a rack.

Sweet Potato Cake

Sweet potatoes are good alongside main dishes but also in desserts. They have a fine dry flavour similar to that of chestnuts.

1 kg (2 lb) sweet potatoes, peeled
2–3 tablespoons butter
5 tablespoons rum
75 g (3 oz) sugar
2 eggs, beaten

Boil or steam the sweet potatoes for 20–30 minutes until tender. Drain, mash and add the butter, rum, sugar and eggs. Pour into a mould and bake for 20 minutes at 175°C (350°F) or Gas 4. Turn out of the mould when cooled slightly.

SWEET POTATO FRITTERS   Prepare a sweet mash as above, very thick. Fry by spoonfuls in oil, dust with sugar and cinnamon and serve hot.

Montecaos
'Little Cakes'

These delicious Spanish cakes have made their way into North African cooking as well.

500 g (1 lb) flour
250 g (8 oz) sugar
125 ml (¼ pint) olive or other oil
½–1 teaspoon cinnamon or vanilla essence

Mix all the ingredients, knead and shape into little balls about the size of walnuts. If desired add a little brandy or water to bind the dough; but the cakes are flakier if you use less liquid. Arrange on a buttered baking sheet. Start baking at 230°C (450°F) or Gas 8 for a few minutes, then lower to 175°C (350°F) or Gas 4. Total baking time should be 15 minutes.

Spanish Cakes

This is a shortbread with a fine, delicate taste.

250 g (8 oz) sugar
250 g (8 oz) lard
1 egg
250 g (8 oz) flour
½ teaspoon cinnamon or vanilla essence

Beat the sugar and lard together. Add the egg, flour, cinnamon or vanilla and knead to make a firm dough.

Divide into balls about the size of walnuts and arrange on a baking sheet. Bake for 20 minutes at 175°C (350°F) or Gas 4. Cool on the sheet.

Bean Cake

This is a great favourite in Latin America.

> 250 g (8 oz) white or red beans, soaked overnight
> 125 g (4 oz) sugar
> ½–1 teaspoon cinnamon
> 2–3 eggs, separated
> Breadcrumbs

Drain the beans, add fresh water and simmer for 2½ hours or until tender. Drain and purée in a Mouli-légumes or blender. Add the sugar, cinnamon and egg yolks, then fold in the stiffly beaten egg whites.

Pour into a buttered baking tin or mould lined with breadcrumbs. Bake for 30 minutes at 175°C (350°F) or Gas 4.

Serve warm or cold.

Pecan Pie

This recipe comes from Louisiana in America's Deep South. The original would be made with Karo (corn syrup) or molasses. Pecans are somewhat similar to walnuts.

> FILLING:
> 3 eggs
> 175 g (6 oz) black treacle
> 175 g (6 oz) sugar
> Salt
> 3 tablespoons melted butter
> ½–1 teaspoon vanilla essence
> 250 g (8 oz) whole or coarsely chopped pecans
>
> CRUST:
> 75 g (3 oz) butter, lard or margarine

250 g (8 oz) flour
2–3 tablespoons cold water

To make the crust cut half the fat into the flour until evenly mixed and granular. Cut the rest of the fat in very coarsely. Add the water little by little, just enough so that the ball of dough will stick together. Leave to rest, covered, in a cool place for at least 1 hour. Roll out thinly on a floured board to make an even disc about 30 cm (12 in) in diameter. Lift carefully by draping over a floured rolling pin and lay gently over a 23-cm (9-in) round pie dish. Gently push the dough down into the corners and crimp the rim by pinching the dough into little peaks at regular intervals, cutting away any excess. Cover the bottom with foil or grease-proof paper, weigh down with dried beans and bake for 1–2 minutes at 190°C (375°F) or Gas 5. Remove beans and paper; leave the oven on.

To make the filling stir the eggs together gently. Mix in the treacle, a pinch of sugar, salt, butter and vanilla essence. Then add the pecans.

Pour into the crust and bake for 15 minutes, then lower the heat to 160°C (325°F) or Gas 3 and bake for 30–35 minutes more.

Serve warm or cold.

Arahara
Millet Drink

The Tuareg, a people of the central and western Sahara, prepare this nourishing drink using *tikamarin* cheese, a hard goat's cheese which may be replaced with *feta* or *pecorino*.

> 150 g (5 oz) dates, stoned
> 750 ml (1¼ pints) water
> 250 g (8 oz) dry goat's cheese
> 125 g (4 oz) millet flour

Chop the dates very finely and add a little water to make a light paste. Crumble the cheese finely.

Mix the date paste and cheese with water and millet flour. The liquid will look like milk and when served chilled is very refreshing. This is also easily made in a blender.

Chicha
Maize Beer

This is an adapted version of the native brew (see page 32) made by Mexican and other Latin-American Indians.

> 125 g (4 oz) dried sweet corn kernels
> 125 g (4 oz) barley
> 4 litres (8 pints) water
> 1 stick cinnamon
> 500 g (1 lb) fresh pineapple, crushed
> 250 ml (½ pint) orange juice
> 1 kg (2 lb) sugar

Lightly toast half the corn and half the barley, then soak these with the rest of the grain in one-quarter of the water for 2 days. Grind the grain in a pestle and mortar or put through a blender and mix with the remaining water together with the cinnamon, pineapple, orange juice and sugar. Keep in a clay pot for 2 days. Strain and serve with ice.

Mexican Chocolate

A fine version of a good, stimulating drink.

750 g (3 oz) unsweetened chocolate
1 litre (2 pints) milk
5 tablespoons brown sugar or 150 ml (¼ pint) runny honey
2–3 cloves
50 g (2 oz) almonds
½ teaspoon cinnamon or 1 cinnamon stick

Melt the chocolate in gently heated milk. Stir in the sugar. Crush the cloves and almonds finely with the cinnamon in a mortar and mix with the hot chocolate. Whip with an egg-beater. Alternatively, melt the chocolate in gently heated milk, put in a blender, add the other ingredients and whip. The blender will chop the nuts and spices finely as well as make the drink foamy. Serve hot.

Clabbered Milk

A tangy drink of pioneer America, clabber was either naturally soured milk or residue from the butter churn (buttermilk). If you have unpasteurized milk available, place a little in a small glass dish or bowl, and leave until it has turned, then refrigerate until ready to drink or use in baking. Since pasteurized milk will not sour properly, but simply spoils, you'll need to resort to cultured buttermilk, commercially available, to make your own clabber, if you have no raw milk of your own.

250 ml (½ pint) skim milk
1 tablespoon cultured buttermilk

Scald the milk (bring just to the boil) remove from the heat and
cool to lukewarm: about 25°C (80°F). Stir in the buttermilk and
cover. Leave to stand at room temperature until 'clabbered' or
turned. Stir or shake until smooth; refrigerate until ready to drink.

Barley Water

Because of the nourishing properties of the barley this used to
be given to invalids, but it is now more common as a refreshing
summer drink, with more lemon or orange added.

125 g (4 oz) pearl barley
1½ litres (3 pints) water
1 lemon, sliced very thinly
5 tablespoons runny honey

Cook the pearl barley in the water for 2–4 hours. Strain, reserving
the barley for soups. Bring the liquid back to the boil and pour
over the lemon and honey. Stir until the honey is dissolved, then
allow to stand for 15 minutes. Strain once more and serve warm or
cold.

Ginger Beer

50 g (2 oz) root ginger, bruised
50 g (2 oz) cream of tartar
4 litres (8 pints) boiling water
500 g (1 lb) brown sugar
Juice and rind of 2 large lemons

1 tablespoon fresh yeast dissolved in 4 tablespoons warm water
with 1 teaspoon sugar

Put the ginger and cream of tartar in a plastic bucket, pour in a
little of the boiling water, and stir until well dissolved, then add
the sugar, lemon juice and rind and remaining boiling water. Cool
to lukewarm, stirring often, then stir in the yeast solution. Leave
in a warm, draught-free place, covered with a cloth, for a day or
two; until the yeast has stopped frothing. Strain through muslin
into clean strong bottles (beer or cider bottles; not wine). Keep
for 3 days before drinking; serve cold.

Wassail

This used to be the traditional festival punch in Great Britain.

750 g (1½ lb) brown sugar
4 litre-bottles of red wine
1 stick cinnamon
3-cm (1½-in) piece of root ginger
10 whole allspice
¼ whole nutmeg
5 whole cloves
12 eggs, separated

Stir the sugar into the wine and heat slowly; do not boil. Tie the
spices into a piece of muslin and suspend them in the heating wine.
Beat the egg whites until stiff; beat the yolks until thick and light
yellow. Fold whites into yolks and place in punch bowl. Pour the
hot spiced wine on to them, first removing the spice bag. Whip
the wassail with a wire whisk until frothy.

Shopping Guide

Wheat flour, rice, corn, chicken, beef, pork, onions, and garlic are used in the recipes of all races, groups and classes of people in almost every country; they present no problem to the Western shopper. Some dishes are exotic to Westerners only because familiar products are used in unfamiliar ways: coconut with chicken, chocolate with rice or peanuts with barbecued ribs. Some products, like seaweed, *molokheya*, and dried malva flowers, are harder to find. Every ingredient in this cookbook can be either bought (or grown or gathered wild) in Britain and North America. It may, of course, take some adventuring which, apart from being enjoyable, is a lot easier than the kind of adventuring that most of the world's people have to undertake to procure the same products.

The best and most interesting places in which to find the ingredients in this cookbook are ethnic markets. Peoples from the over-populated Third World often emigrate, bringing their cooking and necessary ingredients with them. Emigration does not change tastes quickly. One of the best uses of this cookbook, in fact, is as an excuse to go into Chinese, Latin, Italian, Middle Eastern and Indian shops with appropriate requests and questions. Apart from the satisfaction of learning how to distinguish *bamias* from chickpeas and *chayote* from *calabaza*, you literally get the flavour of foreign countries and their peoples without the cost of a plane ticket and hotels. The utensils used in many of the recipes—the *tawas, woks, comals, molcajetes* and associated paraphernalia, are often quite beautiful to look at and practical and can usually be found beside the foods. Using authentic utensils should not, of course, be an obsession. The kind of fire you use to cook the foods affects the taste and texture, but stoves are hard to duplicate. A stone mortar such as a *molcajete* is, on the other hand, easy to find and hard to beat when grinding small quantities of spices or making a chili paste out of soaked chilis. Do not, however, disdain a blender when grinding large quantities of chilis and spices for *mole*, or chickpeas for *hummus*.

Another major and often more convenient source of people's products are the health or natural food shops. The relation of these foods to health apparently depends on the greater simplicity of unprocessed foods. Most Third World peoples, who eat only such foods are found in health or natural food shops, are certainly no healthier than are Westerners with our impressively complex system of processed foods. Still, they do avoid the high incidence of cardiovascular disease and other ailments of affluent societies, and there is much Western man can learn from them.

Although supermarkets usually carry a great variety of bottled spices, it is worth the effort to find a herb and spice shop where you can browse through the even greater variety, educating your nose to the various aromas. Loose spices must be bottled as they lose their pungency quickly, and even bottled they fade, so spices should if possible be bought in regular visits or for the occasion rather than on rare, grand expeditions. Herb and spice wholesalers are good suppliers of some rare products such as dried malva flowers for soup.

If you are not careful, shopping for unfamiliar products can be expensive, especially if you buy huge quantities of a spice you only intend to use once or twice. The best advice is to be prudent;

become aware of which products do and do not stay fresh (dried foods generally keep indefinitely; dried herbs lose their flavour; whole grain flours turn rancid rapidly); try to consult the shop-keeper whenever possible (admittedly this is difficult in some ethnic markets, but it is worthwhile trying to communicate with people from foreign cultures); and most of all, use your own common sense. At any rate, you will not find yourself spending exorbitant amounts on expensive cuts of meats or prepared im-ported delicacies when you use this cookbook. Also remember that experimentation and learning will save you a lot of money in the long run. Some of the products you buy may interest you enough to want to make you grow or make them from scratch—the cheapest and most satisfying way of all.

One good way to organize a meal using this cookbook is to try to feature one or two unfamiliar foods. Or try recipes all from one region or country. That way, you simplify preparation and really get to taste the food. Also, if you are cooking for guests, remember that people tend to be more conservative about what they eat than how it is prepared, so it may be confusing to try too much at once. There really is little reason to be squeamish or afraid—people's stomachs vary less than their religions. It is worth the effort to challenge your habits of taste. Once upon a time, populations in easy reach of despised herring starved to death in Europe.

Indian Shops

The cooking of India varies tremendously from region to region. Indian shops stock many of the items needed for the different regional foods. They always stock *ghee*, which along with coconut milk, garlic and curry spices, is largely responsible for the taste of the most familiar kind of Indian cooking. They also stock mustard, sesame and peanut oils, and sesame seeds which are characteristic of other regional styles of cooking. These shops and markets are the best source of staples like *dhal*, *dhal* flour, lentils, beans, rice, rice flour, *atta* (wholewheat) and *maida* (white wheat) flours. In our supermarkets we are used to very little variety in staples, which in our well-organized nation are nationally and consequently homogeneously marketed; but in these Indian markets, *dhal*, lentils and even rice are available in a surprising diversity of colours, shapes and taste.

Curries are subtler and more delicate if you mix the spices yourself instead of using blended curry powders. Indian shops keep all the spices that make up a curry blend: fenugreek, turmeric cloves, cinnamon, hot peppers, cardamom, cumin, coriander, bay leaves, saffron, black pepper, and fennel. This is an area for imagination—using the above spices selectively, you can develop a complex aroma that matches the dish, instead of the blended single taste of curry powder. Note too that spices get stale more slowly when bought whole instead of powdered so that whole cardamons and cumin seeds ground specially for a recipe have a fresher taste than shelf-dead curry powders. These spices are also available in herb and spice stores.

Other flavourings, such as rose water*, tamarind paste, sesame seeds, sesame paste (*tahina*), raw sugar, and coconut cream, are usually in stock in Indian shops. If you do not feel like making Indian curds or *panir* (drained curds), which are generally not

*also available from good chemists

available at these stores, you can replace the curds with soured milk, sour cream or yoghurt (see page 37) and use grated cheese in place of *panir*.

As for utensils, you can buy a *tawa*, a concave griddle, but not an *enghati*, a wood stove, for making Indian breads. Banana leaves are not generally available, although some Chinese and Latin markets have them; but these too can be replaced without detriment by corn husks, parchment paper, cheesecloth, or even vine or cabbage leaves, depending on the recipe.

MAIL ORDER

The Bombay Emporium,
Radiant House,
Pegamoid Road,
Edmonton, LONDON N18 2NG

The Far East Exotic Supplies,
34 Greek Street,
LONDON W1.

Chinese Shops

Chinese supermarkets have the widest variety of foods available anywhere. Besides the great number of foods and styles of cooking they owe to their immense country and developed culture, the Chinese have mastered so many techniques of preserving food that they can routinely supply very unusual products. Moreover, the Chinese stick to their traditions, even in foreign cities, and continue to cook and sell the same foods they eat in China.

The assortment of vegetables available in Chinese markets is very rich, including: (1) familiar vegetables such as tomatoes, cabbage, bananas, fresh ginger, watercress, radishes, mustard greens, raw peanuts and potatoes; (2) unfamiliar varieties of familiar vegetables such as yard beans (long string beans), Chinese cabbage, black radishes, long white radishes (*daikon*), snow peas, Chinese melons, kumquats, *calabazas* or pumpkins and long cucumbers; and (3) unfamiliar vegetables such as *bok choy*, water chestnuts, bitter melons, winter melons, *taro* (Chinese potato), arrowroot, yam bean, fresh coriander, and bean sprouts. The selection of dried vegetables is even richer, including: mushrooms and fungi, water chestnuts, lotus root, bamboo shoots, grasses, taro, arrowroot, banana and lotus leaves, beans, lentils and soya beans. The markets also stock many pickled vegetables, such as *kimchi*.

All the familiar staples are available: rice, rice flour, wheat flour, cornmeal, water chestnut powder, millet and tapioca. It should be noted in passing that the Chinese commonly use water chestnut powder instead of cornflour or flour to thicken soups and sauces. Wheat, rice, and soya bean noodles come in many shapes and textures. Bean curd, another Chinese staple, comes fresh, fermented, dried and canned, but most of the recipes in this book are best made with the fresh.

The important flavourings sold include: soy sauce, both thin and salty and thick and sweet; sesame oil, which with soy sauce, garlic and ginger, is responsible for the familiar taste of Chinese food; ginger and hot peppers both dried and fresh; rice vinegar, Szechuan pepper and star anise. Peanut oil is the most important cooking oil.

Some of the most picturesque sights of Chinese supermarkets are the dried seafoods used for dishes, sauces and stocks: shrimps, scallops and squid of all sizes, fish ranging from tiny sardines and anchovies to eels, 2-metre sharks and cod and exotic shellfish like sea cucumber and abalone. Fish such as sea bass, eel and shark are also sold fresh—even here the selection differs from that in familiar fish markets, although the fresh fish come from familiar waters. Dried and smoked pork joints and ducks, hams and sausages ornament Chinese shops. Fresh meat is not butchered in the familiar manner in Chinese butcher shops but comes in different

shapes. The ears, feet, tails and other parts of pigs, fowl and beef used in soups are important items, as well as offal.

Chinese utensils, particularly the wok, are extremely useful cooking tools. Make sure you also buy a stand when buying a wok in this country. Other available utensils include: steamers that fit into woks, clay soup pots for slow cooking, chopsticks, frying ladles and chopping knives.

Some Chinese products can be found in ordinary supermarkets: soy sauce, bean sprouts, some frozen vegetables such as pea pods, and canned vegetables such as water chestnuts and bamboo shoots. Frozen Chinese vegetables are tasty but canned water chestnuts, bamboo shoots and noodles often leave something to be desired.

Chinese products are at their best in Chinese supermarkets in Chinatown in no matter what city. Although it may be difficult to make yourself understood, and some of the foods appear strange, the experience of shopping alongside people for whom lotus root is a more familiar taste than potatoes adds to the taste of the dishes and the appreciation of their importance.

Some supermarkets commonly found in urban Chinatowns are maintained by other Oriental peoples and emphasize other Asian cuisines such as Vietnamese, Thai and Indonesian. They usually also stock most of the same staples as the Chinese shops in addition to their national specialities.

MAIL ORDER

Cheong-Leen,
4–10 Tower Street,
Cambridge Circus,
LONDON, WC2

Kwong Tai Yuen,
26 Nelson Street,
LIVERPOOL, 1

Japanese Shops

Japanese shops are not quite as common as Chinese supermarkets but are another excellent source of oriental products. Dried seaweed is a true Japanese staple and available in great variety, including sheet laver for *sushi* and *kombu*. Dried fish, such as flaked tuna (bonito), dried shrimps and rice, especially the fine, wide-grained Japanese rice and rice flour are, other important staples.

These stores also stock soya beans, *miso* (soya bean paste for soups), fresh and fermented bean curd, soy sauce and *tamari* (a heavy soy sauce); fresh vegetables such as *daikon* (Japanese radish), Chinese (celery) cabbage, *bok choy* (like broccoli), ginger and bean sprouts; and often carry fresh seafood including octopus and tuna. Dried Japanese mushrooms are very fine. Hot radish powder for *sushi* and *sashimi* (sliced raw fish), and rice vinegar, as well as prepared foods like rice biscuits with seaweed (*kakimotchi sembei*), many different vegetables preserved in brine or vinegar, including *kimchi* (see page 173) and other Japanese specialities are available.

Japanese shops also stock utensils, including the noble *wok* with its accompanying steamers and paraphernalia, and good knives.

MAIL ORDER

Tokyo Ya,
234 West End Lane,
LONDON, NW6

Latin-American Shops

There may be one or two shops selling Latin-American—Puerto
Rican, Mexican, Cuban, Dominican, Brazilian, Portuguese—produce in some major cities. They routinely stock wide assortments
of staples like dried beans of all colours, green bananas (*platanos*
and *maduros*), yams (*ñames*), sweet potatoes (*batatas* or *camotes*),
taro (*dasheen* and *yautia*), breadfruit, manioc (*yuca*), manioc meal,
dried corn, many grades of maize meal, prepared tortillas, rice flour,
dried cod (*bacalao*), dried beef (*carne seca*), *chorizo* sausage, fresh
and hard cheeses, dried chilis, chocolate and spices like *epazote*.
They may also carry fresh tropical fruits and vegetables such as
chayote, *calabazas*, mangoes, papayas, coconuts, and fresh coriander (*culantro*). Canned chilis, tomatoes, and *mole* sauces are also
available. Some stores stock utensils as well as foods, including
metates (stones for grinding grain), *molcajetes* (mortars), clay dishes
for *paella*, *comals* (griddles), and tortilla presses. Butchers in these
markets carry wide selections of pork products including sausages,
lard, heads, tails, and feet. Spanish shops and West Indian stores
and markets are also worth trying.

Middle Eastern Shops

The markets of the nations on the eastern shores of the Mediterranean stock many products in common, reflecting the still strong influence of the old Turkish empire. For example, Greek stores carry many of the same items as do the Syrian ones.

Relatively unfamiliar staples like bulgur, chickpeas and couscous are commonly available in different grades in Middle Eastern shops, as well as familiar staples like beans, rice and lentils in uncommon variety. Middle Eastern markets are the best source for vine leaves, *tahina* (sesame paste) sesame oil, dried *bamias* and mint. Nuts, ground lamb, olives and dried fruits are central elements of Middle Eastern cookery available even in supermarkets.

Middle Eastern shops carry the same spices as those available in Indian markets, but with a different balance: cumin dominates, especially in Arab markets; and anise, a favourite of Mediterranean France as well as Greece, is important. Cardamom and cinnamon are commonly used in teas and desserts. Middle Eastern shops also carry other flavourings for sweets, such as honey, tamarind paste, orange water and rose water.

The large, heavy metal mortars sold in these markets are useful and handsome utensils.

MAIL ORDER

Lebanese Food Centre,
11 Sloane Street,
LONDON, SW1

Italian Shops

Many Italian products, such as spaghetti and Parmesan cheese, are familiar supermarket items, but you can find greater variety and better quality in Italian shops. For instance, pasta varies greatly in quality—fresh fettucine is delicious, and even spaghetti bought by the kilogram in one of these shops generally tastes better than the mass-marketed brands. Nothing of course tastes better than home-made. Parmesan comes in many grades and is best bought in chunks and grated just before serving.

Italian shops are scattered in most urban centres and stock fine goods like polenta, chickpeas, chickpea flour, pine nuts, Piedmontese rice for risottos, excellent canned tomatoes that are better in sauces than 'fresh' tomatoes out of season, mozzarella, ricotta, Parmesan and other cheese, dried mushrooms and pork products (which, incidentally, are a major source of protein throughout Europe for rich as well as poor, and also a major pleasure). Chestnuts are available fresh in season, dried all year round and sometimes ground for polenta. Italian greengrocers often carry fresh broad beans, fennel, dandelion leaves and other green vegetables, not to mention tomatoes and garlic, the appreciation of which we owe to the Italians.

Health or Natural Food Shops

Health or natural food shops are increasingly common. They owe their name and some measure of their popularity to the whole grains and flours they stock. Supermarkets, unless they have extensive health food sections, do not stock important staples like whole wheat, millet, rye, oats, buckwheat and maize but usually carry only a narrow range of refined flours and meal. Refined flour is a luxury to poor people—white bread is eaten as a treat in parts of eastern Europe—but it is not as nutritious as coarser grains. The protein-rich germ of the grain is milled away in refining because it spoils relatively quickly when ground into flour. The superior nutritive quality of whole grains confers a right to the title 'health' food shop. The superior nutrition is important if the whole diet consists of little else but grains. Perhaps more important here, in a country where varied fresh fruits, vegetables and meats are generally available, is the fact that these whole grains have their own tastes and textures, unrelated to white bread and cakes. The taste and textures of the grains used give much of the character to simple peoples' cooking.

The title 'natural food' depends on a metaphysical distinction. Almost all food is processed before eating, if only by cooking. Some processing is necessary to bring out the nutritive elements of some foods, or to remove poisons. Many peoples' staples, such as manioc, breadfruit and acorns, go through long processing before they are considered edible. *Popoi*, the staple of Tahitians, the most natural of people according to some writers, is made by a fairly lengthy process. What is natural and what is not is a cultural decision. Perhaps the closeness of human hands to simpler processes make those processes more natural. More to the point here is that native people do in fact eat these 'natural' foods, if only because they lack the technology to produce any other kind.

Health food shops are invaluable sources of: whole grains,

including wheat, rye, oats, millet, barley, brown rice of several kinds, and buckwheat; excellent flours made from all the grains; oils including sesame, coconut, and nut oils; beans, soya beans, lentils, raw nuts and dried fruits. They also stock oriental products such as bean curd, soy sauce, *tamari*, *miso*, bean sprouts, dried fish and dried seaweeds such as *kombu*, laver and non-oriental Irish moss (carrageen). They usually carry a wide assortment of spices and herbs, including herbs for infusions such as camomile; and yeasts.

One final note: 'organic' foods are more expensive and not necessarily better quality. There is also no control on the use of the word, so all depends on the honour of the producer and the reliability and selectivity of the retailer.

INDEX